VOODOO MAC

TIPS & TRICKS WITH AN ATTITUDE

Kay Yarborough Nelson

Ventana Press Voodoo™ Series

VOODOO MAC

MAC

TIPS & TRICKS WITH AN ATTITUDE

Voodoo Mac: Tips & Tricks With an Attitude
Copyright© 1993 by Kay Yarborough Nelson
The Ventana Press Voodoo™ Series

Library of Congress Cataloging-in-Publication Data

Nelson, Kay Yarborough
        Voodoo Mac : tips & tricks with an attitude / Kay
    Yarborough Nelson. -- 1st ed.
            p.   cm.
        Includes index.
        ISBN 1-56604-028-0 (pbk.)
        1. Macintosh (Computer) I. Title.
    QA76.8.M3N45 1993
    004.165--dc20   92-38375
                                                              CIP

Book design: Karen Wysocki
Cover design: Thea Tulloss, Tulloss Design; John Nedwidek, Sitzer:Spuria
Editorial staff: Diana Cooper, Linda Pickett, Ruffin Prevost, Pam Richardson
Production staff: Rhonda Angel, Brian Little, Karen Wysocki

First Edition   9 8 7 6 5 4 3 2
Printed in the United States of America

For information about our audio products, write us at Newbridge Book Clubs,
3000 Cindel Drive, Delran, NJ 08370

Ventana Press, Inc.
P.O. Box 2468
Chapel Hill, NC 27515
919/942-0220
FAX 919/942-1140

ABOUT THE AUTHOR

Kay Yarborough Nelson has written a couple of dozen computer books about other operating systems and software, but her first love is the Macintosh. In addition to *Voodoo Mac*, she is the author of *The Little System 7 (and 7.1) Books* and *The Macintosh Performa: A Visual QuickStart,* from Peachpit Press; and *Mastering WordPerfect on the Macintosh* from Sybex. She is also the coauthor of the second edition of Robin Williams's best-selling *The Little Mac Book.* Her books on the Mac and other subjects have been translated into many languages, including French, German, Spanish, Italian, Portuguese, Greek, Dutch and Swedish. She specializes in making computer topics accessible to normal human beings.

TRADEMARKS

ACKNOWLEDGMENTS

For their excellent tips, tricks and Macintosh insights, I'd like to thank:

Eric Apgar
Harry Baya
Peter the Bugman and the guys at Maxis
Bruce Campbell
Mike Chow
Spring Davis-Charles
Gene Garbutt
Robert Gibson
Elise Hannah
John Hedtke
Edward Hirsch
Ron Hovingh
Eric Hustvedt
Brian Kendig
Holly Knight
Jorn Knuttila
Diane Lennox
Joe Morris
Mike O'Connor
Beckie Pack
Marty Silbernik
Rob Terrell
Fred Torres
Dave Waite
Robin Williams

Special thanks goes to Ruffin Prevost, who not only edited the book, but also served as technical reviewer—by working through each tip to test it for technical accuracy—and even contributed several favorite tips of his own.

One more sad acknowledgment...

As this book went to press, my old boss Jack Byrne died of a heart attack. Although I say "old," Jack wasn't; he went too soon. He was an editor of the old school—the crusty, irascible, Perry White, "keep-'em-guessing" type of editor who could make you feel like a copy boy one minute and Clark Kent's alter ego the next. Jack expected—and got—the best, just by being himself. His terrible, legendary temper also helped. Back in 1981, when I worked at SRI International as a writer and editor, Jack got me started in computers by giving me a portable terminal, a photocopied UNIX manual and access to his account on the VAX. Actually, I did more running around than either writing or editing, because Jack believed in returning the scientists' edited reports by waiting until the scientist in question was gone and then putting the report on the chair ("that way, they can *see* them," he'd say with an evil grin). He said a lot more, too...most of it lost in the passage of time, and a large part of it unprintable. But he was kind and generous with his time and advice, and he got me started using these magic boxes, the hard way, as usual. During the past few years, Jack had become a Macintosh man and ran an all-Mac shop at SRI. I had planned to take this book to him when it was done for the usual mixture of ridicule, praise and gut-busting humor.

Thank you, Jack.

EPIGRAM

In 1968, at the Fall Joint Computer Conference in San Francisco, Doug Engelbart[1] of SRI International stood up on the stage and did magic. Using a telephone line wired into one of the large mainframe computers at SRI Menlo Park and a projection TV that showed on-line text and graphics as a computer monitor does today, he moved text around with a cursor, inserted a figure in a page of text that automatically flowed to make room for it, opened another window on the screen to look at some notes about the text (like hypertext), and viewed a few notes about the program (like a help file). It was magic because it was the first public demonstration of these capabilities.

In fact, it was so magical, some people didn't believe it. They argued that the interactive bit had to be a fake—that it was really just a movie of some kind they were seeing.... And even many of those who did believe what they were seeing, and were thrilled by it, didn't see any practical point to it. Why go to all that effort to do interactive computing? Batch computing, with its stacks of punched cards, was much cheaper. Anyway, why would you need to see it on the screen when tomorrow morning you could have it all printed out, with line numbers?

From ERGO, the newsletter of SRI's Engineering Research Group, June-July 1992.

---

[1] Among the mainstays of personal computing which we take for granted, Doug Engelbart is responsible for the mouse, the swiveling CRT, the interactive display of text, hypertext, windows, online help, shared databases, remote workstations and the electronic publishing of integrated text and graphics—all of which has dramatically changed the way people process and work with information.

CONTENTS

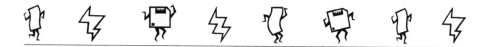

Foreword xiv

Introduction...xv

1 Secrets of the Finder 1
   Alias Tricks 2
   Icon & File Tricks 7
   Selecting Tricks 19
   Trash Tricks 21
   More Finder Tricks..23

2 Menu Magic 31
   Apple Menu Tricks 32
   File Menu Tricks 38
   Tricks for the View Menu 44
   Tricks for the Label Menu 46
   Tricks for the Special Menu 48
   Tricks for the Help Menu 48
   Tricks for the International Menu 49
   Tricks for the Applications Menu 52
   Creating Command-Key Shortcuts for Menus........53
      Assigned Key Combinations 54
      Unassigned Key Combinations 55
      Hexadecimal Alphabetic Equivalents 61

3 Hoodoo Voodoo **63**
Startup Sorcery 64
Easter Eggs 70
FKEY Magic 77
Mixing Sixes & Sevens 79

4 Customizing Your Desktop **85**
ResEdit 101 86
Icon Artistry 104

5 Disk & Drive Tricks **123**
The Basics 123
Floppy Disk Tricks 126
Disk Troubles? 131
Hard Disk & Disk Utility Tricks 133
Miscellaneous Disk Tricks 139

6 Miscellaneous Voodoo Tricks **143**
Control Panel Tricks 143
PowerBook Tricks 153
QuickTime Tips 159
Sound Advice 162
Swapping Keys Around 174
A Grab Bag of Tricks 180

7 Printing Mysteries **191**
General Printing Tips 191
Font Magic 199
Secret Symbols 207
Everyday Symbols 208
Math Symbols 209
Accented Characters 209
More Printing Tricks 211

8 Connectivity Secrets **217**
Networking Magic 217
More System 7 Connectivity Tricks 227
SCSI Secrets 229
Modem Magic 234

9 Memory Demystified **245**
  Mysteries of Finder & Application Memory 247
  Getting More RAM 253
  Using Virtual Memory..256
  Disk Caches & RAM Disks 259
  32-Bit Addressing...262

10 In Trouble? **265**
  Your Emergency Toolkit 266
  Getting Out of Trouble 267

A Installation Tips **281**
  Safe Installation 281
  General Installation Tips.......................................285

B Where to Go from Here.............................**291**
  User Groups..291
  Calling Apple 292
  Online Services 293
  Mail Order Houses 293
  Magazines 294

  Index **295**

FOREWORD

by Robin Williams

It *is* magic, you know. How that programming code gets turned into machine language and how those tiny little chips can hold full-color photographs and fine typography and heavy-duty spreadsheets is a magical mystery, and I just accept it as such. So it made perfect sense when Kay told me she was doing a book called *Voodoo Mac.* Of course— we all become magicians when we work with this computer. Kay, in this book, is giving us apprenticeship lessons so we can make the most of the power we have (literally) at our fingertips. And this is fun power! Kay's resource of tips and tricks does not include complex relational database programming or suggested algorithms for typographical hyphenation and justification. No, this book is full of those irresistible little maneuvers that make our work sing, that make us feel empowered and in control—masters of our computers.

And wedged between the tips for RAM disks and SCSI drives are a few tricks that are ostensibly useless, except they make us smile (and therein lies their value). Take Easter Eggs, for instance: those little hidden messages Mac programmers imbed in their About boxes and other sneaky places. Kay has included the most complete collection of Easter Eggs I've ever seen. What treasures they are. And what a statement of attitude. This peculiar Macintosh attitude (that no other computer has inspired) is embodied in something as simple as an Easter Egg. I cast my vote for the Number One Greatest Easter Egg to WriteNow (well, it ties with Disinfectant's). And if you don't know what I'm talking about, you'd better skip straight to Chapter 3, "Hoodoo Voodoo," to read up on Easter Eggs.

So enjoy yourself with this book—become empowered and inspired. How can you help it?

Robin Williams is the author of The Little Mac Book, The Mac Is Not A Typewriter, PageMaker 4: An Easy Desk Reference *and* Jargon: An Informal Dictionary of Computer Terms.

INTRODUCTION

I f you've gone beyond the point-and-click stage, *Voodoo Mac* is for you. Even if your VCR is flashing "12:00," you'll find plenty of easy-to-use tips and tricks here. Voodoo doesn't mean "hard."

Voodoo Mac presents all sorts of things that aren't in the Mac manuals (which you probably never read anyway). These tricks are voodoo because they deliver quick results, without your having to understand the theory behind them. You'll find tips presented in a format that lets you easily locate the ones that apply to what you're doing, or what you'd like to be able to do, but never had time to search for before. These tricks will also show you a few things you probably never thought possible.

SYSTEM 6 OR SYSTEM 7?

You'll find tips for both System 6 and System 7 (and System 7.1) in *Voodoo Mac*, including tricks for switching back and forth between them. But more and more Mac users (significantly more than half, as of this writing) have upgraded to System 7; it's the system shipped with every new Mac. Increasingly, developers are creating programs for System 7 only. And because of System 7's huge range of features, there are just plain more tricks you can do with it. Few Mac users are going to remain completely satisfied with System 6 for very long. Still, if you're a System 6 user, don't despair. Even though this book features screen shots from System 7 and may assume that the latest version of the Mac's operating system is the greatest, there are plenty of tips and tricks here for you as well. And if you're buying *Voodoo Mac* expecting a lot of System 7, you'll be delighted. By the way, "System 7" includes "System 7.1," too. If a tip can be used only with System 7.1, I say so.

BUT WHAT ABOUT PERFORMAS AND AT EASE?

Performas are shipped with a modified version of System 7 with an easy-to-use interface called System 7.0P or 7.1P. You'll be able to use most of *Voodoo Mac*'s System 7 tips, but you probably won't want to use every one of them, because you're running a slightly different, easier-to-use version of System 7. After you've outgrown System 7.1P, you can purchase System 7.1 from your dealer and install it on your Performa, and you'll have access to all of System 7's capabilities. (For more details on how to do this, see Appendix A.)

Regardless of whether you own a Performa, you may be using a simplified Mac interface called At Ease. It's designed to make your Mac easy to use without using the Finder at all. If lots of different people have access to the Mac you're using, you may find that At Ease has been set up on it. It lets you restrict access to the full range of programs that are stored on your computer, prevents documents from being deleted by mistake (there's no Trash!), and forces users to save their documents onto floppy disks, if it's been set up that way. You'll find tips for using At Ease as well as Performa-specific tips in Chapters 1, 6 and 9, and you can use most of the other tips in the book, too.

JUST THE MAC, MA'AM

Unlike other Macintosh books that tend to be half-filled with details about programs or hardware you don't have or features that were outdated by the time the book went to press, *Voodoo Mac* is pure Macintosh. If you have a Mac—any Mac at all—this book has tips you can use.

Because this book isn't product-specific, you won't find many tips that say, "If you want to do thus and so, go out and buy a $500 application." *Voodoo Mac* is about what you can do with your Mac— right now, right out of the box—without buying a lot of other stuff. On virtually every page, you'll find tips you can use, no matter what kind of Mac you have. (OK, if there's a really great utility or shareware program that does something spectacular or makes a complicated task really easy, I just might mention it.) But, while we're on the subject, if you're interested in shareware, you should pick up a copy of *The Mac Shareware 500*, available from Ventana Press. It's a great guide to all sorts of neat shareware utilities and programs you can get for very little money or maybe even free.

WHAT EQUIPMENT DO YOU NEED?

You need a Mac, of course, and it should be running System 6.0.7 or later. If you're still running System 6.0.5, it's time to upgrade—you can upgrade to System 6.0.7 for free by copying it from your local Macintosh dealer or user group. If you're running System 7, you should have at least 4 Mb of RAM. If you already have (or if you're planning to buy) 4 Mb of RAM, it's time to upgrade to System 7. You don't necessarily need to be using virtual memory or 32-bit addressing, but you'll find some tips for those topics here as well.

WHAT'S IN THE BOOK?

You'll see these sorts of things in the book:

- Tricks for starting your Mac and shutting it down; rebuilding the Desktop without restarting; mixing System 6 and System 7; switching startup disks; bypassing the Startup Items folder; customizing the Apple menu; creating and coloring icons.

- ResEdit tricks for customizing your keyboard; creating a new startup screen; making your own dialog boxes; changing cursors; and more.

- Tricks for using aliases; creating an "office on a disk;" using aliases for long-term storage; fast disk erasing; shortcuts for formatting disks; tricks for the often-overlooked Put Away command; locking disks; throwing away locked files and folders; hiding files and folders; and more arcane mysteries.

- Tips for using PowerBooks on the road, such as saving battery power, getting files from your PowerBook to your main Mac, running on minimal software and turning down that startup sound.

- Finder secrets: hidden sorting; keyboard shortcuts; the Finder in System 6 and System 7; customizing the desktop; Trash tricks.

- Tricks for using the built-in sound recorder; QuickTime tips; transferring files from PCs to Macs; connecting SCSI devices.

- Silly hidden secrets like Easter Eggs, extra sounds, the secret color map in System 7, solving the Puzzle and dozens more.

- Using virtual memory; setting up a RAM disk; making the most of memory, avoiding extension conflicts; dealing with startup problems; using System 7 Tune-Up.

- Printing tips: using TrueType fonts; hidden characters in True-Type; suppressing the LaserWriter's startup page; printing mailing labels; using TrueType on PostScript printers.

- Network tricks: what to do if you've forgotten your password; restricting access; troubleshooting on a net; protecting file sharing; guest access tips; locking folders on a network.

- Desk Accessory tips; using control panels; reorganizing the Apple menu.

- Diagnostic tips: hints for quicker installations; reinstalling corrupted system software; the safest way to install System 7; recovering from crashes; reinstalling System 6.

THE USUAL WARNING

You'll find a lot of tricks here that call for using ResEdit, Apple's resource editing application. You can do some really neat stuff with ResEdit, and you don't have to be a programmer to use it. While most folks may think of ResEdit as the last great domain of the "power users," *Voodoo Mac* will show you how to use it quickly, easily and safely.

WHAT ATTITUDE?

Voodoo Mac is a pretty eclectic collection, but there are a few esoteric topics that it doesn't cover. For example, getting set up for serious multimedia and MIDI (Musical Instrument Digital Interface) sound work is an expensive proposition that most users (including myself) haven't gotten to yet, so there are a few such tips, but not a lot.

And you may be wondering about the "with an attitude" part of this book's subtitle. I originally conceived of the Voodoo series as the Mac approach to computing brought to the DOS world. (Yes, there are *Voodoo DOS* and *Voodoo Windows* books out there; they started this whole series.) In other words, things could be easy if all you had to know was *how* to do them instead of *why*. Believe me, you can be pretty flip about DOS if you take this attitude. So what might seem like "an attitude" to DOS users will probably simply be the reasonable way of doing things for the average Mac owner. If you have a Mac, you probably love it; at least you're probably grateful that you don't have to twirl a wrench to use it! So if you've read the other Voodoo books (which isn't likely, given their subject matter), don't expect lots of Mac-bashing flippancy here—I love the Mac.

HELP US OUT

As part of the process of creating this book, members of America Online, CompuServe and AppleLink were asked to contribute their favorite tips or tricks in exchange for a free book. As you'll see from the tips, quite a few folks responded with their favorites. You may see tips here that you've seen in other places, but that's because Mac people talk to each other. I was amazed at the duplicate tips that came pouring in. So don't take offense if you see a trick here that you think you thought of. But if you have a special tip that isn't here, this offer is open to you, too. If you have a helpful hint or trick you'd like to share, send it in. If your tip is used in the next edition, you'll get that book free and you'll receive a credit line in the book for it, too. Send your tips, tricks, comments and suggestions to

Kay Nelson   America Online: KayNelson
Ventana Press   CompuServe: 72000,1176
PO Box 2468   Internet: KayNelson@aol.com
Chapel Hill, NC 27515   AppleLink: Ventana.Link

phone: 919/942-0220
fax: 919/942-1140

CHAPTER ONE

SECRETS OF THE FINDER

The Finder is a part of the Macintosh that most users simply take for granted. It's the first thing you see after you start up and the last thing you see when you shut down. It's the desktop where you sort folders, copy files and shuffle icons—it's just as important as any application you buy, if not more important. The Finder is a file in your System Folder that loads into your Mac's RAM during startup. It's the Mac's wizard behind the curtain, running the whole show. Under System 7, the Finder is always running, as it is in System 6 under MultiFinder.

Under System 6 (and earlier) without MultiFinder, the Finder closes down when you launch an application and returns when you quit that application. To get just about anything done on your Mac—like launching programs, trashing files or creating folders—you'll find yourself at the Finder. So *Voodoo Mac* begins by taking a look at a rather eclectic collection of Finder tips.

Of course, the most basic Finder secret of all is to organize your folders and windows in the way that best helps you do your work. Some folks like to organize by type of document, keeping correspondence in one folder, spreadsheets in another, and so forth. Others organize by the job. Many people organize by the application (a Word folder, a PageMaker folder, and so on). And some even organize by the month—May 1993, June 1993. No matter what scheme you use, here are some tricks for helping you get the most from it.

ALIAS TRICKS

With System 7 and aliases, you can have an infinite variety of folder schemes. You can create aliases of documents and programs to keep track of files by month and by client and by document type. Just put the aliases in any folders where you think you might want to find them. Aliases don't take up much space on your hard disk (about 3k each), and you can have lots of aliases of the same thing. So we'll start by looking at all the alias tricks I could think of (or have ever seen). If you have another alias trick, send it in! I'd love to know about it.

Use aliases to create an applications folder. System 7's Make Alias command packs a lot of power. Here's a neat trick for getting aliases of all your programs into one easily accessible folder so you don't have to go hunting through a sequence of several folders to start a particular application.

First, use the Finder's Find command under the File menu (or press Command-F)[1] to search by kind, all at once, to gather all your programs (the ones whose kind contains "application"). They'll all be selected, so all you have to do is choose Make Alias from the File menu and drag the aliases to a folder on the same disk (presumably your internal hard drive). Now you have a program folder that you can keep handy on the desktop for starting any of your applications.

---

[1] By the way, "Command-F" means "press the Command key and the F key at the same time." And even though I've used an uppercase F for easier reading, you don't need to (and shouldn't) press the Shift key unless I specify that you should. And if, for instance, you see "press Command-Option-Shift," you should press all three of those keys at the same time. You're probably aware of this standard Mac protocol already, but since I'll be pointing out a lot of keyboard shortcuts in *Voodoo Mac*, I thought I'd lay down the ground rules first thing.

Keep aliases of programs directly on the desktop. Remember, you can open a document by dragging it onto the program's icon or alias, too, so it's often more useful to have a frequently used program's alias handy on the desktop than to have it in an applications folder. If you can't make up your mind which way you prefer things, don't sweat it—make two aliases of the program in question and store one on the desktop and one in your applications folder.

If there are two or three programs that you use a lot, keep aliases of them on your desktop, where you can launch them by either double-clicking on them or dragging a file's icon to them. This is especially handy for a graphics program, for instance, that accepts all sorts of graphics files—EPS, TIFFs, and so forth.

Keep aliases of things you do frequently on the desktop, too. On my desktop, I also keep an alias of my letterhead, an alias of my Navigator CompuServe setup, and an alias of America Online and AppleLink for quickly connecting to those services. There's also an alias of Smokey and Somebody, which are shared disks on my two-Mac network (see Figure 1-1).

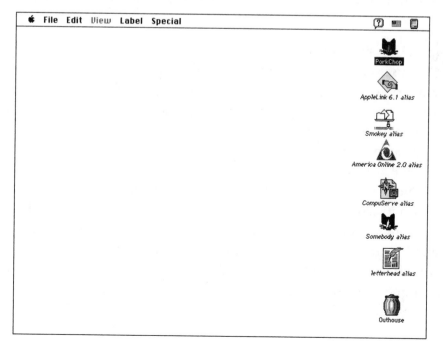

Figure 1-1: Alias icons on the desktop.

Getting to the original of an alias. Ah, this is a sneaky trick.

In a standard Open dialog box, you can press Option and double-click on an alias to go to the original of the alias instead of opening the alias.

Here's another neat way to find an alias's original. Let's say you're rummaging through files on the desktop or in folders trying to find a file you want to copy to a floppy, but you can only find the alias of that file. This isn't much help, because it's only the alias that gets copied to the floppy, not the actual file. Don't despair—it's easy to find your way back to the original file that the alias was made from. Just highlight the alias, choose Get Info, and click on the Find Original button in the bottom right corner of the Get Info box.

Another neat alias trick. If you have a PowerBook, put an alias of your hard drive in your Startup Items folder so you can see the contents of your entire hard drive as soon as your PowerBook starts, even if you closed all your windows when you last shut down. You can do this with a regular Mac, too, not just a PowerBook.

Use aliases to save disk space. If your hard disk is getting full, use this voodoo trick to save disk space: copy the files or programs you don't use very often onto floppy disks. Give each of those disks unique names—don't leave them named Untitled; you'll see why in a second. As an extra precaution, lock them to make sure nothing gets deleted by mistake.

Make aliases of those files and copy the aliases back onto your hard disk. Now, whenever you need one of those programs and you double-click on its icon on your hard disk, the Mac will prompt you to insert the floppy with that program on it. (If you've left all the floppies named Untitled, you may have trouble figuring out which disk to put in the drive.) Be sure to put a paper label on each floppy disk showing its unique name so you can find the right disk later, but let the Mac keep track of the tiny files that are on the disks and save you the trouble of writing and reading every single file on the floppy. Just double-click on the file's icon, and your Mac will tell you which disk to go hunting for.

This is a neat trick for PowerBook users. You can travel with a few floppies and keep those seldom-used programs off your hard disk. By the way, Chapter 6, "Miscellaneous Voodoo Tricks," has a whole section on neat PowerBook tricks.

Put aliases of folders in other folders. Remember, aliases take up very little disk space, so make a lot of them and save yourself time hunting for things. You aren't restricted to making aliases just of programs and documents: you can make aliases of folders, too. If you find yourself constantly switching back and forth between certain folders, make aliases of each one and put them in each folder.

If you make aliases a lot, you'll probably want to assign the Make Alias command a keyboard shortcut, such as Command-M, so you're not constantly pulling down the File menu. See Chapter 2, "Menu Magic," for details on how to do this.

Alias the Trash, too. If you don't like to mouse down to the Trash to delete a file or eject a disk, make aliases of the Trash and put them all over the place. Be creative. If you're always throwing files out of a particular folder, keep a Trash alias in that folder. You can put a Trash alias in your Apple menu, too. Although you can't drag files to the Trash under the Apple menu, you can easily open the Trash this way and see what hasn't been emptied.

Make an alias of your System Folder, too. If you find that you're frequently opening the System Folder, make an alias of it. While you're at it, make aliases of the items you're opening the System Folder to get at, too (like your Control Panels folder or your Apple Menu Items folder). Keep these aliases handy on the desktop so you don't have to scroll through windows to get at them each time you need them. And remember, you can quickly get back to the desktop level from Open and Save As dialog boxes just by clicking on the Desktop button in the dialog box.

Aliases won't work if you put their originals in invisible folders. You can use ResEdit, DiskTop (CE Software) or a shareware utility like DeskZap to make a file or folder invisible. But if you do, any aliases that you've created of that file or folder won't work. Likewise, any file that you store in an invisible folder won't support an alias, either. (For more on using ResEdit, see the sidebar in Chapter 4, "Customizing Your Desktop.")

Don't make aliases from aliases. Always use the original file or folder to make an alias instead of making aliases from aliases. It's the safest way. If you trash a copy of an alias that you've made an alias from, the Mac can lose track of the route back to the original.

Put an alias of the Clipboard in your Apple Menu Items folder, too. If you do a lot of complex cutting and pasting and you're often switching to and from the Clipboard, put an alias of it in your Apple Menu Items folder or on the desktop. Then you won't have to choose Show Clipboard from the Edit menu.

And why not put an alias of your hard disks in your Apple menu? The number of things you can do with aliases boggles the mind. I'm sure you can think of many more than those suggested here. But here's one last alias thought: put aliases of all your hard disks in your Apple menu. You'll have easy access to all the things on them, and you'll save space on a cluttered desktop. While you're at it, you can put aliases of your letterhead (and all sorts of other frequently used items) in the Apple menu. See Chapter 2 for more hints about that Apple menu, especially tips about creating a hierarchical Apple menu. If you have a large hard disk or frequently work with files that are several levels down in your folder structure, you'll really appreciate being able to take one trip to the Apple menu to find aliases of those often-used files.

ICON & FILE TRICKS

You can do all sorts of tricks with icons. The ones in this section are fairly basic, such as making icons invisible, using the infamous white box trick, speeding up the renaming process, and so forth. If you're really interested in icons, check out Chapter 4, "Customizing Your Desktop," to see how to swipe icons from icon collections and learn probably more than you ever wanted to know about them (like what's an icl8 anyway?).

Quick renaming. In System 7, waiting for the Finder to accept a new icon name can drive you nuts. Use this speed trick: click on the icon's name and then move the mouse just a tiny bit immediately after you release the mouse button. Or click on the icon and then press Return. That will put the name in a box, highlighted and ready for retyping. Type the new name and press Return again to make it stick.

Quick un-renaming. Under System 7, clicking on a window and typing the first few letters of a file's name will take you straight to that file. But I'm often not paying attention and I rename icons by mistake this way. This is easy to do if you've clicked on the icon's name and the text appears in a box, but you're not looking at the screen. When you look up, you see that you've renamed the icon. If you notice this interesting (and annoying) effect before you press Return, just press Command-Z (or choose Undo from the Edit menu) to get the icon's original name back.

Look, Ma! No mousing. Under System 7, you can rename an icon quickly without taking your hands off the keyboard. Type the first few letters of the icon's name to go straight to it, press Return to highlight the text, type the new name and press Return again to save the new name.

Renaming an icon doesn't make a copy of it. This is a really dumb thing to do, but I'll point it out here, because some folks have indeed made this mistake. Renaming an icon doesn't create a new copy of it. To make two versions of a file under different names, do any of the following: save the file under a new name using a program's Save As command, copy the icon by dragging it to a different disk or Option-dragging it to a different location on the same disk, or highlight the file in the Finder and use the Duplicate command (Command-D) on it. Then, after you've copied or duplicated it, rename the copy.

Also, be warned that some icons, such as fonts and preference files, shouldn't ever be renamed, or you'll be asking for trouble—their parent programs go looking for those files under their particular original names, so don't confuse things by changing their names.

Arrange items in a list by using spaces and characters in their names. System 7 lets you use spaces at the beginning of a file's name (System 6 doesn't, but there's a voodoo way around that; see the next tip). Your Mac sorts file names alphabetically, with spaces, numbers and certain special characters sorting before file names like "Alice's Spreadsheet" or even "Aaacme Letterhead." So use this trick of inserting spaces, numbers and characters to force icon names to the top of a list. Even under System 6, you can begin a file's name with a special symbol or a number to get it at the top of a list. For example, my WordPerfect folder is named 1WordPerfect, so that when I view the files and folders on my hard drive by name, Word-Perfect appears right at the top of the list instead of way down at the bottom.

You'll see lots of tips for using this feature to arrange your Apple menu in Chapter 2.

Using spaces in icon names with System 6. The voodoo way around the no-spaces-at-the-beginning-of-a-file-name rule in System 6 is easy. Let's say you want to move the file "My Novel" (without the quotes) to the top of your documents folder. For the purposes of this illustration, we'll use an underlined blank space (_)

to represent a space in the file's name. To get a blank space at the beginning of the file name, type a character—any character—and then follow it by a blank space and then the file name. So you'd change "My Novel" to "X_My Novel." Then, just go back and delete the first character (in this case, the X) and you'll be left with a space and then your file name (_My Novel).

Beware of numbers in the Finder. Because of the way ASCII codes work, you'll get strange looking results when the Finder sorts files that use numbers in their names. For example, say that you're listing the chapters of a book:

Chapter 2
Chapter 12
Chapter 25

You want to view them in numerical order, like the above example, but the Finder insists on listing them this way:

Chapter 12
Chapter 2
Chapter 25

To get around this trap, precede single-digit numbers, like the 2 in Chapter 2, with a zero (Chapter 02) or a space (Chapter _2).

Alphabetizing your icons. In System 7, there's a neat hidden sorting trick that makes it easy to alphabetize icons. First, switch from Icon view to Name view (use the View menu). Now return to Icon view. Hold down the Option key and choose Clean Up by Window from the Special menu (only now, with the Option key held down, it will read Clean Up by Name). You can do the same thing to sort icons by Date, Label, Size and so forth. For instance, switch to viewing by Date; then return to Icon view and choose Clean Up by Date (or whatever).

Viewing by Kind will get all your programs (that aren't in nested folders within that window) alphabetized at the top of the window, which is often handy for getting to them quickly.

Don't use colons in icon names. If you put a colon (:) in an icon name, the Mac converts it to a hyphen. That's because colons are used internally by the Mac to designate folder hierarchy. For example, PorkChop:System Folder:Extensions:Quick-Time says that the QuickTime extension is in the Extensions folder in the System Folder on my hard drive PorkChop. PorkChop, by the way, is a cat; a plump (hence Pork) little orange bobtail (hence Chop).

There's a 31-character limit on icon names. Although you can use as many as 31 characters in an icon name, you won't be able to see more than about 20 characters in most Finder views, so you might as well keep names short.

You can copy icon names, too. Here's another hidden System 7 feature: you can copy icon names into your word processing program or onto the Clipboard. This can be useful whenever you need to list a bunch of files in a document you're writing. Just select the icons whose names you want to copy (Shift-clicking works, you can drag a marquee across the names or choose Select All from the Edit menu if you want all of them), press Command-C, and paste them into a word processing program. It's important to note, though, that you can only copy up to 256 characters at a time using this trick.

If you have lots of kids around or if other, less experienced users need access to your Mac from time to time, consider getting At Ease from Apple. Instead of making things invisible to protect them from being altered or deleted (a popular trick I discuss in Chapter 6, "Miscellaneous Voodoo Tricks"), consider getting At Ease. It's a front-end interface that sits on top of your regular Finder, replacing the familiar Finder with a much simpler interface. There's no Trash, so things can't get deleted by mistake, and you can even set At Ease up to save to floppy disks so that your hard disk doesn't fill up with priceless works of art created by your four-year-old.

After you install At Ease, use the At Ease control panel to set up the programs that you want other users to have access to, just by clicking on them. When you restart with At Ease enabled, the desktop has only two folders. The applications you've chosen to be available go into an Applications folder, and there's a single folder where newly created documents are automatically stored, making everything extremely simple to find (see Figure 1-2).

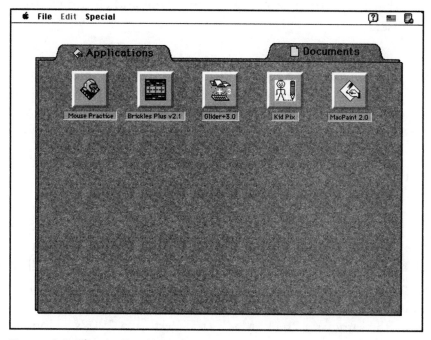

Figure 1-2: The At Ease interface is even easier to use than the normal Finder.

With At Ease installed, you still have access to System 7's full range of features and capabilities, including aliasing and file sharing, just by choosing Go To Finder from the File menu. An optional password protection scheme lets you prevent unwanted users from getting to the Finder, so nobody is going to open or delete anything you don't want them to.

But At Ease isn't just for keeping your children out of your important records. An added bonus of At Ease is that it takes up less memory than the normal Finder under System 7.0 or 7.1, so it's a good choice for installing on your PowerBook when traveling. With documents all in one folder, they're easy to find, and the large buttons are easy to locate, even in dim lighting.

On the other hand, if you have young children, they'll find At Ease a great introduction to the Macintosh. With large icons to click and no complex series of folders to hunt through, it's an ideal learning tool. There's also a Mouse Practice tutorial (with animation and sound) that gets little fingers used to dragging and clicking with the mouse.

Don't confuse At Ease with the Performa's operating system. At Ease is a lot simpler to use than the basic Performa operating system (System 7.0 or 7.1P), which is almost a full-fledged System 7. At Ease runs on "regular" Macs as well as on the Performas.

Don't confuse At Ease with Easy Access, either. I do that all the time. Easy Access is for using your Mac without a mouse.

Want a new Mac? Check out the Performa. In fact, because the Performa comes bundled at a competitive price with so much software in addition to its in-home technical help and toll-free support number, you may want to buy a Performa and then sell off the things you don't want. The hardware on the Performa series is basically the same as a "real" Mac's (the Performa 200 is a clone of the Mac Classic II, the 400 is a renamed LC II); the only significant difference is in the operating system. And if you know much at all about the Macintosh, you can get around saving in the Documents folder and opening applications from the Launcher, which is the way things are set up for the Performa. Look for Performas in Sears and Circuit City, not at your friendly computer dealer.

If you want the "real" System 7 on your Performa, you can buy it separately and install it on your Performa, replacing its System 7.0P or 7.1P.

Create dividers in windows viewed by icon. Here's a neat System 7 trick for creating dividers in windows where you're looking at an icon view. First, create a new folder and "name" it by using symbols such as dashes or bullets (Option-8 creates a nice bullet). Now, the secret: go to your drawing program and create a white rectangle with no border. All you need to do is use the marquee tool to select some white space. Make it big enough to cover the folder's icon in the Get Info box and copy it to the Clipboard.

Now highlight the folder and choose Get Info from the File menu (or press Command-I). Next, click once on the folder's icon in the upper-left corner, and then paste the white box (see Figure 1-3). Since there's no folder outline, all you'll see now will be the folder's name in icon view (Figure 1-4).

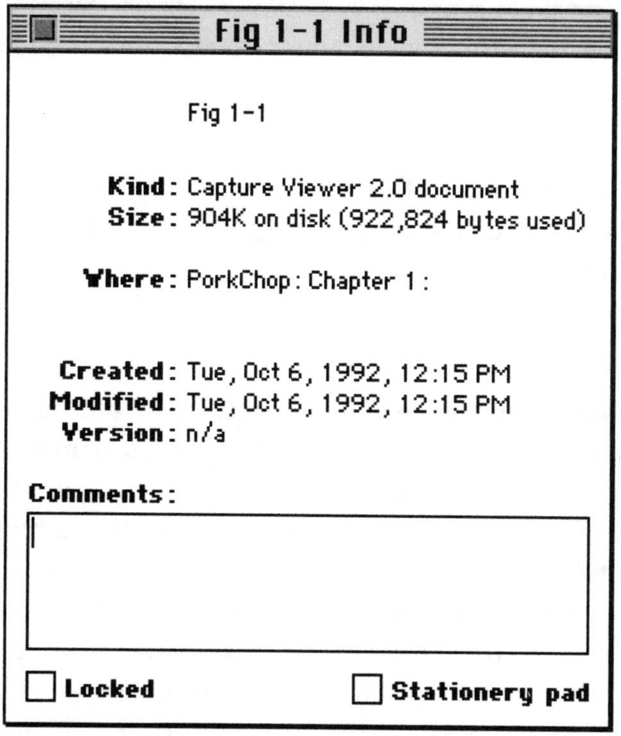
Fig 1-1 Info
Fig 1-1
Kind: Capture Viewer 2.0 document
Size: 904K on disk (922,824 bytes used)
Where: PorkChop: Chapter 1:
Created: Tue, Oct 6, 1992, 12:15 PM
Modified: Tue, Oct 6, 1992, 12:15 PM
Version: n/a
Comments:
Locked
Stationery pad

Figure 1-3: When you paste the white box, the icon disappears.

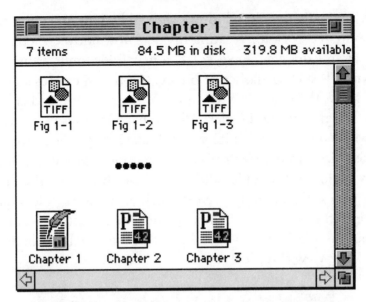

Figure 1-4: Use invisible folders named with symbols as dividers.

(I thought only those of us who cheated at PageMaker knew the old white box trick, which is so dear to us sloppy users and so dreaded by PageMaker purists. Don't ask—it's really not a nice thing to do to your pages.)

Get more desktop real estate with the white box trick. You can create icons that appear with just their names showing on the desktop by using the white box trick in the preceding tip (see Figure 1-5). If you like to have lots of icons on the desktop (or if you only want a folder's name to show inside a window, even when Viewing by Icon), this trick will let you fit about six icons in the space that two occupied when the whole icon was showing. Double-clicking on the name works just like double-clicking on the icon—in fact, you'll have to double-click on the name after you replace the icon with a white box—double-clicking in the space where the icon used to be does nothing.

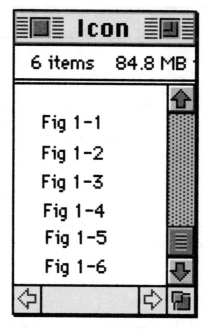

Figure 1-5: Using icon names
only saves lots of real estate

This is also a clever way to keep a "launch pad" area on your desktop where you can open frequently used applications easily. Just stack their names, sans icons, over on the left side of the desktop, along the top, down near the Trash—wherever you want your launch pad.

Thanks to Robert Gibson, Ontario, Canada.

Another use for the white box trick: Post-It notes. If you ever want to leave yourself a reminder or two out on the desktop (see Figure 1-6), use this variation of the white box trick. In your drawing program, create a borderless white box with the marquee tool (if you find yourself doing this a lot, keep a white box in your Scrapbook). Copy it, go to the desktop, and create a new folder (Command-N). Then paste the white box into the folder's Get Info window. Instead of giving the folder a name, as in the previous trick, type your message (up to 31 characters).

Figure 1-6: Creating desktop notes with the "white box trick"

Another way of leaving yourself messages. If you like having a To-Do list to start off the day, you'll appreciate this trick, because it lets you view a list when you start your Mac. There are excellent shareware programs that do this and more, but if all you want is a daily reminder list, why not check out this trick?

Put an alias of the Note Pad in your Startup Items folder. Then make your To-Do lists in the Note Pad, and you'll see them each time you start your Mac.

You can use the Startup Items folder for all sorts of things.
While we're discussing clever uses for the Startup Items folder, I should point out that lots of folks are under the misconception that the Startup Items folder is just for launching applications after start-up, and don't realize that sounds will play, QuickTime movies will run, spreadsheets will find and launch Excel and open themselves, and so forth. Put any document you want to work with every day in your Startup Items folder, such as your letterhead or your fax sheet, and it will open automatically when you start your Mac. To keep the things in your Startup Items folder from activating after your turn on your Mac, hold the Shift key down just before the desktop appears following startup. (Holding the Shift key down like that will also close any windows you left open in the Finder.)

Another way for secret file protection: a variation on the white box trick. Here's another way to make files invisible when you're viewing by name: use System 7's Labels feature instead of the white box trick. In the Labels control panel (not the Label menu), double-click on a label color. Then choose white from the Color Picker. To get white, slide the scroll bar all the way to the top and click in the middle of the wheel. Delete the label's name.

Now, back in the Finder, choose the file you want to make invisible. Assign it that white label and rename it by using spaces instead of a name. Instant invisibility!

Actually, if you look at the very top of your Finder listing by name, you'll see where the invisible file is.

Replacing generic icons. Rebuilding the desktop[2] will usually replace those plain-vanilla, generic icons with icons that identify the application (the icon of a hand holding a pen or pencil in front of a diamond background). But you'll often get just one or two of those generic icons, especially when you decompress a file you've downloaded. Instead of rebuilding the desktop (which can be a time-consuming process) just for a couple of icons, use this quick voodoo to try to get the right icon to show up.

Open the item's Get Info box (Command-I) and select the icon. Now copy, paste and cut. This will sometimes bring back the missing icon.

Losing comments in the Get Info box. When you rebuild the desktop, not only does the Finder replace those generic application icons with the correct ones, it also deletes any comments you might have written in a file's Get Info box. This unfortunate side-effect was supposed to have been fixed with the release of System 7,

---

[2]Rebuilding the desktop is a procedure you should do on a regular basis to keep your Macintosh in good running order. Chapter 10, "In Trouble?", discusses the hows and whys of rebuilding the desktop in detail.

but it wasn't. There are various schemes and even shareware programs designed to preserve your Get Info comments, but as a rule of thumb, you should never store information in those boxes that you can't afford to lose if—or when—the desktop is rebuilt.

Getting cute icons. To spruce up your System 7 desktop, change those ho-hum text page icons that represent documents to something zippier. All you need to do is open a file's Get Info box, copy its icon, and paste it in another file's Get Info box. You can get pretty creative here. (There are lots more tricks on this subject in Chapter 4.) Of course, this trick works on almost everything on your Mac that has an icon, not just documents. If, for some reason, you'd like your copy of TeachText to have a frog icon, as long as you can copy a frog picture from somewhere to the Clipboard, you're in business.

You can't do this in some Get Info windows, though. For example, the System file's or Finder's icons can't be changed by copying and pasting, nor can the folder icons for the the Apple Menu Items, Extensions, Control Panels and Startup Items folders. Also, the System Folder has a special icon that can't be changed this way—look closely at the icon of the System Folder that's in effect, and you'll see a tiny Mac icon on it, indicating that it's "blessed."

You can't change icons of open documents or applications. If you should decide to try the previous trick on a document that's currently open, you'll be disappointed. The Finder won't let you change or replace the icon of a document (or application) that's open at the time (the Paste option simply won't be available when you try to replace the icon).

Custom folder icons, the (relatively) easy way. Tired of all those boring plain folder icons? With just a little trick or two, you can change your folders so they show the icon of the program that created the documents stored in them.

Get Info on a folder icon and copy the blank folder that shows up in the Get Info window. Now open your handy color painting program and paste the blank folder icon. Find the *small* icon of the program you want to put on the folder (view by Small Icon to see this version of a program or document's icon). When you find the one you want, take a screen shot with Command-Shift-3. Make sure the icon isn't selected, so it isn't highlighted, and be sure to get the mouse pointer out of the way!

Double-click on the screen shot (it'll be named Picture 0, Picture 1, and so forth) to open it in MacPaint (System 6) or TeachText (System 7). The image should be stored at the main level of your hard drive, but for an easy way to find it in System 7, press Command-F for Find; then search for Picture.

Select the program's icon and copy it. Just click with the mouse in TeachText, and you'll get a selection cursor; in MacPaint, use the selection marquee. Then go back to the color paint program, where your blank folder icon is patiently waiting, and paste the small icon. Now color the folder and its small icon the way you want it. (If you don't have a color paint program or a color monitor, the trick still works for black-and-white Macs, it just doesn't look as nice.) When you're done, use the marquee tool to copy the icon. Paste the copy into the folder's Get Info window. If the application icon is too small, try enlarging it within the paint program and paste again.

If you do this sort of thing often, you should probably keep a backup file with all your color folder icons in it, just in case you lose a folder icon. That way, you won't have to go back and recreate everything again, you can just open the file, copy the icon and paste it into a new folder.

SELECTING TRICKS

Selecting is another Finder operation that you do all the time, so why not try out some magic that can make a boring chore more fun? These tricks are easy but often overlooked.

Select several icons at a time by dragging. Instead of Shift-clicking on individual icons to select them, try this speed trick to select icons that are next to each other. Click just a little bit outside the first icon and then drag over the others. You'll see a marquee selector around them. This trick works in both Systems if you're viewing by Icon, and in System 7 you can use it when viewing by Name, too.

More marqueeing magic. Combine the previous trick with this one to do some major selecting. Once you've selected a group of icons by marqueeing them, Shift-click to add other icons that aren't next to your original selection.

You can press Shift and marquee another set of side-by-side icons to add it to the icons you've already selected. Likewise, if you accidentally selected an icon or two that you didn't want to include, you can simply Shift-click each one to deselect it.

Stopping a dragging operation. A little-known but useful trick: you've selected a bunch of files and you're dragging them, say, to the Trash. But then, before releasing the mouse button, you decide you don't want to do that after all. Just drag them to the Finder's menu bar and they'll all go back where they came from.

The tip of the pointer is all that matters. It's easy to forget, especially when dragging a huge group of files around the Finder, but it's only the very tip of the mouse pointer that your Mac is concerned with. Don't be distracted by the outlines and shadows of huge groups of files and folders. Just remember to put the tip of your mouse pointer right on top of where you want to move things, and everything else, no matter how large or unwieldy, will follow.

If you want to change the "hot spot" on tools like your insertion cursor or the crosshairs, you'll learn how in Chapter 4.

Selecting with the keyboard (System 7). System 7 has several keyboard shortcuts for selecting icons. You can press Tab to move to the next icon (in alphabetical order) or select the first icon in the window or on the desktop. Shift-Tab moves you backward (in reverse alphabetical order). Also, you can use the arrow keys to move to the icons just above or below or to the right or left of the currently selected icon. If an icon hasn't been selected, pressing the right or left arrow keys will select the last or first icon in the window, or the last or first item in a Finder window that you're viewing by name.

And of course you remember that typing the first letter of an icon's name takes you straight to that part of the alphabet, so I'll try not to mention that again.

TRASH TRICKS

The Trash works differently in System 6 and System 7. In System 6, it automatically empties whenever you start a new application or restart or shut down your Mac. In System 7, it doesn't empty until you tell it to. Here a few more Trash oddities.

Instead of ejecting a floppy disk by dragging it to the Trash, use a keyboard shortcut. Dragging the icon of a floppy disk to the Trash dismounts the disk (ejects it and removes it from memory). This is just about the most basic Mac trick of all. But here's a refinement for it: press Option-Command-E (in System 6) or Command-Y (in System 7) to do the same thing. You'll save a lot of time by not dragging disk icons to the Trash to eject them. Unlike the Eject Disk function (Command-E), which leaves a dimmed image of the disk on your desktop and holds the presence of the disk in memory (which may mean you'll be asked to insert it again later—what a pain), this handy trick works just as if you'd dragged the disk to the Trash.

Open a Trash window. Sometimes it's convenient to be able to see what's in the Trash. It's also nice to have a larger target to hit than a tiny trash can, especially if you're junking large groups of files. In System 7, you can open the Trash and put its window anywhere you like, any size you like.

Some people like to open a Trash window and widen it across the bottom of the screen so they can drag items straight down into their own sort of Trash maw from any point on the screen. You can tell what's in the Trash at a glance, too. With System 6, this is a good trick for major housekeeping sessions, but since System 6 returns the

Trash back where it was when you restart, it's not a permanent change. System 7, however, leaves the Trash where you put it even after you restart.

Retrieving trashed items. With System 6, what's in the Trash gets automatically emptied, as explained earlier. (You can usually get things you've trashed by mistake back with a utility program like Symantec's SUM or Central Point Software's MacTools Deluxe.) But in System 7, there's an easy way to retrieve trashed items and put them back where they originally came from at the same time. Open the Trash, select what you want to retrieve, and press Command-Y, the keyboard shortcut for the Put Away command on the File menu.

Bypassing the Trash warning. In System 7, you normally get a warning message when you empty the Trash, telling you how many items are in there and how much disk space they occupy. If you're sure you want to empty the Trash, just press the Option key while you choose Empty Trash. You won't see an ellipsis after Empty Trash (Empty Trash...) in the Special menu because no dialog box will come up.

To turn off the warning message completely, select the Trash icon and press Command-I for Get Info. Then uncheck the Warn before emptying box (see Figure 1-7) and press Command-W to close the dialog box.

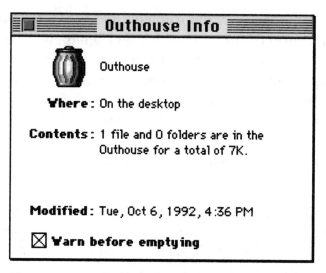

Figure 1-7: Uncheck the Warn before emptying box
to suppress the Trash's warning dialog box.

Yes, I know I've gotten cute in Figure 1-7; you'll see how to rename your Trash and all the messages about it in Chapter 4, "Customizing Your Desktop." Stay tuned.

A Trash trap. In System 7, if you're trying to copy files onto an old floppy and you keep getting a message that there's not enough room, check to see if you've left something in the Trash. System 7 doesn't empty the Trash until you tell it to, and the same holds true for floppies and other removable media. It's easy to throw out a few files and then forget to empty the Trash.

You can get a freeware program called TrashChute if you want your Trash to work the way it did in System 6, when it got emptied automatically. For this and other neat Trash shareware utilities, see *The Mac Shareware 500* (Ventana Press, 1992).

MORE FINDER TRICKS

And here are a few eclectic Finder tricks that quite simply wouldn't be easily categorized anywhere else. In this section, you'll find dialog box tricks as well as tips for using windows (the lowercase kind, of course) and your mouse.

You can open several documents at a time from the Finder and control the order in which they open. Applications open documents in the order you select them in the Finder. So if you're highlighting several documents to open from the Finder and you want a particular one to be on top, after all the others have opened, make sure you select it *last*, just before you choose Open from the Finder's File menu or press Command-O.

Thanks to Robert Gibson, Ontario, Canada.

Try opening by dragging and dropping. With System 7, you can drag a document's icon onto an application's icon and drop it to open the document. Just click and hold over the icon you want to open, drag it onto the application you want to use to open the document (until the application becomes highlighted), and release your mouse button. This may be obvious, but what's not obvious is that often you can open a document in a program that didn't create it by using this trick. For example, if you drag a TeachText document icon to the Microsoft Word icon and drop it, the document will open in Word.

Thanks to Robert Gibson, Ontario, Canada. Robert loves Finder tricks.

Stopping opening! The magic shortcut Command-period will abort an opening document if you suddenly decide midway through opening it that you don't want to open it after all.

Hidden ways to navigate the Finder. You can Command-click on a window's title to display a pop-up menu that shows the folders leading back to the main disk folder—on your hard disk, that's the hard disk itself. For a quick trip back to another folder above the one you're in, Command-click on the folder's name in the title bar, drag to the name of the folder you want to reach, and release the mouse button.

Also, shortcuts lurk in Open and Save As dialog boxes. Clicking the Desktop button in the Open or Save As dialog will take you to the desktop, obviously. But you can click on the downward-pointing arrowhead next to the name of the folder you're looking in to see a pop-up menu listing the folders that will take you back to the main disk level—or to the desktop as well. And here's another neat trick: click on the tiny icon of your hard disk in an Open or Save As dialog to go directly to the main level of that disk. (Sorry, this trick doesn't work with floppies.) Click that icon again to go to the desktop. Voodoo.

Use Command-W to close an open window. This neat keyboard shortcut closes the active open window not only in the Finder, but in most Mac programs and dialog boxes, too.

A very handy use for it is when you're searching for a file in System 7, using the Find command. If you're looking for something with, say, "chapter" in it, often you'll be taken to a window that has Chapter 1, Chapter 2, Chapter 3 and so on up to Chapter 26 or whatever, but those chapters in that folder aren't the "chapters" you're looking for; the ones you want are in a completely different folder. Just press Command-W to close that window and then the Finder will go on searching with Command-G (for Find Again) starting with the *next* folder.

Hide windows for faster performance. In System 7, use the Application menu and choose Hide Others so you'll see only the windows of the program you're working in. This speeds up your Mac's performance, especially with virtual memory on, because hidden windows (that would normally be visible in the background) no longer have to be redrawn each time you rearrange your foreground windows or close a dialog box. It also reduces the amount of desktop clutter you have to look at.

One drawback to Hide Others is that you have to remember to select it every time you switch from one program to another. An easy shortcut is to simply press the Option key while you select the next program to switch to from the Applications menu. This will automatically reveal the windows for the application you're switching to while at the same time hiding the windows from the application you just left.

Change the Window color to Black & White. To speed up the Finder and get System 6-style windows (without three-dimensional scroll bars), open the Color control panel and choose Black & White for the Window color. This will make your windows black-and-white while leaving everything else in color. Of course, drawing color icons slows the Finder down, so to see an even greater increase in the Finder's speed, go to the Monitors control panel and set your color monitor to Black & White.

Mouse hung up? Here's a voodoo trick. If you've got Easy Access in your System Folder, you may still be able to save a document if your mouse freezes. Instead of shutting down your Mac, just press the Shift key five times in a row. Then press Command-Shift-Clear. Now you can use the numeric keypad to control the mouse and save the document you were working on. See Chapter 5, "Disk & Drive Tricks," for more details about the amazing Easy Access—it isn't just for those who can't (or don't want to) use a mouse.

Copying in the background. With System 7, you can copy files in the background while you work in another program. The trick is to start the program you want to work in before you begin copying files, because once you start the copy process, you can't start another program. You can switch to another program that's already running, though, so launch any programs you might want to work in before you begin a monster copy or backup session.

Moving unsightly dialog boxes. If System 7's Copy, Find and Trash dialog boxes are usually just where you don't want them—obscuring the part of the screen you want to see, such as the disks you've got mounted or Finder windows that are open—drag them by their title bars to another part of the screen. The next time you use one of these dialog boxes, it'll open in the new position.

Hitting that tiny radio button or check box in a dialog box.
The secret is: you don't have to. Just click on the text next to
the button or the box to turn the selection on or off.

Getting to the desktop—and to another drive. In System 6, to
get to the desktop you have to click the Drive button in Open
and Save As dialog boxes (and in other directory dialog boxes, too).
In System 7, you can click the Desktop button to go to the desktop,
where you can choose another drive. Command-D is a nice hidden
shortcut for this. In fact, all the buttons in directory dialog boxes
have keyboard shortcuts. The secret to finding them? Press the Command key to see them (see Figure 1-8).

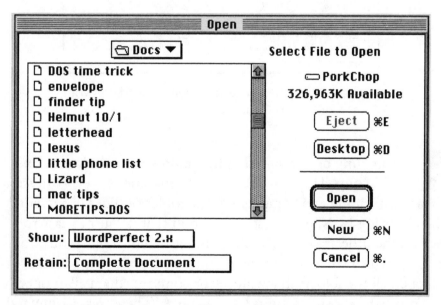

Figure 1-8: Press the Command key to see keyboard shortcuts in
directory dialog boxes.

Clicking on the tiny disk icon next to the name of the disk will
take you to the desktop, too.

Use Geneva for your fastest Finder font. Although you can
choose other fonts as your Finder font by using the Views
control panel (see Figure 1-9), keep it Geneva to get the most speed

out of your Mac. Choosing a different TrueType or ATM font can slow things down, although it's usually not a major difference in speed.

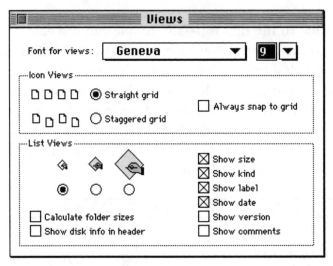

Figure 1-9: For the quickest screen draws, keep your Finder font set to Geneva.

Expanding or compressing the folders in a window in one fell swoop. There are a couple of little-known keyboard short-cuts for expanding and compressing the folder outlines in a window when Viewing by Name. Personally, I find that it's just as easy to click on the little arrowheads to expand or compress individual fold-ers as I need to see what's inside them, but these keyboard shortcuts will open all the folders in a window or compress them all at once.

To use the shortcuts, press Command-A. Then press Command-Option-Right arrow to expand the folders in the window or Com-mand-Option-Left arrow to compress them all at once.

Option-click on a window's close box to close all open Finder windows. Remember this one! System 7 has so many keyboard shortcuts, but this one's really handy. Option-click on any one window's close box, and all your open windows go zipping closed and you're looking at a clean, uncluttered Finder.

For a keyboard shortcut, use Option-Command-W. That closes all open windows, too (try it and see).

Don't calculate folder sizes unless you need them. In System 7, you can use the Views control panel to have the Finder continuously calculate the size of each folder and show it to you automatically (see Figure 1-10). But calculating each folder's size can slow down your Mac, too. So don't use this feature unless you really need to continuously keep track of folder sizes. Turn it off and on selectively. If you only occasionally need to check the size of a specific folder, highlight it and Get Info (Command-G) on it instead. Its size will appear in its Get Info box, regardless of whether you have your Mac set to calculate folder sizes.

Name	Size	Kind	Label	Last Modified
▷ ☐ Icon stuff	280K	folder	—	Sat, Sep 26, 1992, 8:46 AM
☐ INVOICE.DOC	7K	document	—	Fri, Jul 3, 1992, 11:06 AM
◈ LaserWriter Utility	280K	application program	—	Thu, Aug 8, 1991, 12:00 PM
☐ LETTER	20K	WordPerfect docu...	—	Sat, Oct 3, 1992, 8:51 AM
▷ ☐ Macintosh Electronic Ref...	3,114K	folder	—	Tue, Apr 28, 1992, 7:08 PM
▷ ☐ Macintosh® Basics	1,255K	folder	—	Tue, Apr 28, 1992, 7:08 PM

PorkChop

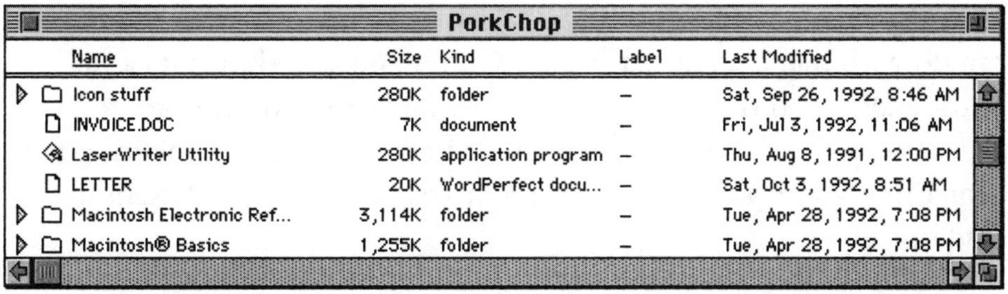

Figure 1-10: Notice that even the folders in this illustration have a size shown, when normally only a dash (—) is given for a folder's size.

You can drag folders to your System Folder, too. You probably already know that System 7 lets you drag control panels, extensions, fonts and so forth to the System Folder, where it magically figures out where they belong (this feature is called, appropriately enough, the Helping Hand). Well, you can drag entire folders to the System Folder, too, and the invisible Helping Hand will store its contents appropriately. Just drag a folder of fonts (a suitcase, too), or a folder of control panels or extensions, and it will send the items to the appropriate folder inside the System Folder. (But it only searches one folder level deep.) If all the items in the folder were moved to other folders within the System Folder, the original folder will be deleted. If the Helping Hand can't find an appropriate spot for one or more items, it leaves them in the original folder on the main level of the System Folder.

If there are only suitcases in the folder, you may see a message that the suitcase shouldn't be deleted because it contains items that are in use—but don't believe it. The suitcases will be deleted and the folder will remain.

Thanks to Eric Apgar, Apple Worldwide Technical Assistance.

MOVING ON

We've covered a pretty wide range of subjects in this chapter, all the way from easy stuff like closing and hiding windows to some really mind-boggling tricks you can do with aliases and white boxes. The next chapter, "Menu Magic," takes a look at another basic part of the Mac: the menu system. You'll see all sorts of neat voodoo tricks you can do with menus, like setting up Command-key shortcuts and putting aliases in the Apple menu. So whether you're hungry for more tricks like the ones we've covered here or you're hankering for something more powerful still, Finder tricks are just the beginning—read on.

CHAPTER TWO

MENU MAGIC

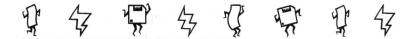

The first thing I did when I got my 128k Macintosh back in 1984 was sit down and create a cookbook of my favorite recipes, which I gave to family and friends for Christmas. It was all done in MacWrite and MacPaint. Looking at a copy of it today—tattered and greasy—I can remember what I went through to get it all done. No hard drive, just a single floppy drive! (Reading it now, years later, I also notice how much it looks like a bitmapped font sampler—each recipe has a different layout and design. Oh well, we all make that mistake....) I still use that cookbook today, especially at holiday time for looking up old favorite recipes when I'm working on a traditional family menu. Well, this chapter's about a different kind of menu—the kind you pull down and use to give commands to your Mac.

The Mac's Finder menu system differs slightly, depending on whether you're running System 6 or System 7. With System 7 you'll find Help and Application menus on the right side of the screen, and the Color menu has become the Label menu. Also in System 7, the File menu now features the Find command (formerly the Find File desk accessory) and a new Sharing command when file sharing is enabled. The View menu has also changed a bit, bringing you more flexibility in how you want to arrange files and folders in Finder windows. Otherwise the menus are pretty much the same (with a few subtleties, which we'll cover), so users of both systems will find lots of great tricks in this chapter.

We'll start with the left-most menu—the Apple menu—and work across to System 7's Application menu on the far right. At the end of the chapter, you'll find detailed instructions for the technique of adding Command-key shortcuts to the menus, both in System 6 and System 7.

APPLE MENU TRICKS

Before System 7 came along, the Apple menu simply presented a list of all the desk accessories you'd installed. With System 7, this menu is a lot more flexible: you can rename and reorder the items on it, and it will list all the items that are in your Apple Menu Items folder, including files that aren't desk accessories and even folders. The About the Finder option has become About This Macintosh, and it displays information about how your Mac and your open applications are using RAM. Since most of the neat things you can do with the Apple menu are possible only in System 7, System 6 users are out of luck in this section.

Put aliases in the Apple menu. Under System 7, put aliases of everything you use most often in the Apple menu—documents, programs, folders, file servers. You'll save real estate space on the desktop, and you won't have to hunt for the items you use every day. You can use aliases to organize your Apple menu, too, so that frequently used items are near the top and seldom-chosen options fall at the bottom of the list. (See the tip on using spaces in Apple menu item names below.)

Make an alias of the Apple Menu Items folder if you're often adding things to your Apple menu. An Apple Menu Items folder alias, kept conveniently on the desktop, can save you a lot of clicking for changing what shows up on your Apple menu.

You can also keep an alias of your Apple Menu Items folder in your Apple menu, so you can easily add things to and delete them from the Apple menu.

Keep an alias of the Apple Menu Items folder in your Startup Items folder. Wheels within wheels. If you do put an Apple Menu Items Folder alias in your Startup Items, the Apple Menu Items folder will open when you start up, and you can easily go straight to the menu items that you've handily put on the Apple menu.

Use the Apple symbol in your Apple menu items. Option-Shift-K produces the Apple symbol ( ). To group files together in your Apple menu, you can rename them and add the Apple symbol to the beginning of each of their names (see Figure 2-1). I use that symbol to move seldom-used items like the Puzzle to the bottom of the menu.

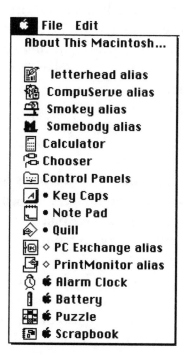

Figure 2-1: You can use all sorts of symbols to group items in your Apple menu.

Use diamonds and bullets in the Apple menu, too. Using a diamond in front of an item on the Apple menu is a nice touch, too. Press Option-Shift-V for a diamond, or get a bullet with Option-8 (see Figure 2-1).

Consider buying a "submenu" program for your Apple menu. While this tip gives you a powerful hierarchical menu system, it does require that you at least purchase a $15 shareware program. For the next-best free alternative, see the tip below on using spaces in your Apple menu. You can get third-party utility programs such as NowMenus (a part of Now Utilities), HAM (from Microseeds) or the shareware program MenuChoice (by Kerry Clendinning) that give you true hierarchical Apple menus—that is, at each point in your Apple menu where there are nested folders or multiple options, a submenu appears allowing you to immediately access the items inside that folder or application. For instance, you can stick an alias of your hard drive in your Apple menu and use the submenus to quickly navigate through several levels of nested folders to select exactly the item you want, without opening a single folder.

Use spaces in Apple menu item names to force them into different positions on the menu. Files whose names begin with a space are put at the top of the Apple menu's list. So use this trick to put the items you use most often near the top, where they're easier to reach.

For example, you might want a few often-used programs or folders to start off the menu. In Figure 2-2, you can see that I've forced several frequently used aliases to the top of the list: PC Exchange, Print Monitor, and my hard drives come before aliases for Compu-Serve and other things that I usually use when I first start my Mac. Begin the names of the top-of-the-list items with three spaces. For the next set of items—say, programs you use a lot—use two spaces at the beginning of each name. Start another group beginning with one space. The items you don't rename, or those that you name with

symbols, will appear at the bottom of the menu. You can get fancy
and use dividers, too, as I've done in Figure 2-3 (see the next trick).

You can also use sets of symbols, such as periods, to group items,
too. For example, you can start one set, say, of disk utility programs,
with ".." (like "..Disinfectant" and "..Disk First Aid") and another
set of desk accessories with "." (like ".Calculator" and ".Key Caps").
The ones with two periods come first, followed by the those that
begin with one period. The Mac will sort these sets alphabetically, so
you'll get each set in alphabetical order.

Or, if you're trying to force a new alphabetical order within one
set of items, use a period to bring that item to the top of its set. You
might want to get Word to the top of a list by beginning it with a
period, for example (see Figure 2-3). Those tiny dots hardly show at
all on the screen, so they're very convenient for reordering items.

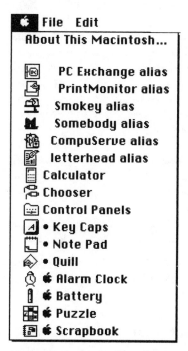

Figure 2-2: Arranging the
order of Apple menu items
is easy if you use spaces and
special characters.

Use dividers in your Apple menu. If you'd like an at-a-glance, neatly ordered Apple menu, put dividers between the categories of different items in the menu. Just add a few empty folders, judiciously named, to your Apple Menu Items folder. Use dashes for the name of one, bullets for the name of another, and diamonds for the name of a third. Then select each folder icon, press Command-I for Get Info, and paste one of those infamous white boxes over the folder's icon. (For more details on this trick, see Chapter 1, "Secrets of the Finder.")

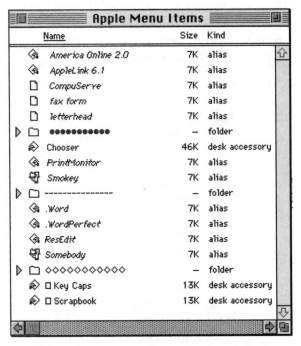

Figure 2-3: Putting dividers in your Apple menu makes it easier to find things you need quickly.

Color-code your Apple menu, too. You can use label colors to color-code your newly reordered Apple menu. This doesn't really add anything to its usefulness, but it's a nice touch.

Starting a big project? Put it on the Apple menu. By putting an alias of a new document in the Apple menu (perhaps at the top of the menu, too), you can easily find it to work on it every day. (You might consider putting it in the Startup Items folder, too.)

Keep an Applications folder in your Apple menu. If you put aliases of the programs you work with frequently in an Applications folder (or Games folder?) inside your Apple Menu Items folder, it'll be easy to find those programs (or games) by using the Apple menu.

If you put that Applications (or Games, or whatever) folder in your Startup Items folder instead of in your Apple Menu Items folder, it'll be open and available each time you start your Mac, no matter how you left Finder windows arranged.

Keep a Desktop folder in your Apple menu. If your screen is usually cluttered with windows and you have a hard time uncovering your hard drive and Trash icons, make a folder called Desktop and put it in your Apple menu. In the Desktop folder, put aliases of your hard drives—and the Trash, of course. Now you can easily find things or throw them away with a little help from the Apple menu.

Remember that you can Option-click on one window's close box (or press Command-Option-W) to close all the open Finder windows, if you get lost looking for a single, elusive window.

You don't have to keep control panels in the Control Panels folder—put them on the Apple menu. If there's a control panel you use a lot, make an alias for it and put it someplace where it's convenient, like out on the desktop or in the Apple menu. Or in both places. If you find that you're tuning your Mac's volume up and down frequently, maybe the Sound control panel is a good candidate for this trick.

With System 7, you get a new alert sound. There's a freebie alert sound in the System 7 Scrapbook file. Open the Scrapbook and scroll to the sound (you'll recognize it by the familiar icon that looks like a speaker with sound waves flowing out of it). If you'd like to hear the sound now, click on the Play Sound button. Copy the sound (just choose Copy from the File menu or press Command-C), open the Sound control panel and paste it. You'll be asked to give the sound a name. Be creative. The Quadra's freebie sound reminds me of a rusty tricycle hooter.

Get a free color world map, too. The System 7 Scrapbook also comes with a beautiful color world map. You can copy it from the Scrapbook to the Map control panel. Press Command-C when the color map is displayed; then open the Map control panel and press Command-V. You'll be asked if you want to replace the old map with the picture that's on the Clipboard, so click Replace.

Can't find the color map? If you can't find the map or new sound, here's what's happened. When you install System 7, the Installer doesn't touch your Scrapbook file if it finds one already there, left from System 6. To get the new map and beep, move your old Scrapbook out of your System Folder and then copy the System 7 Scrapbook into its place. Open the new Scrapbook; copy and paste the new sound and map into the Sound and Map control panels. Then, if there's anything in your old System 6 Scrapbook you'd like to keep, drag it back to the System Folder, replacing the new System 7 Scrapbook. Otherwise you can just trash the older Scrapbook and use the new one.

FILE MENU TRICKS

The File menu changed a bit from System 6 to System 7. The change I like best is a subtle one: new folders are called "untitled folder" and they appear where you can see them, instead of being called "Empty Folder" and popping up way up there in the Es instead of appearing in the Ns where one would rationally suppose a New Folder to appear. (I never did get used to that Empty Folder stuff. However, if you really want each new folder to be called a System 6-style "empty folder" instead of "untitled folder," it's possible. See Chapter 4, "Customizing Your Desktop.")

The tips in this section cover several commands on the File menu, but other File menu tips are discussed elsewhere. You'll find tips on the File menu's Sharing command in Chapter 8, "Connectivity Secrets," because it's used with networking, and you saw quite a few suggestions for using aliases back in Chapter 1. So we'll start by exploring the File menu's feature for finding things (after all, that's what the Finder's for). Although the Find command on System 7's File menu can be used to do all kinds of sophisticated searches, it's more limited in System 6 (where Find is a desk accessory), so there's only one lonely tip for you System 6 users. Sorry. Here it is.

Getting a found file to the desktop (System 6). I used System 6 for years without realizing that once a file's been found with the Find File desk accessory, a new Find File command appears on the menu bar. You can choose the Find File menus to select Move to Desktop so that the file appears on your desktop, ready for you to check and see if it's really the file you're looking for.

You can even highlight the newly found file and use the File menu's Put Away command (press Command-Y) to put it back where it came from when you're through with it—you don't have to remember which folder it was in. This can save you a lot of time if your file belongs in a folder several levels down, or worse, if you've forgotten just exactly where you stored it.

Refining your searches (System 7). Here's an idea of the kind of searching you can do in System 7. I should warn you that it may close or rearrange the views of a few of your Finder windows, but it doesn't change their position, and you can easily switch things back to the way they were once you've finished your search. This is a complicated trick, but it's an absent-minded person's best friend, so it's worth learning—I promise.

Say you're looking for a document, and all you remember about it is that it has "memo" in its name and you know the one you're looking for was created after February 16, 1993 (maybe you recall it was a memo you wrote a few days after a Valentine's Day party). It was a pretty short memo, too, so you can look for any documents that are smaller than 5k.

To search for the first criterion, press Command-F and click More Choices. Fill out the dialog box (see Figure 2-4) with the part of the name you're looking for (in this example, "memo"), pick the volume you want to search and check the all at once box.

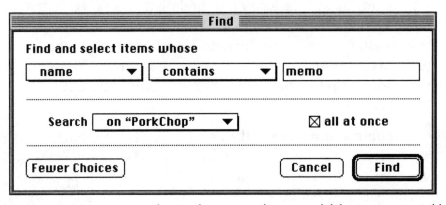

Figure 2-4: You can use the Find command's powerful features to quickly search for a specific file.

When the search is done, all the files that meet that criterion will be selected and the folder windows they're in will be opened, but you probably won't be able to see them all. Be sure not to click your mouse pointer anywhere, or you'll deselect all the newly found files, which you don't want to do yet (see the trap below). Now you can press Command-F again and search among those highlighted (or selected) files for the one that matches the date of creation of the file you're looking for. From the pop-up menus at the top of the Find dialog box, choose "date created" and "is after" and set the date to 2/16/93 by clicking on the date and changing it with the up and down arrows. Choose "the selected items" from the other pop-up menu and click OK (see Figure 2-5).

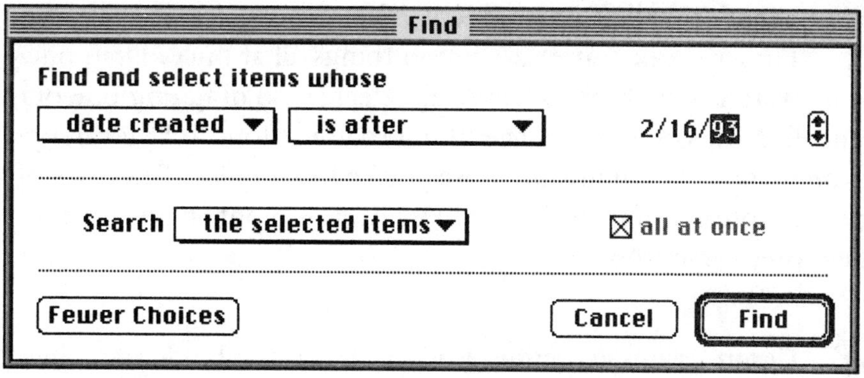

```
┌──────────────────────────────────────────────────────────────┐
│                             Find                               │
│ Find and select items whose                                   │
│   ┌─────────────────┐  ┌──────────────────┐                   │
│   │ date created  ▼ │  │ is after      ▼  │      2/16/93   ▲▼  │
│   └─────────────────┘  └──────────────────┘                   │
│ ···········································································  │
│        Search │  the selected items ▼ │      ☒ all at once    │
│ ···········································································  │
│   ┌──────────────┐                    ┌────────┐ ┌────────┐   │
│   │ Fewer Choices│                    │ Cancel │ │  Find  │   │
│   └──────────────┘                    └────────┘ └────────┘   │
└──────────────────────────────────────────────────────────────┘
```

Figure 2-5: You can search for a file with a specific creation date.

When you've got that list of found documents (which should be smaller than the last list), select "size" and "is less than" from the pop-up menus and enter **5k**. Again, choose "the selected items" from the pop-up menu and you'll narrow the field down to only a few items—probably just the one file you're looking for.

Don't click on a file or folder during a selective search. If you're in the middle of a complicated, multiple-criteria search and you click anywhere—on another file or folder icon, for example—you'll deselect all the files that have been found so far, wrecking the search scheme. So don't do it.

If you search for several criteria, you can't search more than one volume at a time. Normally, when you're performing a simple search using the plain-vanilla Find command (fewer choices mode), you can either limit the search to any single drive you've got mounted (like just your internal hard drive, for instance) or choose to include all drives you have access to—including the floppy drive, if there's a disk in it. Unfortunately the new, improved Finder won't let you search several disks at once if you're hunting for several criteria. You'll have to search first one disk and then the other.

Searching all at once. Here's the easy way to see what the Finder's found after it's found things all at once. Drag one of the items to the desktop. They're all selected, so dragging one drags them all. Now you can see everything that was found. You can open the ones you think might be those you're looking for. Select them again and press Command-Y (for Put Away) to put them all back where they came from.

Compressing expanded folders. When the Finder searches "all at once," it expands the folders where it finds items. Here's a neat trick for compressing them again: choose by Icon from the View menu; then go back to viewing by Name. The expanded folders will magically be compressed again.

The Finder doesn't search your System file. With Systems 6 and 7, you can't find screen fonts and sounds with the Finder because they're in your System file. But with System 7.1, which puts screen and printer fonts together into a Fonts folder, you can use the Find command to find them. The short of it: the Finder doesn't search the System file. (Naturally, if you use a third-part font utility like Suitcase, the Finder will be able to locate your screen fonts in their respective folders.)

Use Find before you do batch copying or deleting. Haven't you ever wanted to be able to copy (or delete) all the files created by one program, or all the files with QTR in their names?

With System 7's improved Find command, you can do just that. Click More Choices and search for all the files whose kind contains MacPaint, or whose name contains QTR (or whatever else tickles your fancy). When all the files are located, they'll all be selected, and you can drag just one of them to the Trash to delete them all or press Command-D to duplicate them all at once.

You can use the Find command to do backups without buying a backup program. Lots of people spend big money on fancy incremental backup programs, and in many cases this is justified. But if you're doing quasi-recreational work on your Mac or working on something that doesn't have to be backed up, but you'd still like to make a reliable, regular backup of it, you can use the Find command for good incremental backups. First, back up your entire hard drive (let's say to an external hard drive), and then move all the files into a single folder (with no nested subfolders) on that external drive. The next day (or whenever you next back up), use Find to search for all files of any kind modified since the day before (or whenever). This will collect not just all documents, but all files (like data, preferences, resources, and so forth) that were modified since you last backed up. Copy them to the folder on the external drive that has all your files in it, replacing any files with the same name (since they'll be old, out-of-date files). Then do another search to find all at once all the files created since the last backup. Copy them to the same folder on the Syquest. This will add all the new files to your backup drive. This is a fairly reliable (and free) scheme for backing up your files on a regular basis without having to copy your entire hard drive.

Find TeachText! And delete all but one. Just about every time you buy a new application, TeachText is included on its disk so you can read that application's Read Me files, and it usually gets copied onto your hard disk when you run the installer or copy the application disk. Why not take the time now to search for all those extra TeachTexts and get rid of them? You only need one TeachText. (Remember, search for them all at once and then drag one to the Trash; like lemmings, the others will follow.)

Option-Open to open a file and close the active window. If you press the Option key when you choose Open (or press Option-Command-O), you'll open the folder or file that's selected and close the active window at the same time. This is a neat trick for keeping your desktop uncluttered.

Closing all the windows. Press Option as you select the File menu, and you'll see a Close All command (instead of a Close Window command) that will close all the open windows. You can also do the same by Option-clicking in any window's close box or pressing Option-Command-W.

TRICKS FOR THE VIEW MENU

System 7 added more functionality to the View menu by adding a Views control panel that lets you specify what you want to see when you View.

Use System 7's Views control panel to change your icon arrangements. The Views control panel that comes with System 7 (see Figure 2-6) lets you do an important thing: get rid of overlapping icon titles. Isn't it irritating not to be able to read them? Just use the Views control panel and click Staggered grid. Click Always snap to grid if you like things neat and orderly—whenever you move an icon, it will be automatically integrated into a grid alignment that matches all your other icons.

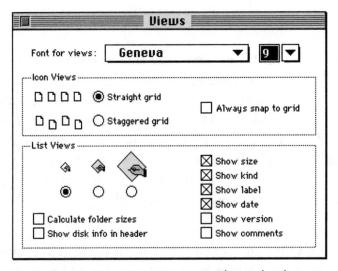

Figure 2-6: System 7's Views control panel enhances the power of the View menu.

If you've turned on Always snap to grid, you can Command-drag an icon to put it exactly where you want it, not on the grid (see the next tip).

Turn off the invisible grid (System 6). In System 7, it's easy to turn the invisible grid that icons "snap to" as you drag them around (just use the Views control panel). In System 6, turning off the grid is a little harder. You can get a freeware program that will do this (check CompuServe and other services for LAYOUT, by Mike O'Connor, one of my favorite tipsters), or you can use the "easy fix"—rearrange your icons with the Command key held down, thus temporarily bypassing the snap-to-grid feature.

Squinting at the Finder? Switch fonts with the Views control panel. Most people don't realize that they can use the handy Views control panel to change the font that's being used by the Finder to display file names, sizes and other data. You can change the font size, too. So if you find that things like icon names are hard to read, try a combination like 12-pt New York, as Figure 2-7 shows.

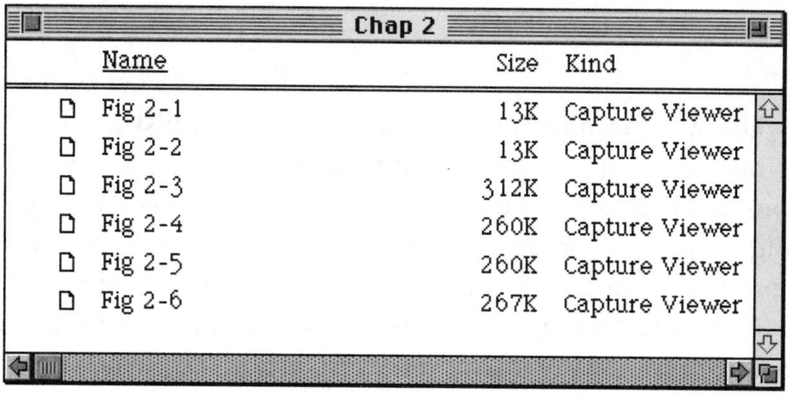

Chap 2		
Name	Size	Kind
Fig 2-1	13K	Capture Viewer
Fig 2-2	13K	Capture Viewer
Fig 2-3	312K	Capture Viewer
Fig 2-4	260K	Capture Viewer
Fig 2-5	260K	Capture Viewer
Fig 2-6	267K	Capture Viewer

Figure 2-7: Try new font and point size combinations in the Finder.

Which font size to use? Choose a font size that appears in outline form in the Views control panel. They're the ones that will look best on the screen.

Change views by clicking on the column heads. In System 7, you can switch views of Finder windows just by clicking on the heads at the tops of columns; you don't have to make a trip to the View menu at all. Click Size to sort the window listing by size, Last Modified to see the files you worked with most recently at the top, and so on; you'll know which view you're in because its corresponding name will be underlined. A real time-saver. Note that for this trick to work, you can't be viewing a window's contents by Icon or Small Icon—you must first switch to one of the other options.

TRICKS FOR THE LABEL MENU

The Label menu replaces System 6's Color menu. You either use it or ignore it (which lots of folks do); a lot of people think it's a worthwhile tool for organizing your files. If you use it, here are some tricks for it. See Chapter 10, "In Trouble?", for a trap that using the Label menu can cause.

Use the Labels control panel to change the colors on System 7's Label menu. I mention this one here because I had a hard time figuring it out. The Labels control panel is also the place where you change the system of labels you use.

Use a color-matching system for icons and disks. If you're neat and tidy, you may want to set up a color-matching system for icons and disk labels. For example, you could choose yellow for painting/drawing programs, red for system/utility stuff, blue for word processing, and so forth. Use the Labels menu (System 7) or Color (System 6) to assign colors to icons; then buy sets of disk labels in the right colors. A very neat way to see at a glance which disks hold what kinds of files.

Thanks to Jorn Knuttila, Bemidji, Minnesota.

To change the set of colors used for labels, click on a color and then choose a new color from the color wheel (see Figure 2-8).

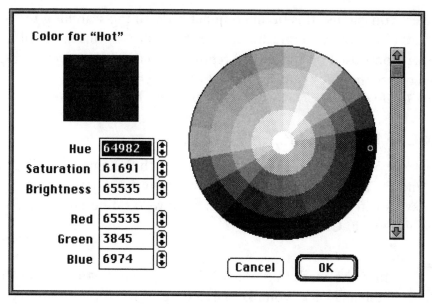

Figure 2-8: Use the color wheel (also called the color picker) to choose new label colors in System 7.

Although you can choose from 16 million colors on the color wheel, you'll see only 256 of them in the Finder unless you've got a 24-bit video card. See Chapter 6, "Miscellaneous Voodoo Tricks," for more interesting trivia about using the color wheel.

Use labels to help categorize, find and sort fonts. You can use the Label menu to help categorize similar files within single folders. For instance, if you work with fonts a lot and you're constantly gathering all your sans-serif faces, or scrounging around for all your display faces, you know what a pain it can be to make sure you've found all of them. Nested folders aren't always the answer (that often just complicates the matter), and you shouldn't add spaces or special characters to font names, since it can hinder their operation with other programs. Why not use the Label menu to categorize your fonts?

You might color all your sans-serif fonts blue and label them "Sans Serif." You can label all your display faces accordingly and color them orange, and so forth. Another method is to label fonts (or other files, for that matter) by job, client or whatever other subjective scheme you prefer. You can use this tip in conjunction with the searching techniques discussed earlier in this chapter to gather, for instance, all the display fonts used on the annual report project, without ever having to separate those fonts from the rest of your collection.

Thanks to Spring Davis-Charles, Durham, North Carolina.

TRICKS FOR THE SPECIAL MENU

Well, the Special menu looks the same in both Systems 6 and 7, but behind the scenes, there are big differences in the way the Trash works, as you saw in Chapter 1. Clean Up works differently, too, as you also saw in Chapter 1.

Move the Trash in System 7. With System 7, you can put the Trash anywhere you like. Drag it up to the top of the screen next to the files you're trashing to cut down on drag time.

Can't Trash a folder? Sometimes the Trash won't let you delete a folder. It keeps telling you that a file was busy, or that a folder wasn't empty, even though you know that's not the case. What's usually happening is that you haven't quit the program that created the document. You can throw the document away, but the Finder won't let you delete the folder that contains it.

To get around this, open the folder, select everything in it with Command-A, and throw everything in the Trash; then choose Empty Trash. Now you should be able to trash the folder, too. If that does not work, see Chapter 10 for heavier-duty trash-nuking techniques.

To delete a locked file, press Option while you drag it to the Trash. This saves you having to respond to a dialog box or unlock the file and is much, much faster.

TRICKS FOR THE HELP MENU

There's not much to say about the Help menu except two things. First, check out the Finder shortcuts if you haven't done so already.

There are lots of neat, useful shortcuts you can use in the Finder. Second, turn on Balloon Help and find a few Easter Eggs, as described in my favorite chapter, Chapter 3, "Hoodoo Voodoo."

Balloon Help is good for something. Most of the time, all Balloon Help is good for is getting in your way. But if you turn on Show Balloons and go to the Apple menu and choose About This Macintosh, you'll be able to see how much memory each application is using by clicking on the bar graphs.

TRICKS FOR THE INTERNATIONAL MENU

The international version of System 7.1 includes the International menu, a third icon at the far-right end of the Finder's menu bar. It indicates which keyboard layout you're using. In Figure 2-9, you can see that I'm using the U.S. keyboard layout.

Figure 2-9: The International menu shows which keyboard layout you're using.

Bring up the International menu in System 7. To get the International menu even if you're not running the international version of System 7.1, use ResEdit on a copy of your System file—be sure to work only on a copy of any file you alter with ResEdit—that way, if something goes wrong, you can always go back to the original. (For more on ResEdit, see the sidebar in Chapter 4, "Customizing Your Desktop." Open the itlc resource (see Figure 2-10) and double-click on the line that reads 0   48. Then scroll to Always show icon (see Figure 2-11) and click the 1 radio button. Save and exit from ResEdit. Rename the System file something else, like Old System, and then rename the System copy as System. Restart, and you've got the International menu. Whenever you're working on the System file in ResEdit, you might want to save the old, untouched copy under a different name and in a different folder for a while, just in case your Mac starts misbehaving and you think it might be a result of your ResEdit work.

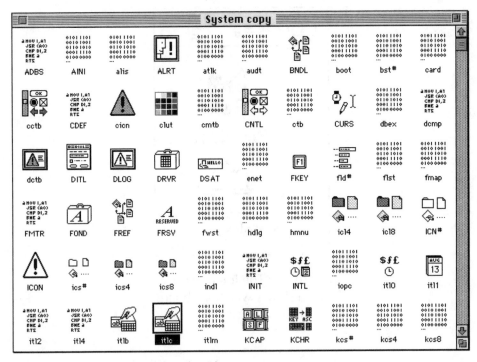

Figure 2-10: Double-click on the itlc resource.

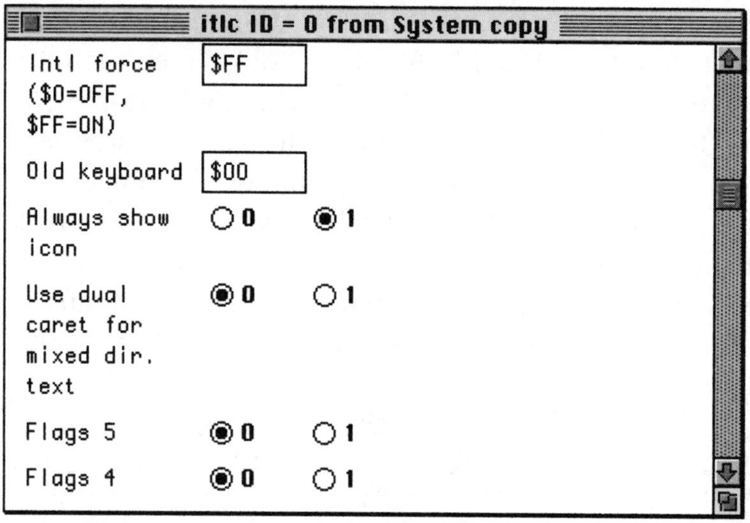

```
┌─────────────────────────────────────────────┐
│ ▣▤▤▤▤▤  itlc ID = 0 from System copy  ▤▤▤▤▤ │
├─────────────────────────────────────────────┤
│  Intl force    │$FF        │              ▲  │
│  ($0=OFF,                                    │
│  $FF=ON)                                     │
│                                              │
│  Old keyboard  │$00        │                 │
│                                           ▒  │
│  Always show    ○ 0    ◉ 1                   │
│  icon                                        │
│                                              │
│  Use dual       ◉ 0    ○ 1                   │
│  caret for                                   │
│  mixed dir.                                  │
│  text                                        │
│                                              │
│  Flags 5        ◉ 0    ○ 1                   │
│                                           ▼  │
│  Flags 4        ◉ 0    ○ 1                ▣  │
└─────────────────────────────────────────────┘
```

Figure 2-11: Find the Always show icon buttons and click on 1.

If you've got other keyboard layouts installed, such as a foreign-language keyboard for typing in Greek, you'll be able to quickly switch to them by using this colorful menu bar icon showing the country's flag instead of opening the Keyboard control panel .

Switching international keyboards (System 7.1). The big news about System 7.1 is that it lets you easily switch to a different language (of course, you have to purchase the language module from Apple first). To use the WorldScript feature (which is only available if you're running System 7.1), drag the Text control panel, the Script Switcher control panel and the WorldScript icon from the System 7.1 installation disks to your System Folder. The WorldScript 2 icon is for Japanese, Korean and Chinese—the double-byte languages, where each character requires two bytes of information to represent it. The WorldScript 1 icon is for the rest—Greek, Thai, Arabic and so on. Then drag the script file and the font suitcase for the language you want to your System Folder.

When you restart, you may think something's wrong, because your menus will be in English. But if you look closely, you'll see that there's a new flag between the Help and the Application menus showing the nationality of the language the Mac has switched to and that dates, times, and so on in Finder windows are in new formats (Figure 2-12 shows my other Mac, which is switched to Greek—check the dates and times). Check the Key Caps desk accessory to see that you've really switched to the new language; press Shift, Option and Command to see which additional characters are available.

	Somebody				
Name		**Size**	**Kind**	**Label**	**Last Modified**
ResEdit		622K	application program	—	06 Δεκεμ 1990, 12:00
▷ System 7.1 art		—	folder	—	26 Αυγου 1992, 09:53
▷ System Folder		—	folder	—	10 Σεπτ 1992, 17:05
System Picker 1.0b11		30K	application program	—	14 Αυγου 1992, 08:49
TeachText		36K	application program	—	25 Απριλ 1991, 12:00
▷ WordPerfect 2.1		—	folder	—	28 Αυγου 1992, 09:17

Figure 2-12: Switching to the Greek keyboard reveals dates and times in Greek characters.

TRICKS FOR THE APPLICATIONS MENU

I personally find System 7's Applications menu tiresome because I have to mouse up to that tiny icon to switch to another program if I can't see its window. There are a couple of freeware programs that handily replace that Applications menu. The first is named ApplicationMenu, and it's available from America Online's Mac Shareware 500 library or directly from its author, Larry Rosenstein, 182 Muir Avenue, Santa Clara, CA 95051. When you press a hot key combination and click anywhere on the screen with the mouse, ApplicationMenu gives you a pop-up menu of the programs that are running. It works with System 6, too.

The second is Applicon, and it's only for System 7. You can get it on America Online or from its author, Rick Holzgrafe, Semicolon Software, PO Box 371, Cupertino, CA 95015. Applicon shows a NeXT-style tile for each program you've got running, so you don't have to remember which programs you've started—you can simply click on a tile to switch to another program.

Both of these utilities are discussed in more detail in *The Mac Shareware 500* from Ventana Press. I mention them here because they're free, and because I don't like using the Application menu.

Use keyboard shortcuts instead of the Application menu's Hide and Show commands. Instead of mousing up to the Applications menu to hide programs, use these neat shortcuts:

- Option-click on another open application window to hide the application you're working in and make the other application active.

- Option-click on the desktop to hide the application you're working in and make the Finder active.

Likewise, if you hold the Option key down as you switch between applications using the Application menu, the application you're leaving will become hidden as you switch to the new one.

Flashing Application menu? Weird symbols on the menu bar? If the PrintMonitor icon in the upper-right corner of the screen flashes, PrintMonitor needs your attention (you may not have enough free memory to print, or your printer may be out of paper). If you see a U-shaped icon there, Easy Access is on.

At the other end of the menu bar, if the Apple menu flashes, it means the Alarm Clock is ringing. If you see the Finder icon (a compact Mac) flashing while you're working in an application, it means that something has happened in the Finder that requires your attention (the Finder will sometimes close windows, for instance, to free up extra memory).

CREATING COMMAND-KEY SHORTCUTS FOR MENUS

It's easy to add keyboard shortcuts to the Finder's menus if you have ResEdit. (Okay, it's relatively easy. If you want the really easy solution, get a macro program like QuicKeys or Tempo II, or a shareware program like Finder 7 Menus.) For example, you might want to designate Make Alias as Command-M. I can't live without Shut Down as Command-K (for Kill or Kwit or Kay); it saves me reaching for the mouse as that last step. (If you'd like more information on what ResEdit is, how it works and where you can find a copy, see the sidebar in Chapter 4.)

Whether you're running System 6 or System 7, be sure to edit a copy of the Finder, not the one that's running the show. Believe me: you can make changes that you don't intend to, no matter how careful you are. Keep that emergency disk handy for restarts, too. See Chapter 10 for details on how to make an emergency startup floppy that you can use to access your Mac's hard drive in case you make a mistake using ResEdit (it also comes in handy in other situations).

General rules for editing the Finder: highlight the Finder in the System Folder and press Command-D to duplicate it. Make a new folder somewhere outside the System Folder with Command-N (to hold the "good" Finder later on while you test your new one). Then use ResEdit to work your magic on the Finder copy. When you're done, save your changes and quit ResEdit. Drag the old, "safe" Finder to the untitled folder and rename the altered copy of the Finder as just "Finder," placing it in the System Folder. Now restart. If all goes well, you can later trash the untitled folder with the former Finder in it, once you've had a chance to test out your new, improved version.

Which Command-key equivalents are available? If you try any of these tricks, be sure not to assign keys that are already being used. For instance, don't try to assign Command-A to the Make Alias command, since that key combination is already used for Select All. Here are the keys that the Finder has assigned:

Assigned Key Combinations

Combination	Meaning
Command-A	Select All
Command-C	Copy
Command-D	Duplicate
Command-E	Eject Disk
Command-F	Find (System 7)
Command-G	Find Again (System 7)
Command-I	Get Info
Command-N	New Folder
Command-O	Open
Command-P	Print
Command-V	Paste
Command-W	Close
Command-X	Cut
Command-Y	Put Away
Command-Z	Undo

Here are the keys that are normally unassigned, so you can use these for your own shortcuts:

Unassigned Key Combinations

Combination	Combination
Command-B	Command-Q
Command-H	Command-R
Command-J	Command-S
Command-K	Command-T
Command-L	Command-U
Command-M	

Again, with either system, always work on a copy of the Finder—not the real thing. In fact, version 2.1 and later of ResEdit won't even let you work with the active copy of the Finder.

Keep a spare Finder on hand. One other general rule: once you've tweaked a Finder the way you like it, make a copy of it and store it on a floppy so you can reinstall it later without repeating your tedious editing when—not if—the Finder becomes corrupted.

System 6: Changing Finder menus. If you have System 6, editing the Finder's menus is a snap. All you need to do is use ResEdit on a copy of the Finder, open the MENU resource, open the menu you want to edit (see Figure 2-13), and click on the menu item you want to assign a shortcut to. You'll see a Cmd-Key box (see Figure 2-14). Type the key you want to assign to the function in that Cmd-Key box. Here I've assigned Command-R to Restart.

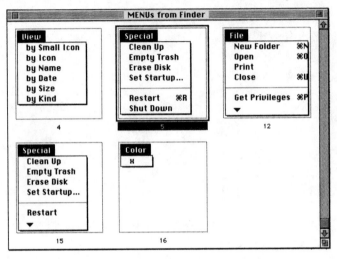

Figure 2-13: Under System 6, use ResEdit to open a copy of the Finder and pick the menu you want to edit.

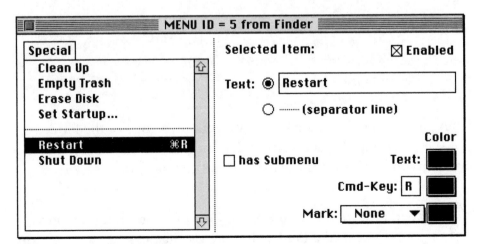

Figure 2-14: Type the new command letter you want to use in the Cmd-Key box.

Then, of course, save your changes, exit ResEdit, swap Finders as outlined above, and restart.

System 7: Changing Finder menus. With System 7, it gets harder. The Menu resource becomes the fmenu resource, and ResEdit opens it in hexadecimal format, so you have to type in hex code to make changes. Fortunately, Res Edit will convert what you type into hex—if you do it exactly right. "Exactly right" means that you replace one character with another (you don't delete it and then type the new one) and that you press the Shift key to get the capital letter, not the lowercase one. (Now you know one reason why bugs exist in computer programs!)

In the System Folder, locate the Finder and press Command-D to duplicate it. Now go on to the next tips, which will show you how to assign specific key shortcuts.

Assigning Command-M to Make Alias (System 7). Start ResEdit and open the copy you made of the Finder. Then double-click on the fmenu resource (see Figure 2-15). Locate ID 1252 and double-click on it. In the column on the right (see Figure 2-16) you'll see the text used in some Finder menu items, such as New Window and Put Away. Locate Make Alias and then replace the third character before the M in Make Alias with a capital M. Warning: select only the third character before the M so that it reads "M box box Make Alias." (Look at New Window or Put Away to see the pattern.) If you don't replace exactly the right character, your Mac may not reboot with that Finder, and you'll have to start up from the Disk Tools disk, or from your emergency startup floppy.

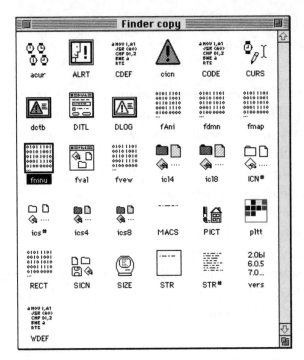

Figure 2-15: Under System 7, copy the Finder and open the fmenu resource.

000078	1002 0000 0853 6861	00000Sha
000080	7269 6E67 C900 7364	ring...0sd
000088	7570 1002 4400 0944	up00D00D
000090	7570 6C69 6361 7465	uplicate
000098	7361 6C69 1002 0000	sali0000
0000A0	0A4D 616B 6520 416C	0Make Al
0000A8	6961 7300 7370 7574	ias0sput
0000B0	1002 5900 0850 7574	00Y00Put
0000B8	2041 7761 7900 7878	Away0xx
0000C0	7830 0000 0000 012D	x000000-
0000C8	6669 6E64 8110 4600	findÅ0F0
0000D0	0546 696E 64C9 6669	0Find...fi
0000D8	6E6E 8100 4700 0A46	nnÅ0G00F
0000E0	696E 6420 4167 6169	ind Agai

fmnu ID = 1252 from Finder cop!

Figure 2-16: Open ID 1252 to add a keyboard shortcut to the Make Alias command.

Now save; then quit ResEdit. Again, follow the directions above for swapping Finder files and saving a "fail-safe" copy and restart your Mac. Now you should see Command-M as a keyboard shortcut for Make Alias listed on the File menu (see Figure 2-18 for an example).

Assigning Command-K to Shut Down (System 7). You may ask "Why Command-K?" I used that letter for an obvious reason, but you can think of it as Command-Kwit or Command-Kill. I never could get Command-S to work: my Apple menu disappeared when I assigned Command-S to Shut Down. I guess it's voodoo.

This shortcut is really useful. It's the trickiest one, too, because of how the fmenu resource is displayed. Here's how to do it.

Open the Finder copy with ResEdit. Then open the fmenu resource and ID 1255, which is the Special menu. Scroll to the very end of the box. Line 000088 in the left column is the Shut Down part (see Figure 2-17; it just says "shut").

Highlight the third character before the last s in the far-right column and type a capital K. You'll see over in the column immediately to the left that two of the characters change to 4B. That's because 4B is hexadecimal for K.

Quit ResEdit, saving your changes. Swap Finders and restart. Now you should see Command-K next to Shut Down on the Special menu (see Figure 2-18).

```
▓▣▓ fmnu ID = 1255 from Finder cop!
000028    7074 8006 0000 0C45   ptÄ000DE
000030    6D70 7479 2054 7261   mpty Tra
000038    7368 C900 7878 7830   sh...0xxx0
000040    0000 0000 012D 7365   00000-se
000048    6A65 1002 4500 0A45   je00E00E
000050    6A65 6374 2044 6973   ject Dis
000058    6B00 7365 7261 1002   k0sera00
000060    0000 0B45 7261 7365   000Erase
000068    2044 6973 6BC9 7878    Disk...xx
000070    7830 0000 0000 012D   x000000-
000078    7265 7374 8100 5200   restÄ0R0
000080    0752 6573 7461 7274   0Restart
000088    7368 7574 8104 4B00   shutÄ0K0
000090    0153                  0S
```

Figure 2-17: Locate the Shut Down string at the bottom of
the far right column.

Figure 2-18: The new Special menu
now has a keyboard shortcut for
Restart (covered later) and Shut
Down.

Other command-key shortcuts (System 7). Here are some other shortcuts you may want to assign.

To add Command-R to Restart, locate the line 000078 in ID 1255, the same ID as the Shut Down command. Find Restart (in line 000080), highlight the third character back (a box), and type R. Hex for R is 52, so you'll see the four zeroes in the column to the left change from 0000 to 0052. Now quit and save, swap Finders and restart, just as above.

How about Command-T for Empty Trash? Find line 000028 in the same ID (1255), count back three characters before Empty, and type T (hex: 54). For Command-U for Clean Up, find line 00018 (still in the same ID window), highlight the third box before Clean, and type U (hex: 55).

Table 2.1 Hexadecimal-Alphabetic Equivalents

Letter	Hexadecimal	Letter	Hexadecimal
A	41	N	4E
B	42	O	4F
C	43	P	50
D	44	Q	51
E	45	R	52
F	46	S	53
G	47	T	54
H	48	U	55
I	49	V	56
J	4A	W	57
K	4B	X	58
L	4C	Y	59
M	4D	Z	5A

Table 2.1 shows the hexadecimal equivalents for the uppercase alphabet, just in case you want to experiment with more command shortcuts.

You can try highlighting the appropriate characters in ResEdit and typing in the straight hex, but I haven't had as much success with that method as typing in the letter I want and letting the Mac figure it out.

MOVING ON

Now that you've seen tricks for all the menus from Apple to Application, get ready for a lot more fun stuff in Chapter 3, "Hoodoo Voodoo." It's got tips about the Easter Eggs (secret tricks and messages left by mischievous programmers) that are found on all Macs and in most applications, plus secrets for switching from System 6 to System 7, arcane ways to start up and shut down your Mac, and more.

CHAPTER THREE

HOODOO VOODOO

K ids of all ages! This is the chapter that defies all categorization. If you love weird, you'll find it here. Mac users love to tinker and toy with their machines, add stupid, useless things...just generally goof off at their computers. That's one reason why using a Mac is so much more fun than using any other kind of compter. These fun things are addictive, too. If you've used a Mac for very long, you may remember Talking Moose, which was a moose head that appeared at random and could be made to say outrageous things. You can spend hours customizing modules in After Dark, the screen saver from Berkeley Systems, or using ClickChange from Dubl-Click Software, which lets you make your Mac's desktop look like a NeXT computer or even a DOS box. SoundMaster, which lets you assign sounds to events, is another non-productive but extremely popular utility. I have a very realistic sound of a toilet flushing as my shutdown sound—it really surprises people when I'm on the phone and shut down my Mac. (I suppose I should explain that to them some day....)

So get ready for the fun stuff in this chapter. And while most of the fun Mac gimmicks that people rave about will cost you a chunk of change, here are loads of neat tricks you can do without spending any money. Of special interest to most children in adult bodies are the famous Easter Eggs, the little surprises programmers leave behind for users to find. You'll also see all (or at least all I could collect) of the arcane keyboard shortcuts used to start your Mac in different ways, rebuild the Desktop without restarting, and so forth. That's not all! Want to change your shutdown message or switch back and forth between System 6 and System 7? Now that is weird.... System 7 is harder to get used to, but it lets you do so many neat tricks that I can't imagine going back to System 6.

STARTUP SORCERY

There are all sorts of different ways to start your Mac by holding down certain keys or key combinations during the startup process. You might want to photocopy Table 3.1 to use as a quick reference guide; it will help you remember many of the the following tips.

Table 3.1: Startup Key Combinations

Hold Down	To
Shift	Disable INITs—in System 7, that's whatever's in the Extensions and Startup Items folder (as well as some special control panels).
Mouse button	Bypass any disk in an internal floppy drive.
Command-Option-Shift-Del	Bypass the internal hard disk and start from the first SCSI device.
Command-Option-Shift-Backspace	Bypass the internal hard disk (ADB keyboard).
Command-Option-p-r	Clear the PRAM (System 7).
Command-Option-Shift and choose the Control Panel DA[1]	Clear the PRAM (System 6).
Command-Option-Esc	Rebuild the Desktop without rebooting.

---

[1] See Chapter 9 for variations, depending on your model, and for what the PRAM is.

Rebuild your Desktop without restarting your Mac. Every once in a while, you should rebuild your Desktop. This doesn't involve a hammer and saw—it's a simple technique to help make your Mac run better. When should you rebuild the Desktop? See Chapter 10, "In Trouble?", for all sorts of hints for getting and staying out of trouble.

If you have a lot of extensions (which you may remember were called INITs in System 6; a lot of us long-time Mac users can't call them anything else), you know how long it can take your Mac to restart. Instead of restarting when you need to rebuild the Desktop, try this voodoo trick. At the Finder, *with no applications running*, press Command-Option-Esc. Click on the Force Quit button; then hold down the Command and Option keys. When you're asked if you want to rebuild the Desktop, click OK.

Uh oh. You've got no Esc key? (Some keyboards don't have one.) Try Command-Option-tilde instead.

Thanks to Eric Apgar, Apple Worldwide Technical Assistance, for the tilde trick. Dave Waite provided the basic trick.

Be careful with Force Quit. Don't use the Force Quit method (see the preceding tip) to arbitrarily exit from programs, or you'll lose anything you haven't saved. Use Force Quit to exit from a program only when it's really stuck and you have no other options.

Also, be aware that Force Quit isn't the most graceful way to get your Mac to exit a particular program. If you have to Force Quit one program to avoid crashing the others that are open, it's a good idea to save all your work right away and then restart.

Rebuilding the Desktop (System 6). If you're running System 6 without MultiFinder, you can press Command and Option when you quit a program to rebuild the Desktop. Alas, here's one tip that works with System 6, but not with System 6's MultiFinder or System 7.

Split-second timing on startup to rebuild the Desktop. You can wait until all your extensions (INITs) load and then rebuild the Desktop. Just let the Happy Mac face go by and let your extensions load. As soon as the last one has loaded (watch the bottom of the screen) and before the menu bar and desktop appear, press and hold Command and Option to rebuild the Desktop.

Bypassing a startup floppy disk. If there's a disk in the floppy drive that you don't want your Mac to waste time trying to read during startup, hold down the mouse button while you reboot. This ejects the floppy, even if it has a valid System Folder on it.

Another arcane startup key combination. To bypass your internal hard disk or the SCSI drive you've picked as the startup volume and instead use the System Folder on the next SCSI drive that your Mac finds, press Command-Shift-Option-Del as you start up. When you see the flashing question mark icon, let go of the keys. Your Mac will start from the first SCSI device it locates with a System Folder on it.

Command-Shift-Option-Del is a hard sequence to remember. If you rearrange the order of the keys for this arcane combination, they spell "docs," or "cods." Depending on how your mind works, one or the other of these combinations may be easier to remember.

Now here's a weird one. Your computer comes on by itself. If you have a modular Mac with a slotted power button in the back, that power switch is lockable, and it can get locked in the On position. Apple provided this feature for Macs that are going to be used as file servers so that they'd stay on all the time and come back on if the power went out. If your Mac's not functioning as a dedicated file server, you'll probably want it to stay off when you turn it off. If it's been coming on mysteriously, check the power switch. In the Off position (unlocked), the power switch's notch should be horizontal, not vertical—depending, of course, on whether you've stacked your Mac's box horizontally or vertically.

Hold down the Shift key to disable all your extensions. You'll see this one often in this book, because unruly extensions are usually the cause of strange and frustrating problems with your Mac. Under System 7, to disable them so they don't cause trouble, start up with the Shift key held down—you can release the Shift key once you see the message "Welcome to Macintosh. Extensions disabled." This is an excellent way to diagnose what's going wrong on your Mac because it deals with the whole class of extension problems at once.

If you're a System 6 user and you're looking for an equally elegant solution, you might try Apple's Extensions Manager (which works with Systems 4.2 through 7.1). Written by Ricardo Batista, it's a free control panel that lets you turn INITs or extensions on and off selectively, turn them all on or all off, or revert back to the way they were. (See Chapter 10 for a few more strategies for isolating problem extensions.)

Hold down the Shift key to disable what's in your System 7 Startup Items folder, too. Keeping the Shift key down also turns off whatever's in the Startup Items folder. However, it doesn't turn off 32-bit addressing. That's done with the Memory control panel (and a restart).

Press Command-period to stop opening startup items. If you forget to press the Shift key to bypass startup items and extensions, press Command-period. That will stop any remaining items from starting up if the startup sequence has already begun.

Slow startups. If booting seems to be taking forever, hold that Shift key down to disable extensions. Since they won't load, you'll speed up startup. Also, a very slow boot could be a sign that you need to rebuild your Desktop (see the previous tips). A final reason for a slow startup could be trouble with any attached SCSI devices. See Chapter 8, "Connectivity Secrets," for more on the mysteries of SCSI.

Change the Shut Down message. Here's a ResEdit trick (for more on ResEdit, see the sidebar in Chapter 4, "Customizing Your Desktop.") for those of you with compact Macs and external hard drives. It's easy to forget to switch off the external drive when you've finished work for the day, so add that reminder to your normal Shut Down message. The secret is to use 44 characters for the message, no more, no less (but you can cheat with spaces).

First, of course, make a copy of your System file. Then open the copy of the System file in ResEdit and find the DSAT resource, which contains various startup, warning and shut down messages (see Figure 3-1).

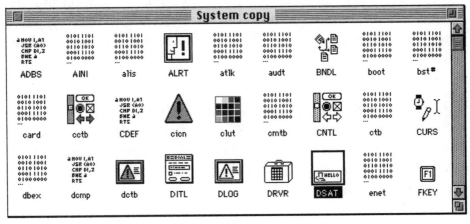

Figure 3-1: The DSAT resource is highlighted in this copy of the System file.

Double-click on the DSAT resource and then locate ID 2 and double-click on it. Locate the regular Shut Down message, "It is now safe to switch off your Macintosh."

DSAT ID = 2 from System copy					
0000E0	2069	6E73	6572	7420	insert
0000E8	7468	6520	6469	736B	the disk
0000F0	3A00	B177	0032	005E	:▯±w▯2▯^
0000F8	0072	4974	2069	7320	▯rIt is
000100	6E6F	7720	7361	6665	now safe
000108	2074	6F20	7377	6974	to swit
000110	6368	206F	6666	2079	ch off y
000118	6F75	7220	4D61	6369	our Maci
000120	6E74	6F73	682E	0000	ntosh.▯▯
000128	B176	006E	005E	0072	±v▯n▯^▯r
000130	4974	2069	7320	6E6F	It is no
000138	7720	7361	6665	2074	w safe t
000140	6F20	7377	6974	6368	o switch
000148	206F	6666	2079	6F75	off you

Figure 3-2: Edit the DSAT resource to change the Shut Down message.

Then highlight the whole message by dragging over it and type your new message. Here's a suggestion:

Switch off your Mac and then your hard disk.

Don't forget the period, to make the message exactly 44 characters. If you use a different message, add enough spaces or symbols to total 44 characters.

Now quit ResEdit and restart your Mac with a floppy (see Chapter 10 for more on how to create a startup floppy, or use the one that came with your Mac—either the System Tools disk in System 6, the Disk Tools disk in System 7, or the Utilities disk if you have a Performa). Replace your old System file with the new System file (which you should rename "System") you just created (rename the old one something besides "System" and put it in a different folder on your hard drive so you can get it back later, if you need to). Now restart your Mac again (take the floppy out of the drive) and then choose Shut Down to see your custom message.

For more ResEdit tricks, stay tuned for Chapter 4.

Do you hear the *Twilight Zone* theme when you start up your Quadra? If you do, you're in deep voodoo. Your Quadra hasn't passed its startup routine tests, and there's something wrong with the hardware. Some folks at Apple had fun with this one. Advice: call your friendly computer-repair technician or dealer.

While we're on the subject of startup sounds... Different models of Macs have different startup sounds. For you trivia buffs, here they are. On Pluses, Classics and SEs, the startup sound is a beep. The IIs, the SE/30, the LC and the PowerBook 100 play a chime (actually, it's C, F and the C an octave above). The Quadras and the rest of the PowerBooks play a C-major chord. If you hear anything else, it's an error tone. For example, if your Mac is supposed to play a startup chord and you hear the individual notes, an error has been detected during the startup hardware diagnostic tests.

EASTER EGGS

No hoodoo chapter is complete without directions to the Easter Eggs—the infamous "tricks" that you can get your Mac to pull—left there by the original programmers. I won't always describe here what happens when you discover each Easter Egg—that takes away half the fun of finding them—but I'll give you enough to whet your appetite. These are just plain fun! If you know of a choice Egg that's not listed here, let me know so I can include it in the next edition of *Voodoo Mac*. See the Introduction for how to get in touch. Most of these work only in System 7, but some work in System 6, too. But remember, half the fun of finding Easter Eggs is the hunt itself, so experiment and enjoy.

Finding the main Mac Easter Egg. If you're running System 7, press the Option key and choose About The Finder under the Apple menu (you'll notice that with the Option key held down, the familiar About This Macintosh has become About the Finder). You'll see a mountain landscape. Wait a bit, and you'll see credits scroll by at the bottom of the hill.

That's not all. Repeat the trick, only now hold down both the Command and Option keys—you'll see an unusual pointer.

 More weird Easter Eggs. I love these Easter Eggs. They're useless, but fun! Try these:

- On Macintosh IIci, set the date to 09/20/89, set your monitor to 8-bit color, restart, and hold down Command-Option-ci as you reboot. A color picture of the machine's design team appears.

- On a IIfx, set the date to 03/19/90 (its release date). Restart with Command-Option-fx to see a surprise.

- On a Mac Plus, locate the programmer's switch. It's the funny-looking piece of plastic that was in the box when you got your Mac. Look in your machine's manual to see how to put it on or locate it if it's already on your Mac. With no applications open, press the rear part of the switch and you'll see a blank window. Enter G 40E118 to see a "Stolen from Apple Computer" message. To get out of the debugger (you'll have to restart your Mac Plus to do so), press the front part of the programmer's switch.[2]

- On a Macintosh SE, you have to follow a different procedure but you're rewarded with a different Egg. Press the interrupt switch (the button with the broken circle on it, on the back left side of your Mac). That takes you to the debugger. Then type G 41D89A. You'll see pictures of the Mac development team.

- On a Classic, hold down Command-Option-ox as you start up. If you wait long enough, the Mac creates an internal ROM disk (System 6.03, Finder 6.1x). If you then use a utility like ResEdit that lets you see invisible folders, you'll see a list of the folks who worked on the Classic in the ROM disk's System Folder.

---

[2] See Chapter 10, "In Trouble?", for more about the programmer's switch, also called the interrupt switch.

- On a PowerBook, turn on Balloon Help, press Caps Lock and point to the up arrow in the menu bar. You'll see a balloon with the original code names of the PowerBooks.

- In System 7, turn on Balloon Help and then point at various items in the Extensions folder. You'll see some interesting messages for QuickTime and MacsBug.

- In System 6.0.7 or 7.0, look in the data fork of the System file. (You can open it in Microsoft Word or any similar word processor.) At the end of the file is a secret notice, a variation on the Chinese fortune cookie factory message.

- In the Cache Switch control panel (version 7.0.1), press Option and click on the version number. Watch as its creator's name is revealed.

- In System 7, go to the Memory control panel and turn on virtual memory. Then hold down the Option key and click on the box under Select Hard Disk. You'll see a list of programmers; look at the submenu next to each one for some irreverent comments.

- In System 7, click and hold on the sample text in the Color control panel. Click and hold again for more.

- In System 7, delete all the labels in the Labels control panel and restart. The labels change so that they now read ALANJEF when you read down from the top label to the bottom.

- In the System 7 Monitors control panel, click and hold on the version number. You'll see the names of the developers (also known as Blue Meanies) of this control panel. To get an interesting effect, quickly tap the Option key several times.

- You can paste any picture in the System 7 Puzzle to create a custom puzzle. Try the graphic that's supplied with the Clipboard. To cheat and see what the custom puzzle is supposed to look like after it's solved, look at the Clipboard.

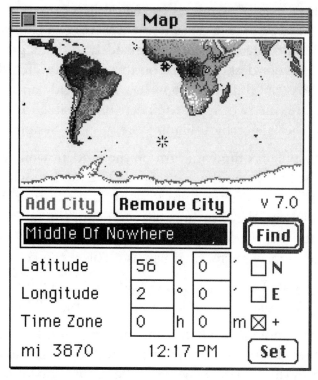

Figure 3-3: Discover the Middle Of Nowhere in the Map control panel.

- The Map control panel in System 6 or 7 has *lots* of Easter Eggs. Open it with the Option key down (double-click and then quickly press the Option key) to get a close-up view of the world. Then try it pressing the Shift key after you double-click. Shift-Option magnifies the map even more. Type **mid** as the location; then click Find to see the Middle Of Nowhere (see Figure 3-3). Click on the version number to see the author's name. Option-click on Find to go alphabetically to every city the Map has stored, starting from wherever you are. (Starting from the Middle Of Nowhere will take you to Minneapolis.) Click in the map and drag it to a border to scroll around the world. Paste the color map from the Scrapbook to get a nice color map. Click and hold on the version number (v 7.0, for example) to see the Map programmer's name. (For even more Map tricks, see Chapter 6, "Miscellaneous Voodoo Tricks.")

- Rename a floppy disk exactly to any of these names: KMEG JJ KS (eight uppercase letters and two spaces) or Hello world JS N A DTP. Eject the disk with Command-E so that a grayed icon of it stays on your desktop. Click on the disk and watch the request dialog box (tip: dnf and ksct are David N. Feldman and Kenny S. C. Tung, the two Apple engineers responsible for the extensions to the Hierarchical Filing System under System 7).

- On the Apple fax modem, turn on the modem while you hold down the button on the front panel. The modem will beep three times. After it beeps the third time, press the button three times, in rhythm with the first three beeps. If your timing is right, you'll hear the modem speak digitally recorded voices of the three developers saying their names. (This is too cool.)

- In Microsoft Word 4, press and hold the Command key in the About Word dialog box. Click on the "flying W" logo.

- In Word 5, hold down the Command and Shift keys and choose Preferences from the Tools menu. Scroll to the last item in the list, which should be a new Credits icon that you've never seen before (see Figure 3-4). (If the Credits icon doesn't appear, close the Preferences dialog box and try again.) Click on it to watch a color display. To stop the display, click again.

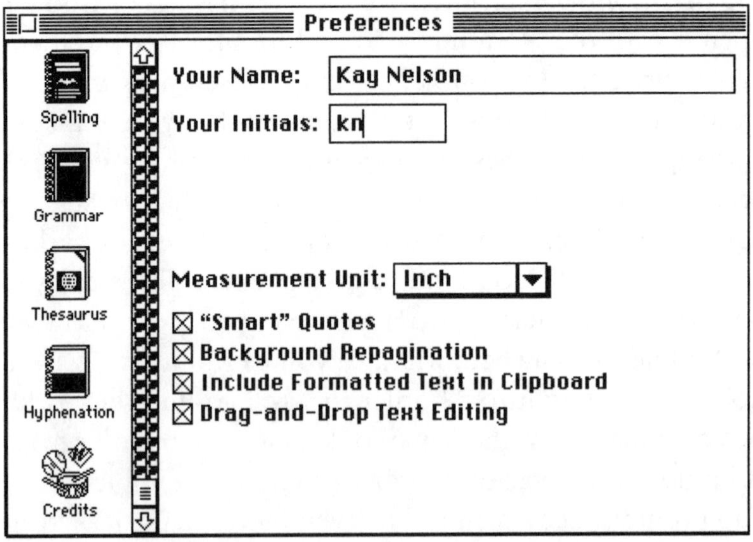

Figure 3-4: Click the Credits icon to see a neat color display.

- In TeachText, press Option and choose About TeachText from the Apple menu.

- In WriteNow 2.2, choose About WriteNow in the Apple menu. Then hold down the Option key and click on the names of the program's authors.

- In Excel 3.0, choose Style from the Format menu, type **excel**, choose About Excel, and click on the big Excel icon. In an Excel spreadsheet, press Command-Right arrow and Command-Down arrow to go to the bottom-right cell. Make the column width and row height zero. Then click on the down arrow and right arrow in the scroll bars in the bottom right of the window until no cells are showing. Click on the gray rectangle in the window's upper left.

- Here's another one for Excel 3.0: from the Format menu, choose Style and type **excel**. Then choose About Excel from the Apple menu and click on the Excel logo.

- In Photoshop, Option-select About Photoshop to see the names of the original designers.

- In the QuickTime Simple Player, press Option while you select About Simple Player from the Apple menu to see some nice cats.

- In QuicKeys^2, click Open. Then click on the QuicKeys logo to see the credits. Wait a bit, and you'll see a variation on the Energizer bunny, complete with sound effects.

- In ResEdit 2.1, press Shift, Option and Command while you select About ResEdit from the Apple menu (see Figure 3-5). (No, you don't want to go into pig mode because it slows ResEdit down, but it sure is fun to hear the pig oink.) If you do enter pig mode and you want to exit, just press Shift, Option and Command and again select About ResEdit. To see who created ResEdit, press Command and Option as you choose About ResEdit.

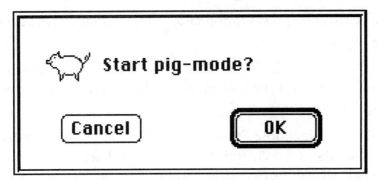

Figure 3-5: Finding the secret pig mode in ResEdit actually has a practical application if you're a programmer.

- In SimAnt, type at any point:

    will to make the yellow ant invincible.

    jenn to make the yellow ant never go hungry.

    susi to make the black colony always healthy.

    jeff to start a black colony in each sector.

    ZHEA to set the black colony health to zero.

    zhea to set the red colony health to zero.

    hole to dig 64 new holes on the black field.

- Here's a great one! In Disinfectant, select About Disinfectant from the Apple menu and wait a few seconds. You'll soon hear John P. Sousa's "Liberty Bell March." It's addictive; I keep hearing it in my head. Sometimes on a gray, rainy day I start Disinfectant just to hear it again. Keep watching the parade of viruses to see a funny tribute to "Monty Python's Flying Circus."

- In HyperCard, hold down the Option key while you choose About HyperCard from the Apple menu. You'll see your name, if you've entered it in the Chooser, and (in HyperCard 2.1) a screen listing information about your Macintosh, such as the version of the system software you're running, the ROM version, total memory size and so forth.

I love these Easter Eggs. If you know more, send them in (see the Introduction)! I haven't included all the programming-oriented eggs or some for the less widespread applications, but Brian Kendig (whose Internet address is bskendig@phoenix.Princeton.edu) keeps a master list of a lot them. I've seen some of these eggs described in various publications and on bulletin boards, with all sorts of different people credited as the discoverers. The folks I've credited here either sent tips to me, or the tips were in Brian Kendig's master list; he most graciously allows us to distribute information about them freely.

Thanks to Brian Kendig, Joe Morris, Eric Apgar, Fred Torres, Rob Terrell, Peter the Bugman and the guys at Maxis, and many others for finding more Easter Eggs than I could imagine.

FKEY MAGIC

A lot of folks aren't aware that the Mac has built-in function key combinations that are part of the system software that comes with every Macintosh. You use them by pressing Command-Shift and a number key. The number keys 0 through 4 were the original Mac FKEYs (System 7 doesn't use Command-Shift-4). Here's a list of the key combinations and what they do:

Command-Shift-0   Ejects a floppy disk from the external drive if you have two internal drives. If you don't have this setup, it works just like Command-Shift-1.

Command-Shift-1   Ejects a floppy disk from the internal drive, leaving the grayed disk image like Command-E does.

Command-Shift-2   Ejects a floppy disk from the second external drive.

Command-Shift-3   Takes a snapshot of the screen. In System 7, this screen dump is saved as a PICT file (named Picture 1, Picture 2, and so forth) that can be opened and printed using TeachText.

Command-Shift-4   Sends a snapshot of the screen to an ImageWriter, where it is printed (System 6). In System 7, Command-Shift-4 doesn't work any more.

You can assign other FKEYS to the number keys 5 through 9, as you'll see in the next tricks.

Interested in FKEYS? Check out shareware. Although FKEYS have sort of fallen out of favor, being replaced by more versatile macro programs like QuicKeys and Tempo, there are lots of shareware programs that provide FKEYS. For example, you can download DateKey from a bulletin board or online service. This shareware FKEY will insert the date into whatever text document you're working on whenever you press Command-Shift-6. Shareware FKEYs often come with their own installer, or you can use a shareware installer utility.

No installer? Here's the voodoo way to get an FKEY into your System file. Use ResEdit to open the FKEY file. Then locate the FKEY resource, select it, and copy it (press Command-C or choose Copy from the File menu). Now use ResEdit to open a copy of the System file and select its FKEY resource. Paste the copied FKEY. If there is an ID conflict, ResEdit will offer to renumber things for you; let it do so. Make note of this number, for this will be the number you press to invoke the FKEY. Now save and quit, swap System files, and restart.

You can install an FKEY in the Fonts folder in System 7.1. Here's an easy way to install a new FKEY in System 7.1 so that it'll be enabled on startup. Just drag it to the Fonts folder inside the System Folder. Open the FKEY in ResEdit and choose Get Info from the File menu. Then change the file type to FFIL (or ffil), which identifies it as a font file.

There are differences between FKEY screen shots in Systems 6 and 7. You can edit screen shots taken with the System 6 FKEY in MacPaint (they're saved as MacPaint documents named Screen 0, Screen 1, and so forth), but other than cropping, you can't edit screen shots taken under System 7 in TeachText. In System 6, you can crop screen shots in MacPaint; in System 7, open the screen shot with TeachText, click on the image with the cursor and it turns into a crosshair that lets you select and copy portions of the image.

In Chapter 6 you'll see how to direct screen dumps to a different drawing program instead of the regular TeachText or MacPaint, and you'll also learn more about TeachText's shortcomings.

If you need to make lots of screen shots of windows (or anything less than a full screen) under System 7, get a program like Capture from Mainstay. Capture also lets you convert PICTs to TIFFs (Tagged Image File Format) that show multiple levels of gray (like the ones you see in this book). A respectable shareware program for making screen shots is Flash-It.

There's a 10-picture limit in System 6. After you've taken screen shots 0 through 9, you can't take any more in System 6. You'll know, because your Mac will beep at you. The solution? Drag Screens 0 through 9 to another folder, or rename the files as something other than Screens 0 through 9.

MIXING SIXES & SEVENS

One subject that you seldom find much useful information on is the arcane art of switching back and forth between System 7 and System 6. But it's not as difficult as you might think, and since there are times when it's convenient to be able to use one System version or the other without a major hard drive overhaul, here are a few tricks that can help you figure out what's going on, and show you how to switch in the safest possible way. There are several different ways to do it, and the one you pick depends on your hardware and how often you switch.

Switching between System 6 and System 7. Yes, you can alternate between starting up with System 6 and with System 7. The pitfall to avoid is trying to have two System Folders on the same disk (but see the next tip). Instead, partition your hard disk into two separate disks. If you have an Apple hard disk, you can partition it using the Apple HD SC Setup utility (which is on the system software disks that came with your Mac); if your disk is a third-party model—

Apple HD SC Setup doesn't recognize disks made by other manufac-
turers—you can use the formatting software that came with the drive,
or you can use a third-party utility (like Software Architects' Formatter
Five). Then you can alternately start up with the different volumes by
using the Startup Device control panel (System 6) or Startup Disk
(System 7) to select the one you want to start up with.[3]

If you don't want to repartition your hard disk (repartitioning
involves erasing everything that's on a disk, so you'll need to back up
the whole thing first or else reinstall everything later), read on.

If you have an external hard disk, just put a System 6 (or 7) System Folder on it and a System 7 (or 6) System Folder on your internal
hard disk and select the one you want to use as a startup disk.

And here's one more neat way to switch between 6 and 7. If you
have System 6 on your internal hard drive and System 7 on an external
hard drive, just start your Mac holding down the Command, Option,
Shift and Delete keys to bypass the internal drive and start from your
external System 7 hard drive (remember the docs/cods trick from
earlier in this chapter?). When you see the question mark disk icon, let
go of the keys.

A more elegant solution is to use Kevin Aitken's System Picker,
available free from online services or user groups. Using System Picker, all you have to do is click on the folder that has the system you
want to use when you restart (see Figure 3-6).

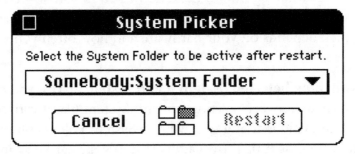

Figure 3-6: Use System Picker to switch easily between
systems.

---

[3]Unfortunately, you can't switch startup disks via a control panel on a Mac Plus. But
you can usually use whatever program you partitioned your hard drive with to select the
startup volume.

If all you want to do is switch to System 6 once in a while, create a System 6 startup disk. The two essential files you need to be able to boot up from a floppy are the System and Finder files. You can even use the Disk Tools disk that comes with System 7 as a startup disk; it has the bare essentials of System 6 on it. And if you want to keep your favorite fonts in System 6, stick them into a font suitcase and put it on the startup disk. Of course, don't try to cram all the normal luxuries you store in your System Folder onto a startup floppy—it should simply be a tool for quick, limited trips "back" to System 6.

There are freeware and shareware extensions and utilities that let you switch systems, too. Check out SwitchBoot if you have access to an electronic bulletin board.

Use your startup disk when all else fails. Playing around with different System Folders and startup disks can sometimes be frustrating and even risky. Sometimes your worst fears are realized and you find yourself staring blankly at the dreaded "questioning floppy" icon when you start your Mac. No matter what you try, you can't get your hard drive or any attached drives to come up. Don't panic! Just reach for your handy startup disk, pop it in your floppy drive and you're back in business. This will at least get your Mac to start up all the way so you can poke around your system and try to figure out what's gone wrong. For more on using a startup disk to get out of sticky situations, see Chapter 10.

Run Disk First Aid after you switch from System 6 to System 7, or vice versa. To be really safe, run Disk First Aid (which is on the disks that come with your Mac) each time you switch systems. I've heard reports of a bug that can cause problems after you switch from 6 to 7, but I've never experienced it, and so I can't even describe what it is. Running Disk First Aid after switching systems is supposed to prevent this mystery bug from occurring.

Two Systems, no partition. You may not be able to or want to partition your hard disk right now (after all, partitioning does wipe out everything on it). If you're careful, you can have two

Systems on the same disk. The trick is to watch for the System Folder that's "blessed" (it has a tiny Mac icon on it—see Figure 3-7). That's the System Folder that's currently in use.

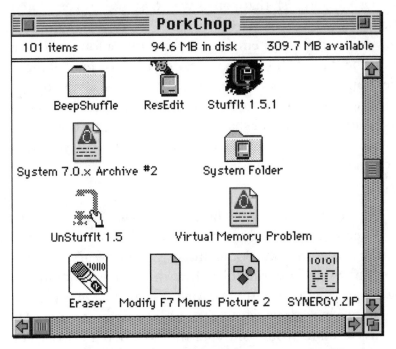

Figure 3-7: The "blessed" System Folder sports a tiny Mac icon.

Your Mac will start up from any folder that has a functional System file and a Finder file in it. That folder doesn't have to be named the System Folder. Yes, you can cause confusion by having a Finder file and a System file in the same folder, but the trick is to avoid putting them in the same folder until you're ready to use them. Keep your System 6 System file in a folder named something like "6 System folder" and the System 6 Finder file in a "6 Finder folder." Then, when you're ready to switch from System 7 to System 6, put them together in a folder and move the System 7 Finder and System files to separate folders within another folder somewhere else, naming them carefully so you can find them when you need them. To put the different system in effect, do this:

1. Double-click to open the System Folder you want to switch to, whatever it's named.

2. Drag the System file out of it.

3. Close the System Folder.

4. Drag that same System file back into it.

5. Then restart your Mac. Check to see that the right one is blessed.

The little icons all look alike, and it's easy to get confused, so stay alert. Better yet, get System Picker.

Extra folders get created when you switch to System 6 from System 7. When you leave System 7 and restart under System 6, two new folders are created because of the difference in the way the two systems deal with items on the desktop and in the Trash. Switching to System 6 leaves you with a Desktop and Trash folder that hold what was on the desktop and what was in the Trash when your were running under System 7. Open them in System 6 to see if there's anything in there you need.

Avoiding rebuilding the Desktop when you switch from 6 to 7. When you switch from System 6 to System 7, your Desktop file (a special invisible file that keeps track of some of the Mac's file management and housekeeping chores) gets rebuilt. This can take a while, but there's a way to avoid it. Install the Desktop Manager extension into your System 6 System Folder. The Desktop Manager doesn't use the Desktop file that System 6 uses, so your Desktop won't have to be rebuilt when you switch back to System 7. However, some people report that they've lost icons after putting the Desktop Manager into a System 6 System folder, so be warned.

Don't try to make a System 7 startup disk. System 7's just too big to fit on a floppy disk. Any tiny version of it that you can possibly create is too small to do much good. Instead, use System 6 as an emergency startup system.

Unexpected system switches with System 6, no MultiFinder. If you start with a System 6 floppy disk which isn't set up to run MultiFinder and then you launch an application from a hard disk with a System Folder on it, your Mac will start using that System Folder. To avoid this unwanted switch, press Option while you open the application that's on the different disk. But if MultiFinder is available and running on the startup floppy, the Mac won't switch startup disks.

Still can't switch to the right startup disk? If the SCSI drive you choose as a startup disk doesn't spin up and become available before the other SCSI drives in the chain, you may not be switching to the startup disk you wanted because the Mac is instead using the first System Folder it found on another disk. Change the numbers of your SCSI devices around to avoid this trap. (For more tricks with SCSI devices, see Chapter 8.)

MOVING ON

Had enough fun yet? Just wait for Chapter 4, "Customizing Your Desktop." There you'll learn how to modify icons and create new ones as you continue to explore the strange world of ResEdit and discover all sorts of ways you can edit resources to control the appearance and feel of your Mac. If you don't know a resource fork from a dessert spoon, don't worry. I'll tell you the basics of what you need to know to work effectively and safely using ResEdit, and besides, Chapter 4 has a few things you can do without ResEdit, too.

CHAPTER FOUR

CUSTOMIZING YOUR DESKTOP

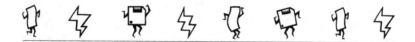

This chapter is for those of you who sometimes get a wild urge to rearrange all the furniture in your living room—not for any reason in particular— just for a change of pace. If you're the kind of person who doesn't feel at home in a new place until you've hung pictures and tacked up posters, you've probably also wished you could make your Macintosh look more like your own individual computer and less like all the others that rolled off the production line. The good news is that there are all sorts of things you can do to personalize your Mac— some serious, others fun.

Here's your chance to personalize your desktop in all sorts of ways. The tips and tricks in this chapter show you a few of the things you can do to customize your Mac, such as changing the patterns used in scroll bars, switching icons from one program to another, and even changing things like the messages you see in alert dialog boxes.

RESEDIT 101

Many of the tricks discussed in this chapter require using ResEdit, Apple's resource editing application. If you aren't familiar with ResEdit, don't worry—I'll take you through each trick step-by-step and teach you just what you need to know to get the job done safely and easily. And while I know I promised not to indulge in long and useless technical babble in *Voodoo Mac*, I've included below a brief discussion of what ResEdit is, how it works and where you can get it. Those of you already familiar with ResEdit will no doubt want to skip ahead to the tricks. If you're new to ResEdit, read on.

ResEdit allows mortal users like you and me to do tricks that normally are left to programmers. Because of the way Macintosh files are structured—with a *data fork* containing data and a *resource fork* containing all the other stuff, such as menus, dialog boxes, messages, and so forth—you can change those things classified as "other stuff" without actually writing programming code. In most cases, all you do is click or drag; sometimes you may have to do a little typing.

Resources are classified into resource *types*, all of which have four-character names, such as 'MENU' or 'snd '. Notice that a blank space is part of the 'snd ' resource's name. That's why programmers put single quotes around resource names—to indicate where these blank spaces are. We aren't programmers (at least I'm not), so I won't bother with the single quotes.

But just because you're not a programmer doesn't mean you can't use ResEdit. Lots of people know about ResEdit but fear using it because they may have heard that it's possible to damage your Mac if you make a mistake while using ResEdit. I'm happy to report that, for the most part, ResEdit-phobia is an irrational and unfounded fear. It's about as easy to use as any other Mac application, and shouldn't be restricted to programmers and so-called "power users." ResEdit can't alter any of the hardware on your Mac, and as long as you're careful, you can't do any permanent damage to any of your software. You need only follow a few easy and basic rules:

- Back up your hard drive regularly. This is just good advice for any computer user, regardless of whether you intend to work with ResEdit.

- Always use ResEdit on a *copy* of what you want to change, never the original. Just press Command-D to duplicate whatever file you're planning to edit before you start, and work on that copy. Then, if something doesn't work right, you can always get the original back. (This advice is doubly true for editing the System and Finder files. In fact, starting with version 2.1, ResEdit won't even let you work with the active Finder.)

- Keep a startup floppy disk handy, just in case your hard drive doesn't appear and you need to boot from a floppy. (You can start from the System 7 Disk Tools disk or System 6 Utilities disk that came with your system software, or see Chapter 10, "In Trouble?", for details on how to create your own startup disk.)

You can edit a program's resources to customize it, or—as I'll discuss in this chapter—edit the Finder or the System files to customize your Mac's desktop. To edit a file in ResEdit, start ResEdit and then click in the splash screen that shows the jack-in-the box. That will take you to a standard Open dialog box, where you can choose the file whose resources you want to edit.

If you like, you can use this trick instead to open a file for editing: since, in System 7, dragging a document onto an application's icon launches the application and opens the document, just drag a file onto ResEdit's icon, and ResEdit will open it, ready for resource editing. This is often a lot more convenient than going through the Open dialog box, especially if you keep an alias of ResEdit on your desktop.

Now, since this is a tips and tricks book, that's about all the technical ResEdit stuff you ought to be burdened with. Don't expect the rest of this chapter to feature a long and detailed discourse on the theory and practice of using ResEdit. All you'll get are tips that say "do this; then do that." If you want a book to help you explore ResEdit and understand what's going on behind the scenes, get BMUG's guide to ResEdit, *Zen and the Art of Resource Editing.* It's available from Peachpit Press (800/ 283-9444; $24.95). Or, if you want to get more information of the sort that programmers use, check out Peter Alley and Carolyn Strange's *ResEdit Complete*, from Addison-Wesley (617/944-3700; $29.95).

If you'd like a custom desktop but you don't want to fool with ResEdit, consider getting ClickChange, a commercial program from Dubl-Click Software. It's compatible with System 6 or 7 and it gives you all sorts of neat ways to customize your Mac, including adding colors to window elements, choosing animated cursors and more. You can even make your desktop resemble a PC with ClickChange (but who would want to?).

Another candidate for changing the System 6 desktop without editing resources directly is Michael C. O'Conner's LAYOUT program, available from most online services, bulletin boards and user groups.

Adam Stein's Insanely Great Software System 7 Pack! is a bundle of shareware programs, including one for customizing the System 7 desktop without using ResEdit. You can get the System 7 Pack! through the usual shareware outlets, or you can order it directly from Adam at 800/242-4775 (or call 908/549-0590 for information).

While there is a wide array of other programs, both shareware and commercial, that let you customize your Macintosh, the tricks in this chapter are for things you can do without buying any programs—other than ResEdit, of course.

Always work on copies of special files when using ResEdit.
A lot of the tips that tell you how to customize your desktop
require you to edit the System file, which is one of the most important files on your Mac. Since even the most experienced voodoo
practitioners can make a mistake now and then, it's always a good
idea to make a copy of any file you intend to alter using ResEdit, and
it's vital that you follow this rule when working on something important like the System file. That way, if things don't turn out the way
you wanted, you can simply throw out the altered copy and replace it
with the original. Here's how to safely tweak your System file. (This
same procedure works when editing the Finder file, too. Follow
exactly the same procedure when making changes to the Finder, only,
of course, using the name Finder instead of System.)

First, duplicate (Command-D) the System file to make a copy of
it. Then open ResEdit and edit the *copy*. When you're through, save
your changes and quit ResEdit. Now drag the original System file
(the one named System) out of the System Folder; you can put it
anywhere except in the Trash—you can't trash it because it's still
active. (But you can trash it after you restart.)

Then rename the copied file you altered in ResEdit—named
System copy or, in System 6, Copy of System—as just plain System;
be sure to name the file exactly with no typos or spaces. Restart and
check to see how your changes look. You can then trash the old
System file—but it's a good idea to keep it around (or at least back it
up to a floppy) in case you need it later on (see Chapter 10 for more
tips about keeping spare parts on hand).

And remember, it's not just special files like the Finder or System
files that you should make safety copies of before changing with
ResEdit—it's just a smart policy to copy any file whose resources you
intend to edit.

Change the resolution and design of your desktop pattern.
You'll need to use ResEdit for this trick, because it's not at all
the same thing as changing the desktop pattern with the General
control panel. (That control panel limits you to the system colors—
the ones that come up on the wheel when you double-click on one of

the pattern palette colors—and restricts you to patterns created using an 8-by-8 pixel grid.) To begin, make a copy of your System file and experiment on it.

Open the System copy with ResEdit (remember that under System 7, you can open a file and launch ResEdit at the sime time by dragging and dropping the file onto the ResEdit icon). You'll see the resource picker window, where the resources are arranged in alphabetical order and each one is represented by an icon. Find and double-click on the ppat resource (it has a patterned icon); you may have to scroll around to find it (see Figure 4-1). Now, double-click on the resource that has the current desktop pattern; it should be ID = 16 (that is, it should have an identifying number of 16 below it). You'll see a pixel editing screen (see Figure 4-2).

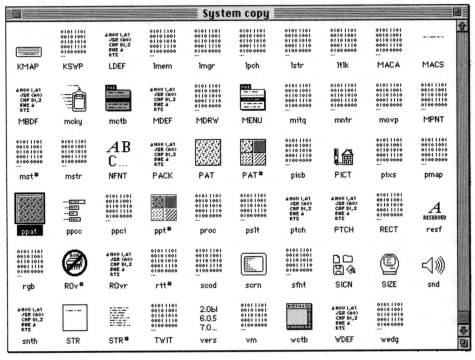

Figure 4-1: Locate the ppat resource in the resource picker window; it's the one highlighted in this illustration.

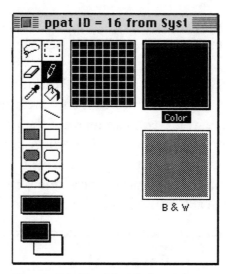

Figure 4-2: Double-click on the pattern (ID = 16) resource to get to the editor shown here.

Click on the color boxes at the bottom of the screen to change colors. You can make some very interesting patterns using several different colors by using the dropper, pencil or paint can tools in the pattern part of the dialog box. You can also use the Color menu near the far right of the menu bar to select from a number of different pre-defined color schemes (ranging from the standard 256 colors to Apple's "official" icon colors) or you can choose your own custom color from the color picker wheel. If you have a 24-bit monitor capable of showing the legendary "16 million" colors, you'll have access to each of them (assuming you can tell the difference between them all) via the color wheel. Monitors with other (or no) color capabilities will, obviously, show only those colors or gray shades they are capable of displaying. Hint: Use lighter shades as outline colors to get a 3-D effect. You'll see a miniature of your desktop pattern in the Color box to the right. If you don't like the results, go to the Resource menu and choose Revert this Resource to return things to the way they were when you started.

You can also paste any image you've copied to the Clipboard. If the image is bigger than the pattern size you're working with, you may see only part of the image when you paste it. To get around this, first press Command-A for Select All, and ResEdit will resize the picture for you.

To choose a larger pattern size, select Pattern Size from the ppat menu at the far right of the menu bar. You'll see a different dialog box (see Figure 4-3), where you can increase the pattern size to as large as 64 pixels square. Choose Try Pattern from the ppat menu to see the effects of your new creation. You'll have to choose Try Pattern again—unchecking it—to prevent each new change you make from being automatically reflected on the desktop.

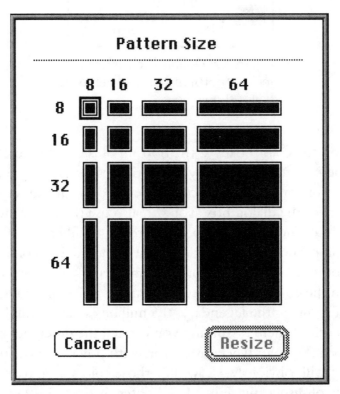

Figure 4-3: Choose Pattern Size... from the ppat menu for a different screen resolution of your desktop pattern.

When you're satisfied, save your changes, swap System files, and restart your Mac. Of course, if you're planning to further customize your desktop, you might want to simply save your changes, but don't replace your old System file until you've made all the modifications you have in mind.

Changing the scroll bar pattern. You can have a custom scroll bar pattern, too. In a copy of the System file, open (double-click) the PAT resource and then double-click on ID = 17, which is the scroll bar pattern (see Figure 4-4). You'll see the PAT editor (see Figure 4-5).

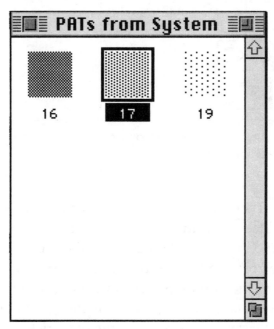

Figure 4-4: ID = 17 is the resource for the scroll bar pattern.

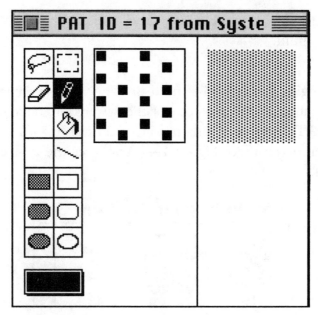

Figure 4-5: The PAT editor lets you change the scroll bar's pattern.

Use the paint tools to create a custom pattern; see Figure 4-6 for a sample. The Mac makes the pattern by taking the design you create and repeating it. Choose Try Pattern from the PAT menu to see the effect of your pattern on the desktop. Don't worry—it's really the scroll bar pattern—it won't replace your desktop pattern! When you've settled on a new pattern, save your changes and either swap System files and restart or move on to the next trick.

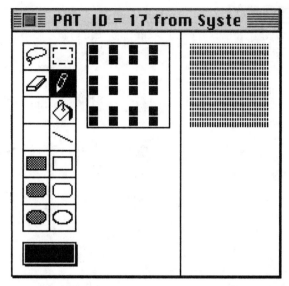

Figure 4-6: A sample custom pattern for the
scroll bars resource.

Customize your cursor. Changing the cursor is another nice
custom touch you can give your Mac. You can personalize the
wristwatch, the I-beam and the crosshair cursors. You can't change
the arrow cursor—it's stored in ROM—so don't go nuts trying.

Applications often come with their own specific cursors, so don't
think you've done something wrong if your custom cursor doesn't
show up when you're using your favorite program. You'll need to use
ResEdit to change that application's cursor resource if you want it to
match the one you created in the System file. (Don't try this trick
with Microsoft Word, because it doesn't have a cursor resource.)

Working on a copy of the System file, open the CURS resource
(see Figure 4-7). Double-click on a cursor to edit it. We'll use the
watch in this example, since it's a neat shape. (If ResEdit asks you if
you want to uncompress the resource when you try to open it, click
Yes.) You'll see the CURS editor (see Figure 4-8).

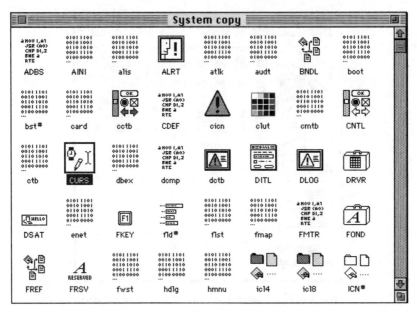

Figure 4-7: Double-click to open the CURS resource in the System file copy.

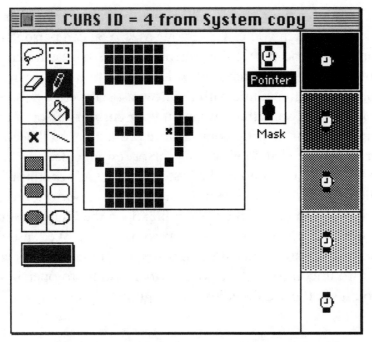

Figure 4-8: The CURS editor lets you change the shape of the watch.

You can edit three different things with this CURS editor: the cursor itself, the mask (which governs how your cursor appears against different kinds of backgrounds), and the hot spot (which is, practically speaking, the pointing part of the pointer or the "active" part of the insertion beam). It's easy to create a mask for your new cursor; when you're through editing it, drag the image in the Pointer box down onto the Mask box, and the Mac should take care of creating a mask for you.

Look at Figure 4-8 carefully (better yet, look at your own screen), and you'll see that an x marks the hot spot. You can change the location of the hot spot with the hot spot tool—the item in the tool palette that looks like an x. Of course, the hot spot is not really an issue on the watch cursor, since you don't use that cursor for selecting, pointing or clicking. But if you wanted to be able to use the top of the crosshair, for instance, to define your selection area, you could move it from the middle to the top (or anywhere in between).

Use the painting tools to edit the large cursor any way you like. For example, you might want to change the watch cursor to a different time instead of the perpetual 9 o'clock, or you could put a pattern on the watchband or make the whole thing into a jack o'lantern if you like—be creative.

When you're done, drag the small cursor (in the Pointer box) over the Mask box. Choose Try Pointer from the CURS menu to see the effects of your editing. When you're satisfied with it, save and try the next trick, or quit ResEdit and replace the old System file with the new one.

Want an animated cursor? You can do that in ResEdit, too (by editing the acur resource), but quite frankly, it's a tricky, tedious process—you have to create multiple versions of the same image, only in different stages of movement—just like a Disney animator. Instead, pick up a shareware program called Cursor Animator—it comes with a nice collection of cursors, and it's easy to create your own. You can get Cursor Animator from most bulletin boards.

Nuking the *alias* in your aliases. Tired of seeing the word "alias" tacked onto the ends of names whenever you create an alias? Since alias names are in italics anyway, you know they're aliases just by looking at them. Use ResEdit to shorten those long names.

Work on a copy of the Finder, as always. (You should note here that we're working on the *Finder* file now; in the past few tricks, we were poking around the *System* file.) Open the STR resource (see Figure 4-9) and double-click on ID = 20502 (see Figure 4-10). Change the string (see Figure 4-11) from the word "alias" to a blank space. (It has to be at least one character, or you'll get a number at the end of each alias.)

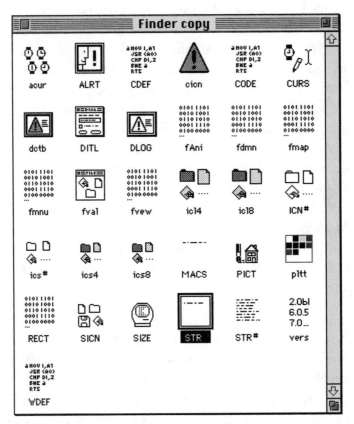

Figure 4-9: Double-click to open the STR resource.

STRs from Finder copy		
ID	Size	Name
11252	7	
11502	5	
12502	7	
12510	136	
12752	5	
13002	9	
13502	9	
14002	6	
14252	15	
14502	5	
14512	59	
14752	16	
14760	183	
15502	14	
15752	24	
17002	9	
17252	20	
17254	34	
19504	42	
19550	7	
20502	6	
27260	15	

Figure 4-10: Scroll down to locate the right ID number and double-click to open it.

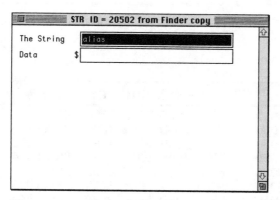

Figure 4-11: Change the alias string from "alias" to a blank space.

Eliminate window zooming in the Finder. While some people are thrilled by the "zoom" effect you see when you open a window in the Finder, not everyone loves it. This handy little trick speeds up your Finder, because you don't have to wait for the window zoom display. Open a copy of the Finder in ResEdit; then open the CODE resource. Open ID 4 (it's OK to decompress it). Now, press Command-F or go to the Find menu and choose Find hex—this is the easiest way to search for a particular line of code and replace it with another (see Figure 4-12). Find hex 4E56 FFE0 48E7 1F38 and replace it with 205F 700A DEC0 3ED0 (see Figure 4-13, and note that those are all zeroes, not the letter O). I'm showing spaces here so that you can easily see what to type and because that's how the code appears in the resource window; you'll actually enter them all in one string, as in Figure 4-12. Be sure to type the letters and numbers exactly as they appear here or the trick won't work properly. Then quit ResEdit, saving your changes, replace the old Finder with the new one, and restart.

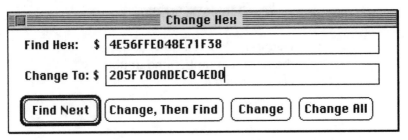

Figure 4-12: Use Command-F to find and replace hex addresses.

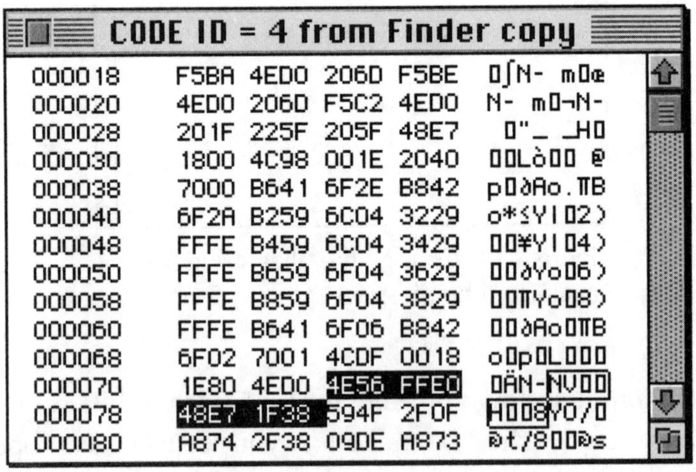

Figure 4-13: Locate the right hex string and change it.

Thanks to Eric Apgar, Apple Worldwide Technical Assistance.

Make your own startup screen. If you're tired of the same old, boring "Welcome to Macintosh" screen that you see each time you start your Mac, replace it with a color image of your own. You can use a painting program like PixelPaint 2.1 or later, Super-Paint 3.0 or later, UltraPaint or Canvas to create a color image that can be used as your startup screen. There are also a lot of shareware programs (such as ColorDesk) that let you create a color startup screen. If you want a black-and-white image for a startup message, as you'll see in this trick, you can use plain old MacPaint 2.0, which even has a handy Save as StartupScreen button in its Save dialog box.

Here's how to do it. First, use a paint program to create the image you want, or import an image. Then select it and choose Copy from the Edit menu. (You can select just part of an image and copy it, too.) If you're not artistically inclined, use the Text tool to create a startup message box instead (Figure 4-14).

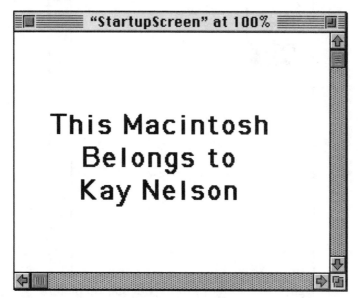

Figure 4-14: Use a paint program to create a custom startup message.

Start ResEdit and instead of editing a file, this time you'll create a new one—if you just launched ResEdit, click New; if you already have ResEdit open, choose New from the File menu. Save the new file in your System Folder under the name StartupScreen and press Command-V to paste the picture you just copied from your paint program. You'll see that it's truly a PICT resource, as opposed to a normal PICT file (see Figure 4-15). Double-click on it; then choose Get Resource Info from the Resource menu. You'll see a new dialog box (see Figure 4-16). Change the ID to 0. Then save the file and quit ResEdit. You'll see your new startup screen the next time you restart—it will appear right after the happy Mac icon pops up. (Note: some extensions clear the screen; if you have one that does this, you won't see your startup screen, or it won't appear for long. Disable the extension or rename it so that it loads later in the startup process so you can be sure to see your handiwork.)

Figure 4-15: After pasting your startup picture, you'll see the icon for a PICT resource.

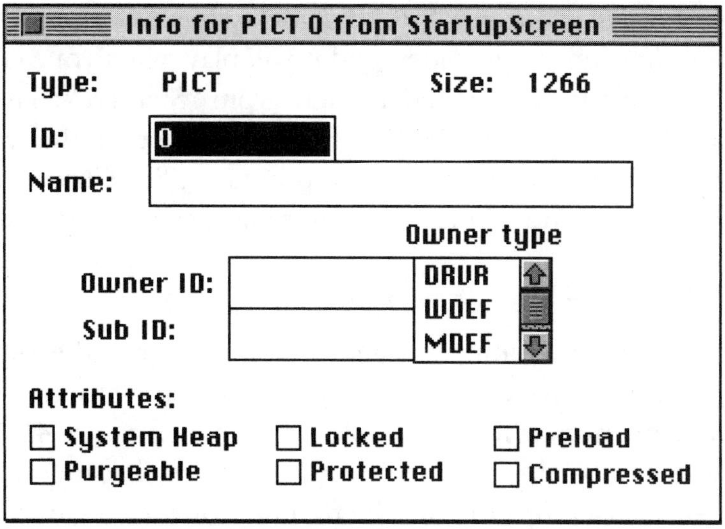

```
┌─────────────────────────────────────────────────┐
│ ▤▥═  Info for PICT 0 from StartupScreen  ═▥▤     │
├─────────────────────────────────────────────────┤
│  Type:     PICT              Size:   1266        │
│                                                  │
│  ID:     │0                 │                    │
│  Name:   ┌──────────────────────────────────┐   │
│          └──────────────────────────────────┘   │
│                             Owner type           │
│                          ┌────────┬───────┐      │
│       Owner ID:  │       │ DRVR   │  ⬆    │      │
│                  │       │ WDEF   │  ▦    │      │
│       Sub ID:    │       │ MDEF   │  ⬇    │      │
│                  └───────┴────────┴───────┘      │
│                                                  │
│  Attributes:                                     │
│   ☐ System Heap   ☐ Locked      ☐ Preload        │
│   ☐ Purgeable     ☐ Protected   ☐ Compressed     │
└─────────────────────────────────────────────────┘
```

Figure 4-16: Change the PICT's resource ID to 0.

Weird colors in your startup screen? If your color startup screen goes weird on you after it appears, you probably didn't create it by using the same set of colors that your system is using (16 colors, 256 colors or millions—check your Monitors control panel to see which setting your system is using). Go back into the program that created it or load it into Photoshop or SuperPaint or another color painting program, switch to a different set of colors (16 or 256), and save it, or switch your monitor setting to match the number of colors your startup screen uses. That should fix the problem.

Want a startup movie? If you are running System 7.0 or later and you have the QuickTime extension installed, you can put a QuickTime movie into your System Folder and name it Startup Movie (one space between the words), and it will play when you start up your Mac. Any startup screen you might be using will appear as the background; your movie will be centered as it plays.

And a startup sound, too. Put any System-7 format sound in your Startup Items folder, and it will play when you start up your Mac. I have Lt. Commander Data (From "Star Trek: The Next Generation") saying "Accessing...." This is an easy trick that you can do without acquiring any other sound programs. See Chapter 6, "Miscellaneous Voodoo Tricks," for more neat tips on using sounds.

ICON ARTISTRY

The science of icons is complex, and a whole book could easily be written about them (one probably has by now)—how to draw them, how to save memory when using color icons, when to use 4-bit color and when to use 8-bit color and so forth. The tips that follow are short, do-it-yourself tips that, in the tradition of voodoo, don't explain a lot about the background of why you're doing what you do. If you're interested in exploring icon science further, get a good book on resource editing (such as Peachpit Press's *Zen and the Art of Resource Editing,* by Derrick Schneider, Hans Hansen and Noah Potkin). Or get the shareware utility iCONtraption by Tom Poston—it's much easier to use than ResEdit.

If you're running System 6, get SunDesk, another shareware program (available on bulletin boards). You won't be able to use the following tips in System 6, but SunDesk will let you use color icons; it comes with complete instructions and a great collection of color icons. (System 7 users should get SunDesk just for the icon collection alone! The later tip "Icon rustling 102" shows you how to hijack them. And get iCONtraption, too.)

A small warning: as you edit color icons, your screen may flash briefly to a perfectly horrible set of colors—pea green and hot pink for instance. This is normal. The Mac is switching colors in the background, and you're seeing the results of that.

You can add color to icons or change an icon's colors. You don't have to be a programming wizard or even own a copy of ResEdit to throw a little color into those drab black-and-white or gray icons. If you're running System 7, all you need is a color painting program. Select the icon you want to paint and bring up its Get Info window with Command-I. Click on the icon in the Get Info window and copy it. Then go to your painting program and paste the icon. Get creative. Use the magnifying glass or a FatBits editor to work out the details of your icon design. Then select your work, copy it, and paste it back in the Get Info window.

You can do this with disk icons or icons for files and folders, too.

Use Photoshop for gorgeous, easy icons. If you're not comfortable with creating icons using a paint program or standard icon editor, consider stealing them from your favorite graphics files. Launch Photoshop and open the graphic that you want to convert to an icon. Make sure your General Preferences (Command-K) are set to Save Preview Icon. Then crop or edit your graphic until it's just the way you want it and save it in any format. Photoshop automatically shrinks the entire image down to a clean, neat icon that it assigns to the file you just created. Select the icon, Get Info (Command-I), select and copy the icon, and paste it into the Get Info box of any file you please.

Easy icon editing. Want to change the boring talking head that comes up in dialog boxes? If you have ResEdit and a willing heart, it's easy to change that and other icons your Mac uses. Open a copy of the System file and double-click on the ICON resource (see Figure 4-17).

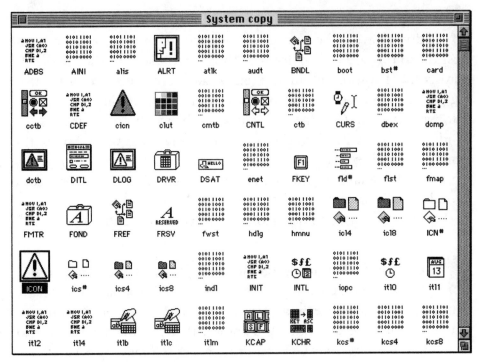

Figure 4-17: Open the ICON resource in the System file to edit all sorts of icons.

Then double-click on the icon you want to edit (see Figure 4-18). You'll be told that the resource is compressed; click Yes to open it anyway. You'll see the ICON editor, where you can easily personalize the talking head or whichever icon you chose (see Figure 4-19) by using the usual painting tools.

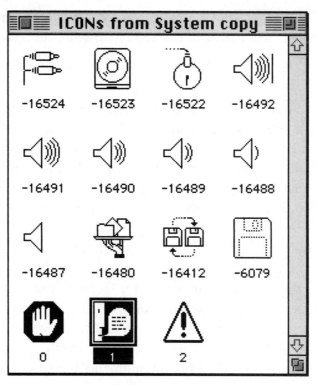

Figure 4-18: Double-click on the icon you want to change.

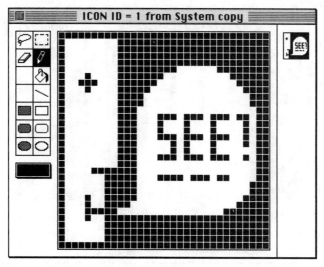

Figure 4-19: Use the icon editor to personalize all sorts of icons.

Save your changes, quit ResEdit, replace the old System with the new one, restart, and you're in business with your new custom dialog box icons.

You can add color to dialog boxes, too. It's easy to assign special colors to your dialog box icons. Open a copy of your System file in ResEdit and double-click on the ICON resource. Then double-click on the icon you want to color and write down its ID number. The alert dialog box icons are 0, 1 and 2, just as in Figure 4-18. Traditional colors are blue for information, yellow for alert and red for warning (the palms-up stop sign).

Now double-click on the icon to open it in the icon editor. Double-click on the marquee tool (or press Command-A) to select the whole thing; then press Command-C for Copy. Close the icon editor and the ICON picker window; then double-click on the cicn resource (for a little more explanation of what this is, if you care, see the next tip). Now choose Create New Resource from the Resource menu (or press Command-K) and then press Command-V to paste your copied black-and-white icon (Figure 4-20). Click on a tool to turn the selection marquee off.

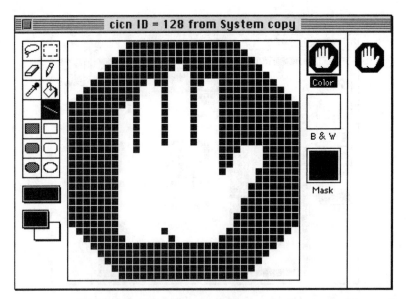

Figure 4-20: Paste the black-and-white icon in the color icon editor.

Click on the color boxes at the bottom of the left side of the editor to get to the color palette. Choose the colors you like, and paint away. Remember that you don't have to redraw the entire icon from scratch—you can just pick a color, click on the paint can tool, and then click on the part of the icon that you want to color. Except for a little touch-up work, this will usually do the trick. (For a few more hints about colorizing icons, see the tip "Another way to color icons" that follows.)

When you're happy with the colored icon, choose Get Resource Info from the Resource menu (Command-I). You'll see the dialog box in Figure 4-21. Enter the number of the original ID in place of the current ID, save and quit ResEdit, swap System files, and restart. When a warning dialog box (which was what was used in this example) comes up, the icon will be in the colors you chose.

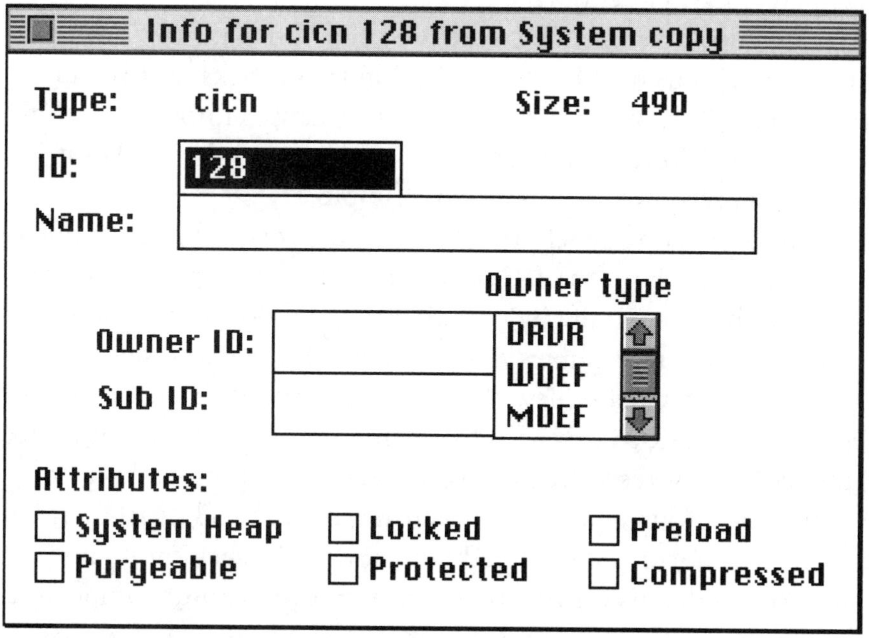

Figure 4-21: Change the ID number of your new color icon to the same number as the old icon in your System file.

Another way to color icons. This way is just a little more involved, but the results can be spectacular. You don't have to have much artistic ability because you swipe the basic icon, either from a collection of icons (like the shareware program SunDesk) or from an application that has the icon. You'll be surprised at how many icons come with the programs you buy, and you can find them with ResEdit, as you'll see.

First, set your monitor to either 256 or 16 colors. If you're using 256 colors, pick icl8 resources in the instructions that follow; for 16 colors, use icl4. If your monitor can display 256 colors but you usually use only 16, go ahead and pick icl8 resources, just in case you'd one day like to see them in 256 colors. To translate these cryptic resource names into something you can remember, think "icon, large, eight," and "icon, large, four," just like Captain Picard orders "tea, Earl Grey, hot."

In ResEdit, open a copy of the program you want to "borrow" icons from. I'm using Microsoft Word in these tricks, not because it has a good collection of pretty icons but because almost everybody has Microsoft Word in one version or another and that makes it a good program to use as a common example.

Double-click on the icl8 or icl4 resource. If you don't see one of these, double-click on the ICN# resource, and then you can create the rest of the icon family by dragging the black-and-white icons into the new color icon resources that you'll create, as you'll see below.

Then choose Create New Resource from the Resource menu, or press Command-K to bring up the icon editor. (If you haven't selected the icl8 or icl4 resource first, you'll get a dialog box asking you what type of resource you want to create; choose icl8 or icl4.) If you want to edit an icon that's already there, double-click on it and answer Yes to the dialog box that asks if you want to uncompress it. That brings up the icon family editor (see Figure 4-22).

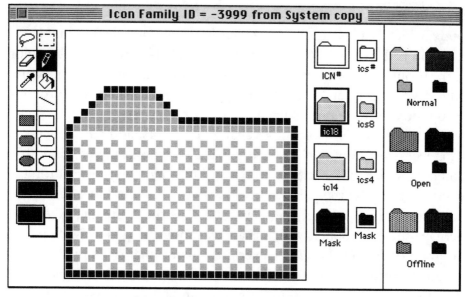

Figure 4-22: The icon family editor lets you edit and create color icons.

Hint: instead of creating an icon from scratch, copy one from another program's icon resources or from (a copy of) your System file and paste it in the blank icon family editor you get when you choose Create New Resource.

At the left of the screen are the usual painting tools (with one exception). At the bottom of the toolbox is a color palette. Although it's probably black-and-white on your screen, just click on either of the two bottom boxes to get to the colors and pick different ones. (Hint: use the Color menu to choose whether you want to paint in 256 colors or in the Apple Icon Colors that Apple thinks are best for icons. You'll probably find that the Apple Icon Colors are just fine— 256 colors are *a lot* of colors to choose from.)

On the right of the screen are representations of how the icon looks under different conditions, such as when it's selected (on the far right) and when it's not. The Offline icons indicate what the icon looks like when the disk they reside on has been ejected but not put away, as you'd do with Command-E.

You see four different kinds of icons here, and without getting into too much detail about any of them (this is voodoo, after all), here's what they are. The ICN# is a representation of how the icon looks in black and white, and it's used with color icons that need a *mask*, which is a background that fills in when you select the icon. The icl8 is the large 256-color icon, and the icl4 is the large 16-color icon. If one of these icons doesn't show up when you open the icon editor, you can create it just by dragging the icon you have to the empty box for its counterpart. That's color icons 101.

To color an icon—or simply change its colors, add fancy effects, whatever—just double-click on it to bring up its editing window. If you drag an icl4 to an icl8 box, that will put the icon in the editing window, too. Use the painting tools just as you would in a paint program. You're probably familiar with all of them already, except perhaps the eyedropper, which is a new tool gaining favor with paint program designers. This is a clever little gizmo that picks up and assigns to your drawing tool the color of any pixel within the icon that you click it on. You'll find it really handy if you've chosen to paint in 256 colors. Just put a few pixels of the colors you're using most often in a corner of the icon and then use them to pick your colors instead of switching back to the color palette every time you want to change a color. In fact, if you press the Option key while you're using any tool, that tool will change into the eyedropper, allowing you to pick a color and then return to your tool so you can apply that new color—a very handy little trick.

A few more coloring tips, and you're on your own. The eraser erases to white. To select the whole icon for copying or deleting, double-click on the marquee tool or press Command-A. You can double-click on the eraser to delete the entire icon, too. Try double-clicking on the lasso tool to select just the outer elements of an icon; this technique doesn't always work perfectly, but it can be a real time-saver when it does.

When you're done, save your work and quit ResEdit. Then, to see your new icons, restart and rebuild the desktop by holding down the Command and Option keys as you restart.

Big hint: before you can copy an icon resource in ResEdit, you have to select it. If you've modified a whole icon family—the icl8, icl4 and ICN#, too—use this shortcut: hold down the Command key and click on the resources you want to select (this works much like Shift-clicking items in the Finder). Then copy, choose Create New

Resource from the Resource menu, and paste. Save your new file of icons for future use.

Stealing several icons? Paste them in the Scrapbook. If you're borrowing a bunch of icons from a collection, copy them one by one and paste them in the Scrapbook. You can then copy and paste from the Scrapbook to get icons into Get Info boxes, and it will save you a lot of time.

Icon rustling 101. I've got to admit that the subject of icons can get complicated. If you've tried to pick up icons from various icon collections, only to be stymied by ResEdit's intimidating interface, just try these simple steps; they should work with any icon collections that are represented by ResEdit icons, such as those in Figure 4-23.

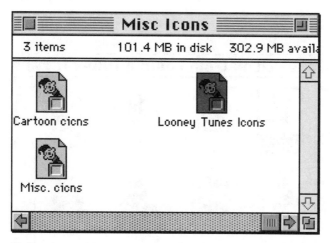

Figure 4-23: It's easy to beef up your icon collection with custom icons from other people's collections

Double-click on the icon of the collection. That will open the icons in ResEdit (see Figure 4-24). Double-click on the cicn resource or, with System 7, double-click on the icl8 or icl4 resources for color icons; choose the ICN# resource for black-and-white icons. You'll then see the icon collection (see Figure 4-25).

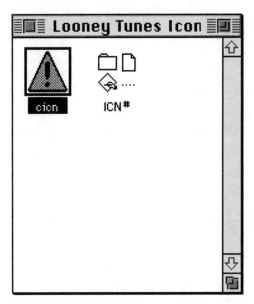

Figure 4-24: Choose the type of icon
resource you want to hijack.

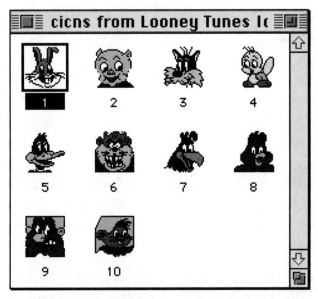

Figure 4-25: Double-clicking on any icon resource
reveals that library's entire collection.

Then pick your icon by double-clicking on it. When the icon editor window comes up, double-click on the marquee tool to select the whole icon (see Figure 4-26); then press Command-C to copy it. Quit ResEdit (unless you want to copy more icons), go to the file whose icon you want to replace, open its Get Info box, select the icon, and press Command-V to paste the new one. Close the Get Info box to see the new icon (see Figure 4-27).

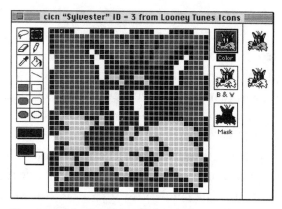

Figure 4-26: Double-click on the marquee tool to select the entire icon.

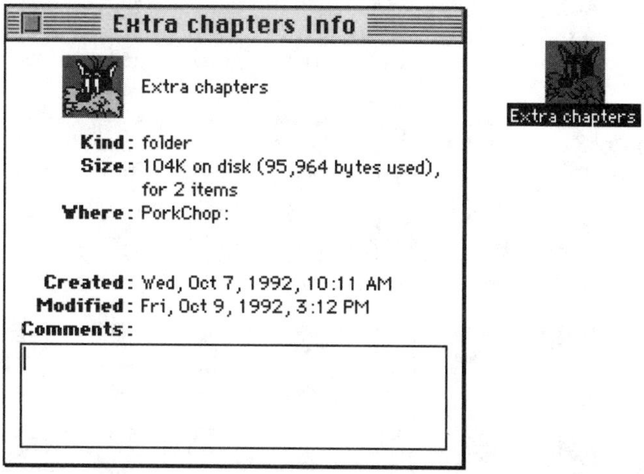

Figure 4-27: The new icon appears on the desktop next to its Get Info box.

If your icon doesn't look good, go back into ResEdit's icon editor and try two things: first, try adjusting the mask to make it a pixel or so larger all the way around. If that doesn't work, go to the original source of the icon you're using as the replacement and copy its black-and-white ICN# resource, too (double-click on the marquee tool when you have the ICN# in the editing screen).

Icon rustling 102. Sometimes ready-made icons don't always come in ready-to-ResEdit form, but they're still pretty easy to work with. Here's how to rustle icons that aren't represented by a ResEdit icon. (Their icons will most likely look like a page with one corner turned down, just like a document icon.) We'll use SunDesk as an example. (System 6 users, don't try this at home. Just use the SunDesk program.)

Open the icon collection in ResEdit, and double-click on the icl8 (or comparable) resource. You'll see the icon collection (see Figure 4-28). Double-click on the one you want; then double-click on the marquee to select it. Press Command-C to copy, go to the Get Info dialog box of your choice, and paste it.

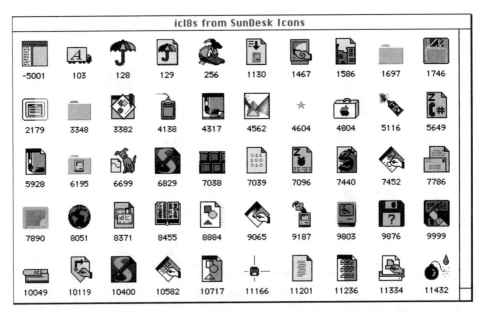

Figure 4-28: With ResEdit, you can choose any icon you like from a custom icon collection.

Substituting a custom Trash icon. The Trash icon is probably the most frequently changed icon of all. There are all sorts of ready-made Trash icons available, from the rude to the ridiculous. But everybody wants to change the Trash icon, so here's the step-by-step method.

Fire up ResEdit and open a copy of your System file. Double-click on the ICN# resource (for black-and-white icons) or on the icl8 or icl4 resource (for color icons). Then find the Trash icon (see Figure 4-29). Double-click on it (say Yes to uncompressing it). Double-click on the marquee tool to select it; then delete the Trash can. (It's important that you delete the current icon *first*, and then insert the new custom icon. My tests showed that performing this trick any other way caused odd problems with my Mac.)

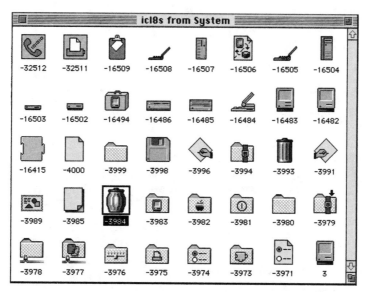

Figure 4-29: Find the Trash icon resource and double-click to open it.

Now open the file that contains the custom Trash icons. (You can find custom Trash icons from user groups, online services and bulletin boards, or you can draw your own using ResEdit or your favorite paint program. There's a neat IBM PC icon you might want to use for the Trash, too.) Double-click on the ICN# resource (for black-and-white icons) or on the icl8 or icl4 resources (for color icons).

You'll see the icon collection you're opening (see Figure 4-30). Double-click on the icon you want—I'm using the infamous toilet in Figure 4-31.

Figure 4-30: Double-click to open the icon collection.

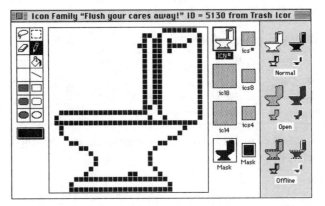

Figure 4-31: Choose the icon you want to substitute for the Trash.

Go back to the Trash icon editor, press Command-A to select all (which should be simply white space, if you deleted the resident icon according to the previous instructions) and press Command-V to paste the new toilet icon. Now drag the toilet to all the little icon windows to replace the trash can with the toilet (see Figure 4-32)— include all the small icons and the mask.

Repeat these steps to replace the full Trash icon with the toilet, too, so that it will show up both when the Trash is full and empty. (Obviously, unless you create two new, distinct custom icons for both the full and empty trash icon resources, you'll have to peek inside the trash to tell if it's full or empty.)

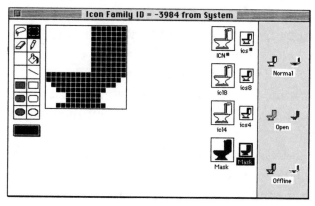

Figure 4-32: Drag the toilet to replace the can icons.

Save your changes and quit, replace the System file, restart, and you've got a new Trash icon (Figure 4-33). To change its name and all the messages associated with it, see the trick "Changing the names of things in the Finder" on the next page. (I've changed the name of my Trash to Outhouse).

Figure 4-33: The new Trash icon
is now a toilet.

Keep a "spare parts" icon collection. If you want to be able to select icons quickly from your icon collection, just make aliases of the files that have those icons. Copy the aliases onto a floppy (they take up very little room, so one floppy can store lots of icons). Now you can copy icons from your icon collection any time you like. Also, should anything disastrous ever happen to your hard drive (and it will, it's only a matter of time), you'll have all the work invested in your custom icons backed up safely to a floppy.

Changing the names of things in the Finder. You can change the names of icons you see and messages you get in the Finder by applying ResEdit to the Finder's STR# resource. Warning: don't change the names of the (invisible) Desktop[1] or the (visible) desktop files, though, or you can cause trouble!

Here are a few ideas for changing Finder names so that you have a consistent look and feel for all the icons you've customized. I'll give you the ID numbers where I found them, but they may be different on your system.

If you've gotten clever and replaced your Trash icon with a toilet or a black hole or some other cute icon, you might want to rename that icon. On my machine, ID 11750 holds the messages about the Trash, which I've changed to Outhouse (see Figure 4-34). Other possibilities are Black Hole (there's an icon for this one available from bulletin boards), Recycler, or, of course, the ubiquitous Toilet (there's a neat flush sound available on most bulletin boards to go with it).

---

[1]The desktop (lowercase) is what you see when you're in the Finder. The Desktop (uppercase) is the invisible file that keeps track of where everything is. Apple capitalizes them this way on purpose to differentiate between the two.

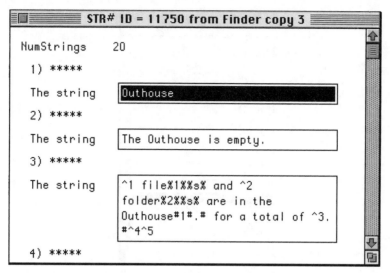

Figure 4-34: You can change messages about Finder icon names, too.

If you don't want untitled folders named Untitled folder, change it to whatever you like, such as Empty folder or Blank folder, or Nothing Here—be creative and have fun. Check ID 112500.

You might want to change those messages about "completely erase disk" and such, which I've found in ID 117500.

After you make your changes, save and quit from ResEdit. Then substitute your modified Finder for the old one and restart.

Once you're tried out a few of the tricks from this chapter and you feel fairly confident using ResEdit, you might try replacing other text strings throughout the Finder. Open a copy of the Finder in ResEdit and double-click on the STR# resource. You'll see a list of resource ID numbers (see Figure 4-35). Go hunting for the words you might like to change.

ID	Size	Name
150	28	
1250	185	
3000	189	
5000	2124	
8750	990	
9000	486	
10000	95	
10250	700	
10500	96	
11000	394	
11250	3159	
11330	577	
11332	917	
11500	1407	
11750	1566	
12000	78	
12250	341	
12750	1653	
13000	1100	
14250	197	
14514	90	
15500	129	

Figure 4-35: Check the strings in these resource IDs to find the ones you'd like to change.

Of course, be sure to change only the text that you actually see when you're in the Finder, as altering anything else is probably not a good idea (especially the stuff that looks like computer code—because that's what it is). And keep a safety copy of your unaltered, working Finder and System files on your hard drive for a couple of days after you've used ResEdit to make major changes to them; if your Mac starts misbehaving, you can always simply replace those two files with their originals to return things to normal.

MOVING ON

The tips and tricks in this chapter are just a few of the things you can do to make your Mac your own, and you'll find many more scattered throughout the book. For example, in Chapter 6 you'll see how to swipe sounds and assign them to events on your computer.

If "Customizing Your Desktop" was a wonderfully frivolous waste of time, the next chapter, "Disk & Drive Magic," proves to make up for it with practical advice and time- and money-saving tricks you can use to maintain your files and do routine chores.

CHAPTER FIVE

DISK & DRIVE TRICKS

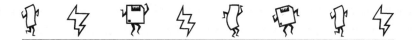

Years from now, we'll probably use a microchip the size of a penny to carry around entire libraries of information—but for now, hard drives and floppy disks are the industry standard. And like everything else in the computer world, they aren't the perfect solution to the data storage dilemma. But you don't have to be a victim of your disks' fickle ways. This chapter will teach you a few simple tricks and techniques you can use to make sure your hard drive and floppies are always working properly. You'll learn powerful tips like how to squeeze more space out of the hard drive you already have, how to use a removable drive for virtual memory, how to back up data reliably, how to fix minor software glitches in hard drives and floppies, and other handy tricks.

THE BASICS

While this chapter has an eclectic collection of tricks for your floppy disks and hard drives, there are a few basic disk tips that you should always follow. They may not be voodoo of the highest order—in fact, they're pretty obvious and elementary ideas—but after all, you're talking about all the work and value you have stored on your drives, and if following a few simple rules can save you hours of agony, frustration and expense, they're worth following.

There's no substitute for regular drive backups. Many Mac users have never experienced a hard drive crash, and I hope they never do. But for most of us, it's not a question of *if* a hard drive fails so much as *when* it will. And half the time, it's not the whole hard drive that goes, it's just the files you need at the moment. You can also experience a corrupted System or Finder file, which throws a monkey wrench into everything else you do. It's a cliché, but I can't stress it enough: back up regularly and thoroughly, and if you can't manage that, at least back up the most important files on your drive. Backing up doesn't mean purchasing a separate backup utility program: if you're willing to reinstall your programs from their original floppies (or copies of those disks), you can just copy documents you really need to keep onto floppy disks and keep those copies handy. The important thing is to make sure you have some sort of backup copies made on a regular basis. For a handy tip on how to use System 7's built-in Find command to perform incremental backups, see Chapter 1, "Secrets of the Finder."

Save early; save often. Of course, all the backing up in the world won't help you if you never get around to saving your work in the first place. There are plenty of horror stories about people who work for hours on a document, forgetting to save it, and then experience a nasty crash, losing all their work. Don't fall victim to the most basic mistake you can make—save your work early and continue to save it often. There are even commercial and shareware utilities that you can set to automatically save your work every 10 minutes or 500 keystrokes, for instance. If you're forgetful about saving, think about picking up an auto-save utility.

Use a little TLC. Though they've come a long way, hard drives are still relatively fragile beasts. They can't take the pounding that your blender or toaster gladly tolerates. Don't toss them around like sacks of flour, don't open an external drive's case unless you know what you're doing and *never* crack open the drive mechanism itself. Treat floppies with the same respect, and don't play around with that little metal shutter on them—dirt or dust from the air or even oil from your fingers can creep onto the magnetic disk inside and wreak havoc with your data.

Likewise, keep any kind of hard drive, floppy or removable cartridge away from strong magnetic fields or electrical devices (this includes stereo speakers, TVs, phones, modems, clocks and anything else with lots of circuitry, a motor or speaker). Random magnetism erases (or at least scrambles) data on disks, so stay away from it. And while you're at it, try to protect your disks from liquids, direct sunlight, excessive heat or cold, dirt, dust, humidity, vibrations or anything else you yourself wouldn't enjoy enduring.

Don't get zapped. Sometimes, a power surge can fry your hard drive or logic board. If other appliances in your home have gotten zapped by power spikes, or if the wiring in your house or apartment is old or of dubious quality, consider buying a power strip or some other kind of surge suppressor or surge protector. If you live in the country, where power outages are frequent, consider getting an uninterrupted power supply. There are two kinds: one gives you a little time to save your work, and the other, more expensive kind, has a battery backup that gives you perhaps a couple of hours of uninterrupted power. I don't have either kind, and I live in the country, but I've been lucky.

Get a SuperDrive and a DOS disk reader. If your Mac doesn't have one already, get a SuperDrive or a high-density disk drive from another manufacturer. (I'm sure that in a very short while, this most basic tip will read "Get a CD-ROM drive," but for now, it's "Get a SuperDrive.") With a SuperDrive, you'll be able to use high-density disks and even read files from DOS and Apple ProDOS disks using Apple's File Exchange utility. If you work a lot in a DOS environment, you might want to pick up a DOS disk-reading utility like Dayna's DOS Mounter or Insignia Solutions' Access PC. You'll be able to mount DOS floppies on the desktop, just like a Mac disk, and you can double-click on PC files and have your Mac automatically launch the appropriate Macintosh application for working with that file. You might also want to consider Apple's Macintosh PC Exchange application. Although you have to purchase it (it doesn't come with your system software, like Apple File Exchange does), it has a few neat goodies like letting you specify which applications on the Mac side are to open documents created by different programs on the PC side.

FLOPPY DISK TRICKS

A really basic tip, but one worth knowing, is how to tell a high-density disk from an 800k disk. Most high-density disks come with "HD" printed on their front left corners, but some don't, especially the kind you buy in bulk from your friendly software-o-rama or by mail order. If you've got a disk of unknown origin, here's how to tell whether it's high-density (1.4 Mb) or double-density (800k): the high-density disks have two square holes in the corners opposite the shutter; double-density disks have only one. Now for some more floppy disk tricks.

Calling for a disk until the cows come home. Although this tip is simple, it's marked as a trap because if you don't know about it, you can go nuts. Here's the scenario: you're through with a floppy disk, and it's been ejected, but the Mac keeps calling for it (you know the all-too-familiar dialog box, "Please Insert the Disk Untitled," or whatever). Here's the trick: keep pressing Command-period until the Mac shuts up and the annoying dialog goes away.

Here's another trick for stopping those calls for Done Disks: if you're not going to be changing anything on them—just reading or copying files from them—lock them *before* you put them in the drive. The reason the Finder wants that disk back is so it can update the disk's invisible Desktop file. If you've locked the disk, the Finder doesn't care about updating that file, because it knows it's not allowed to make any changes to a locked disk.

A basic when-to-lock-the-floppy-disk tip. When you buy a new program, lock the disks before you use them. Then make backup copies and use the backups to install the program from. Even though there's only a small chance that you can harm a program disk simply by running its installer, especially if the disk is locked, it's a good idea to have a backup, just in case. That way, you'll never run the risk of doing by mistake anything irreversible or catastrophic to your master disks.

Quick dual disk erasing. Here's a neat time-saving trick. If you want to erase two floppy disks at once (assuming you've got two floppy drives), put the disks in the drives, highlight both of them and choose Erase Disk. You'll only have to respond to the warning prompts once, and then your Mac will reinitialize both disks.

Quick disk nuking. If you have a stack of disks you'd like to erase, or if there are some disks that keep causing "Disk Initialization Failed!" or "Bad Disk" messages, use a bulk eraser on them. A bulk eraser is a powerful electromagnet that will completely erase any form of magnetic media, including cassettes, video tapes and floppy disks. Every radio station has one, and they might let you use it if you live in a small town.

Thanks to Jorn Knuttila, Bemidji, Minnesota.

Quick disk ejecting. If you're running System 7, select the floppy and use Command-Y to eject it. This method is even faster than dragging the icon to the Trash. Unlike Command-E, which also works in System 6, Command-Y doesn't leave a dimmed disk icon on the desktop, but instead completely unmounts the volume. Pressing Command-Y will unmount any volume except the startup volume.

Thanks to Eric Apgar for fine points in this one.

Mysterious disk sizes. It may sound strange, but 800k disks don't really hold 800k. They hold only 779k under System 6. And if you initialize a double-sided floppy under System 7, they hold only 785k. It's true for erasing, too, which is really just another term for reinitializing the disk.

Cram more on a floppy than you thought would fit. That invisible Desktop file—there's one for every volume—takes up space on a floppy. If you're trying to copy files onto a floppy, but the disk's been used for a while, it has lots of information about files you've trashed still taking up unnecessary space in the Desktop file. Rebuilding the Desktop on a floppy disk will free up some space.

To rebuild the Desktop on a floppy, press and hold the Command and Option keys as you put the disk in the floppy drive.

Much the same thing occurs when you erase a disk that you've been using for a while—since the disk is completely erased, the old Desktop file is wiped clean and a new, smaller one replaces it.

Get Apple DiskCopy. You need it. Apple's DiskCopy utility is becoming more and more of a necessity of life. It lets you copy floppy disks in one fell swoop, without any disk swapping, because it reads the entire disk into RAM and then writes it out in one pass. (As you might surmise, to use DiskCopy, you need 2 Mb of free RAM after your Mac starts up.) With DiskCopy, all the files on a floppy are combined into a single "image" file, which can then be sent conveniently over a modem to a service bureau, bulletin board or online service. You'll also need DiskCopy to convert disk images into usable floppy disks (see the next tip).

You can get DiskCopy free from online services, bulletin boards or user groups. Note, however, that DiskCopy doesn't compress files—that is, it doesn't reduce their file size—it merely combines all the files on a single floppy into one disk image. (For more on file compression, see the tips later in this chapter.) Apple uses DiskCopy because it's the most convenient and reliable method for copying and verifying floppies.

Downloading programs and getting them on floppy disks.
Sometimes when you download from an online service or BBS, you get a disk icon on your hard drive. This is the case with System 7 TuneUp, for example. Double-clicking on the disk image should open it, but if not, use Apple DiskCopy. Fire up DiskCopy and load the image. Then click on the Make a Copy button and insert a floppy disk in your drive. DiskCopy will then create an installer floppy exactly like one that Apple might send you, and you can use that disk to install the software and then store it away safely and conveniently when you're done.

Also, consider getting MountImage if you use DiskCopy a lot or if you need to transfer disk images from CD-ROM disks to floppies. MountImage is a freeware utility that makes your Mac think Disk-Copy disk images are really disks. See Appendix A for neat tricks using it to install things.

Changing the floppy disk icon. If your Mac shows the standard, flat, black-and-white icon when a floppy disk is inserted, follow these steps to give that disk the same neat 3-D icon you see when you install System 7 from floppies.

First, open a copy of the System file with ResEdit. (For more on ResEdit, see the sidebar in Chapter 4, "Customizing Your Desktop." Locate the icl8 resource; then find the neat three-dimensional floppy icon, ID -3998 (see Figure 5-1) and double-click on it. Click Yes to decompress it. You'll see the icon family editor. Double-click on the marquee tool or press Command-A to select the entire icon; then go to the Finder, select the floppy disk icon, press Command-I for Get Info, select the tiny disk icon, and paste. Now you've got a three-dimensional icon for that floppy disk.

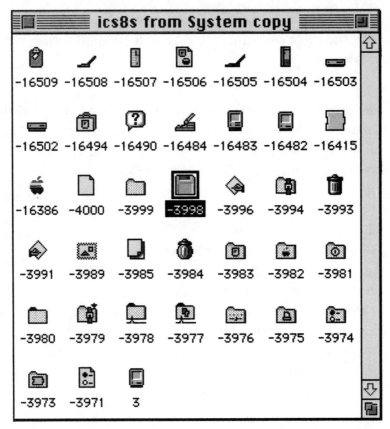

Figure 5-1: Rustle the three-dimensional floppy disk icon from your System file.

You can format PC disks with Apple File Exchange. You can format ProDOS disks, too! The trick is to start Apple File Exchange, shove the disk in the drive, and then choose Erase Disk from the File menu. You'll see a dialog box (see Figure 5-2). Click the 720k button to format an 800k disk as a DOS disk. Not to state the obvious, but, of course, you should be aware that this will erase whatever you have on that disk, and other Mac users may have trouble reading it if you've formatted it as a DOS disk.

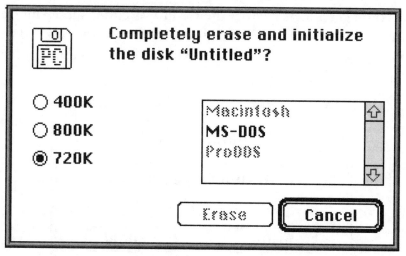

Figure 5-2: You can format DOS disks with Apple File Exchange.

DISK TROUBLES?

Try the repair tricks in this section on disks that aren't working. For more heavy-duty repair techniques, see Chapter 10, "In Trouble?"

Use Disk First Aid! Very often you can repair a disk that's not working right with a simple utility that comes with your system software. Disk First Aid is on the Disk Tools or Utilities disk that came with your system software, and it can often sort out minor problems with a floppy or hard drive. If you don't own a heavy-duty commercial drive maintenance and repair utility like SUM II or Norton, Apple's Disk First Aid can be a life-saver.

To run Disk First Aid, start your Mac with the Disk Tools disk or your emergency startup disk (see Chapter 10 for tips on how to create one of these and what to put on it). Launch Disk First Aid and click Drive (see Figure 5-3) to choose the disk that's causing trouble. Click Open and choose Repair Automatically from Disk First Aid's Options menu. When you click Start, the repair will start. After it's done, you'll get a message that the repair was either successful or unsuccessful, or that Disk First Aid couldn't repair the disk. (If that's the message you get, try again; see "Run Disk First Aid more than once if you need to" below.)

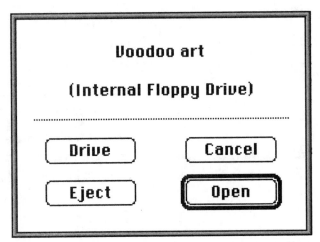

Figure 5-3: Using Disk First Aid to repair minor software problems with drives.

A secret command in Disk First Aid. If you use Disk First Aid, press Command-S after you open the volume; then click Start. You'll see a list of the processes Disk First Aid is going through.

Run Disk First Aid more than once if you need to. Sometimes Disk First Aid tries to make a repair and fails. But you'll often find if you run it again that the second try repairs things a little more, the third attempt fixes things even more, and so on. So if Disk First Aid doesn't completely repair the disk on the first try, run it a few more times.

Can't rename a disk? Have you ever tried to rename a disk, only to find that the Mac stymies you every time? The usual reason for this is that file sharing is on (in System 7). Use the Sharing Setup control panel to turn it off—then rename your hard disk.

If that still doesn't work, try starting from a floppy (in either System 6 or 7). Now you should be able to rename your hard disk.

If that fails, too, your drive's root directory may have had its nameLocked bit set (this is an item that tells whether you're allowed to rename the disk). This bit can get set incorrectly if you're sharing files in a mixed System 6 and System 7 network and a user of System 6 logs on. It can also get set inadvertently when your Mac crashes. There are shareware/freeware utilities called Volume Name Unlocker and UnLockFolder, available on CompuServe and other bulletin boards, that will fix this problem.

Thanks to Eric Apgar, Apple Worldwide Technical Assistance.

HARD DISK & DISK UTILITY TRICKS

In this section we'll take a look at a mixed bag of tricks you can use to manage your hard disk, including using a few disk utility programs that do file compression. You'll see tricks for reinstalling your hard disk driver, formatting a hard disk, getting secret information about it, and so forth.

Get yourself an automatic background file compression utility. If disk space is tight, you might consider investing in an automatic file compression program. All you need to do is install one of these wonderful utilities, and your files will be automatically compressed and expanded as you work with them. I swore not to plug products you have to spend extra money for, but the Mac sadly lacks this built-in capability. Here are three possibilities: StuffIt SpaceSaver (Aladdin), More Disk Space (Alysis) and AutoDoubler (Fifth Generation Systems).

Get StuffIt, too. Don't confuse these automatic background compression utilities—which constantly work to free up space on your hard drive by compressing files while you work—with simple file compression and archival programs, like StuffIt, DiskDoubler or the excellent shareware program, Compact Pro. There's a subtle but important difference between the programs, so check out all the options of any compression product before you buy. Often, you can get a discount if you buy into a package deal (like DiskDoubler, the compression program, and AutoDoubler, its backgrounder companion program).

And if things weren't confusing enough, there's a whole range of StuffIt products out there. Based on software technology first created by Raymond Lau, the products in the StuffIt family are now marketed by Aladdin Systems, which makes StuffIt Lite (a popular shareware program formerly known as StuffIt Classic), StuffIt Deluxe (a commercial compressor/archiver), UnStuffIt (a free utility which only *un*stuffs files), the StuffIt Installer engine and StuffIt SpaceSaver, mentioned above. The StuffIt line is just about *the* compression standard for sending Macintosh files via an online service or bulletin board. StuffIt lets you put several files into one archive so you can transmit them all at the same time (see Figure 5-4). At the other end, someone with a copy of the program decompresses the files so they can be read.

Name	Type	Crea	Size	Date	Saved
Fig 4-1	TIFF	Wdgt	727170	10/9/92	97%
Fig 4-10	TIFF	Wdgt	279416	10/7/92	97%
Fig 4-11	TIFF	Wdgt	322878	10/7/92	98%
Fig 4-12	TIFF	Wdgt	151321	10/9/92	95%
Fig 4-13	TIFF	Wdgt	162872	10/9/92	97%
Fig 4-14	TIFF	Wdgt	230770	10/9/92	97%
Fig 4-15	TIFF	Wdgt	125036	10/9/92	97%
Fig 4-16	TIFF	Wdgt	255900	10/9/92	98%
Fig 4-17	TIFF	Wdgt	727170	10/9/92	97%
Fig 4-18	TIFF	Wdgt	209703	10/9/92	97%
Fig 4-19	TIFF	Wdgt	339434	10/9/92	97%
Fig 4-2	TIFF	Wdgt	162327	10/9/92	96%
Fig 4-20	TIFF	Wdgt	379720	10/9/92	97%
Fig 4-21	TIFF	Wdgt	256324	10/9/92	98%

Current level: 28 items, 8058K decompressed.
1.5.1 Archive is 260K on Voodoo art (824K free).

Figure 5-4: You can use StuffIt to create a single archive of several compressed files.

StuffIt doesn't operate automatically in the background, as the store-bought programs in the preceding tip do. Instead, you create an *archive* file with it and then add files (it can be a single file or as many as you like) to the archive. As StuffIt adds the files, it compresses them, leaving the original uncompressed files on your disk. (You can choose to have the originals deleted after the process is done.)

You can tell that a file has been stuffed because it will have an .sit suffix (like "Annual Report.sit"). A StuffIt archive that contains folders indicates a folder by an *f*, so Book Chapters *f* is the name of a folder called Book Chapters.

You can also create self-extracting (or self-unstuffing) files to send to folks who may not have StuffIt at their end. Self-extracting files have an .sea suffix, and all you do to open them is double-click.

If you're interested in more tips on using StuffIt, check out Chapter 8, "Connectivity Secrets."

Give your hard disk a new icon, too. I've seen lots of messages on bulletin boards from people saying they can't change the icon of their hard disks in System 7, but I've done it (and very easily, too). Perhaps I'm just having voodoo luck, or perhaps there's something I don't understand—but this works. Even on a Quadra. Here's the trick.

You can give your hard disk some personality by pasting a new icon into its Get Info box. HyperCard comes with some neat icons, like the one I use for PorkChop and Somebody[1], real kitties whose names grace the hard disks of my Quadra and Mac II (see Figure 5-5). (My cat Smokey is also a hard disk, but he is being shared at the moment in Figure 5-5.)

The neat cat icon I used in Figure 5-5 is from an old HyperCard Art Bits stack (version 1.0.1—it's dated 1987). Launch HyperCard and from the Home card, click on the Art Bits button. When you find the cat icon, or one you like, pull the toolbox down from the Tools menu. Then use the selection marquee to draw a selection box around the image you want; copy with Command-C. Select your hard disk icon and press Command-I for Get Info. Click the hard drive icon and press Command-V to paste the new image.

---

[1]As in "Somebody is watching you," "Somebody is hungry," "Somebody threw up breakfast," and so forth.

Figure 5-5: These cat hard disk icons are
borrowed from HyperCard's Art Bits stack.

Stories abound about not being able to change the hard disk icon,
so there must be a problem that I haven't encountered.

Hard disks have drivers, too. You probably already know that
the little printer icons in your System Folder represent printer
drivers—software that runs, or "drives," the printer. Well, hard disks
have drivers, too. The formatting software that comes with any new
hard drive you buy puts that hard disk's driver on the disk. If yours is
an Apple hard drive, that formatting software is called Apple HD SC
Setup, and it comes with the system software. If your hard disk is *not*
an Apple disk, but is a third-party disk instead, you should have
received a formatter utility from the manufacturer. (If you didn't, and
somebody else installed the hard disk for you, call him or her and
complain mightily.)

Sometimes you may need to reinstall your hard disk driver if the disk isn't working properly. For example, one source of System 7 trouble is running System 7 with a hard disk driver that hasn't been updated for System 7. Other problems can be caused by damages from power outages or crashes. One tell-tale symptom: the hard disk's icon doesn't show up in the Finder.

To fix this problem, install your hard disk driver again. If you're using Apple HD SC Setup, start up from the Disk Tools disk or from your emergency startup disk. Launch Apple HD SC Setup and click Update. (If you're using a third-party formatter, follow the instructions that came with it.)

Remember, you want to update it, not initialize it. I'm sure you know that if you initialize a disk, the process erases everything on it.

Use Apple HD SC Setup to get information about your hard disk. There's hidden information in your hard disk formatter. Launch Apple HD SC Setup, click Partition and then Details. You'll see a screen like the one in Figure 5-6.

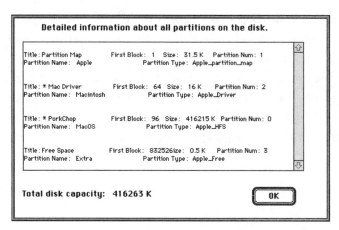

Figure 5-6: Examine your hard disk with the Apple HD SC Setup utility that came with your Macintosh.

You can't always format third-party hard disks with Apple HD SC Setup. Maybe this one is obvious, but it happened to me. I forgot that I had replaced my Mac II's factory installed internal hard drive with a bigger third-party model, and when trouble time came, I tried to format it with Apple HD SC Setup. It kept telling me there were no SCSI devices found, so I figured I was *really* in trouble until I got out the Cutting Edge formatter disk and everything went OK. There are, of course, exceptions to this rule, and you can sometimes get by using Apple's formatter on third-party disks and vice versa, but it's a sound policy to always use the formatter suggested by the drive manufacturer.

Can't eject your Syquest? You can't eject a removable drive like a Syquest with file sharing activated? Turn file sharing off and try ejecting the cartridge again. Always mount Syquest drives after File Sharing is turned on (or leave it turned off the entire time you're working with the cartridge) to avoid this problem.

Switching startup disks. You don't have to always start up using your Mac's internal hard drive. If you have more than one hard drive connected to your Mac, use the Startup Disk control panel (see Figure 5-7) to choose the one you want to be in effect as the startup disk the next time you turn on your Mac. If there's no valid System Folder on the disk you choose, the Mac will start from the same hard disk that it used before.

Figure 5-7: Use the Startup Disk control panel
to indicate which drive you want to boot from.

This Startup Disk control panel is called Startup Device in System
6. It doesn't work on a Mac Plus, by the way. To change the startup
disk on a Plus, you'll need to switch SCSI ID numbers (see Chapter
8 for how to do this). The highest-numbered SCSI disk that has a
System Folder on it will be used as the startup disk.

MISCELLANEOUS DISK TRICKS

Want to use DOS disks on your Mac? Speed up the Finder on your
hard disk? These and other disk mysteries are unveiled in this section.

Using DOS disks. If you need a disk right *now* and the only
ones around are 3.5-inch floppies formatted for DOS, you can
use them on your Mac (as long as you've got a SuperDrive). System
7 will format them for your Mac (erasing them in the process) if you
just stick 'em in the drive and click Initialize (or One-Sided or Two-
Sided if it's a double-density disk).

It can be confusing because DOS formats disks as 720k or 1.2 Mb while the Mac uses 800k and 1.44 Mb capacities, but it's OK. Really, you can use the same disk. Once a disk is formatted for the right type of computer, it's the right capacity. Don't ask me why—this is real voodoo—the sort of thing I don't care to know.

Reclaim storage space on your hard disk. There's extra hidden storage space that you can usually free up on your hard disk, if you have an Apple hard drive and are willing to reformat it. The amount of space you can reclaim ranges from less than a megabyte to sometimes several megabytes. To see how much real estate you can get on yours, use Apple HD SC Setup and choose Partition. Select Custom and Details. You'll see the unused space on your hard disk—the gray area at the bottom. At this point, you can decide whether there's enough reclaimable space to go to the bother of reformatting.

If you think it's worthwhile (users of some large disks have been able to reclaim as much as 15 megabytes, I'm told), *back up what's on your hard disk*, because repartitioning is going to wipe out everything on it. Then launch Apple HD SC Setup again. Click Partition and Custom, select your main Macintosh volume, and delete it. Then click just underneath the top partition and drag all the way to the bottom. In the dialog box you'll see, choose Macintosh Volume and specify the whole drive space. When everything's done, click all the OKs, Dones and Quits, and enjoy your larger hard disk.

Thanks to Eric Apgar, Apple Worldwide Technical Assistance.

Desktops demystified. A lot of folks (and I'm one of them) get easily confused about the desktop and the Desktop. The Desktop (with an uppercase D) is an invisible file that keeps track of everything the Finder needs to know about, such as folder locations and file arrangements. The desktop (with a lowercase d) is what you see when you're in the Finder—all those little icons and windows.

There's a difference between a System 6 Desktop and a System 7 Desktop. There's also a difference between the Desktop on a floppy disk and the Desktop on a hard disk. Stay with me.

In System 6, there is only one Desktop file, but in System 7 there are two—Desktop DB, holding information about where files are stored, and Desktop DF, holding information about the icons that represent those files.

Speeding up the Finder under System 7. There are some obvious things you can do to speed up the Finder as it runs on your hard disk, such as optimizing the disk with a utility like Norton Speed Disk. Here are a few non-obvious tricks that will speed 'er up. Some of them are mentioned in more detail in other chapters, but here they are, all together:

- Turn off file sharing in the Sharing Setup control panel.

- Turn off Calculate folder sizes in the Views control panel.

- Switch to 16 colors or black and white in the Monitors control panel.

- Increase the disk cache in the Memory control panel (see Chapter 9, "Memory Demystified," for details).

- Turn off background printing in the Chooser (although this will mean you can't work and print at the same time).

- Keep a full set of screen fonts installed only for the fonts you use most often.

- Make the window color Black & White in the Color control panel (you'll lose the 3-D scroll bars).

- Eliminate the Finder's zoom rectangles (remember this trick from Chapter 4?).

Thanks to Eric Apgar, Apple Worldwide Technical Assistance.

MOVING ON

Although you've seen all sorts of neat tricks for maintaining your disks and drives in this chapter, be aware that these aren't the last words on the subject. Chapter 8, "Connectivity Secrets," has lots more information about setting up external hard drives (SCSI devices), and Chapter 10, "In Trouble?" talks you through tricky matters like when you should rebuild the invisible Desktop file that's on every disk, as well as discussing how to recover from that dreaded Sad Mac icon, how to make an emergency startup disk, and other things like that which you don't usually want to think about.

We'll get back to the fun stuff in the next chapter, "Miscellaneous Voodoo Tricks." As its name implies, this is the catchall chapter—the one with all kinds of goodies that wouldn't logically go anywhere else.

CHAPTER SIX

MISCELLANEOUS VOODOO TRICKS

n this chapter you'll find all sorts of tricks for everything from using obscure control panels (ever wonder what Mouse Keys was for?) to tips on using PowerBooks to QuickTime and sound tricks. We'll wind up with a grab bag of tricks for doing all sorts of neat stuff like making your own Read Me files, protecting files and folders, using stationery pads and more. If you have a favorite tip or trick that you haven't read about yet, there's a good chance you'll find it here.

CONTROL PANEL TRICKS

Although the tips and tricks in this section may be pretty "easy," they all deal with an often-overlooked area: the little mysteries that lurk in the control panels and desk accessories that come with your Mac.

Group your control panels by renaming them. Normally, control panels are alphabetized, so things like General Controls (which you often use) are about halfway down the list, depending on how many control panels you've got. It only makes sense to put the most frequently used control panels at the top of the list and the ones you never touch at the bottom. Use the Apple Menu Item naming tricks discussed in Chapter 2, "Menu Magic," to reorder your control panels. For example, you can rename General Controls to ..General Controls (adding two periods to the front of its name) to move it to the top of the list. If you use the file sharing control panels often, rename them, too, to get them to the top of the list—they're way down in the S's (Sharing Setup) and the U's (Users and Groups). Some people rename them all with a bullet (Option-8) at the front of their names, for instance, just to group them all consecutively.

And put aliases of your most frequently used control panels in the Apple menu for quicker access. Rename their aliases in the Apple Menu Items folder so they'll appear in the Apple menu where you want them.

Thanks to Jorn Knuttila, Bemidji, Minnesota.

The CloseView control panel doesn't like virtual memory. Maybe Apple has fixed this problem by now, but if you're having problems using the CloseView control panel, turn off virtual memory (if you're using it) and see if that helps.

Turn off extensions before installing desk accessories. Sometimes—a *very few* sometimes—you'll add a desk accessory only to find that instead of being installed, it has disappeared! To get around this problem in System 7, press the Shift key as you start up to disable extensions. Then drag your new desk accessory out of its suitcase. Remember, in System 6 you install DAs by using the Font/DA Mover; in System 7, you just drag them out of suitcases.

Out of memory messages when installing desk accessories. Some bizarre set of circumstances may produce a message that there isn't enough memory to move a desk accessory from a suitcase, even though you know you've got more than enough RAM. If this happens to you, try this trick. Drag the whole suitcase of desk accessories to the System Folder; then go back later and delete the items you don't want installed.

Secrets of the color wheel. The color wheel (or Color Picker, as it's sometimes called) is accessible through System 7's Labels control panel (see Figure 6-1)—not through the Color control panel, as you might think. (The Color control panel in System 7 lets you change the highlight color.) In the Labels control panel, click on any color to go to the color wheel (see Figure 6-2).

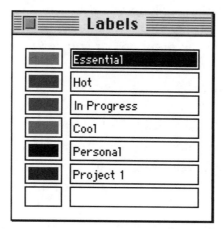

Figure 6-1: The Labels control panel lets you assign a color and category to a file.

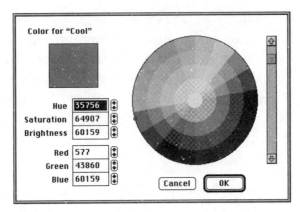

Figure 6-2: Clicking on any label's color block brings up the color wheel.

There are two ways to edit colors. If you look at the boxes at the bottom left of the Color Picker dialog box, you'll see values for Red, Green and Blue and Hue, Saturation and Brightness. You can click on the arrows to change the numbers, or you can type new numbers in the boxes.

While you can use the Red, Green and Blue fields to assign precise increments of those three colors to create a new composite color, you can also use the Hue, Saturation and Brightness fields to assign those specific properties to colors. Higher saturation numbers mean more intense color, while lower saturation numbers make colors duller and grayer. Similarly, the higher the brightness number, the brighter the color.

I find that clicking and dragging within the color wheel is the easiest way to change colors. Click anywhere on the wheel to change the hue and drag the cursor around slowly until you get close to the color you had in mind. The closer you click to the center of the wheel, the grayer the color will be (less saturation). To make a color brighter or darker, drag the scroll bar up or down, respectively.

When you click on a color, you'll see the new color on the top in the "Color for" box in the upper-left corner of the dialog box. The former color is shown below for comparison. Clicking on the former color in the bottom box returns the top box to that same color.

Remember that you can cut and paste between desk accessories and programs, too. This often-overlooked tip can save you a lot of time if you need to get the date and time or the results of a calculation into a program that doesn't have a built-in date/time stamp or a calculator utility. Just copy and paste the date or time from the Alarm Clock, or the results from the Calculator. Copying and pasting this way cuts down on the possibility of making an error when typing a number. You can paste special symbols from Key Caps, too. (Chapter 7, "Printing Mysteries," has more symbol tricks.)

Use the Alarm Clock to set the time. You'll have to reset your Macintosh's internal clock twice a year for Daylight Savings Time. For the most accurate time, use the Alarm Clock desk accessory, not the General Controls control panel. Here's why: when you use the Alarm Clock, your change takes place instantly, but when you use the General Controls control panel, the time change doesn't take effect until you select another option or close the control panel.

Shades of gray Apples! Here's a trivia item for detail fanatics. On a monochrome monitor in System 6, the Apple menu icon was composed of shades of gray. With System 7, the Apple went black. To get your shaded Apple back, use the Monitors control panel and choose Color, even though you don't have a color monitor.

Using Mouse Keys instead of the mouse. A little-known feature called Mouse Keys in the Easy Access control panel lets you use the numeric keypad on your keyboard to control the cursor instead of the mouse. If you need to fine-tune graphics by nudging them one pixel at a time, or if you're simply more comfortable using the keyboard all the time, you may find this feature handy.

To turn on Mouse Keys, make sure the Easy Access control panel is installed and press Command-Shift-Clear (Clear is on the numeric keypad). See the Sticky Keys tips below if you can't press all three keys at once.

With Mouse Keys activated, the 5 key on the numeric keypad works just like a mouse button. Press it three times to double-click and once to click. Use the other keys to move the pointer. The 4 and 6 keys move it left and right, the 8 and 2 keys move it up and down and the four keys in the corners move it diagonally.

To "click and drag the mouse" using Mouse Keys, press the zero key twice to lock the mouse button down (like a click-and-hold), and press the decimal point key twice to unlock the mouse button.

For folks who are computer-inclined but not artistically adept, Mouse Keys can become a secret weapon in draw and paint programs. It's a much more precise and powerful way to create drawings than using the mouse alone.

One other hidden advantage of Mouse Keys: if your mouse freezes up, you can use Mouse Keys to save the file you're working on, exit the program and restart your Mac.

Use Sticky Keys for one-handed typing. In System 7, Sticky Keys is part of the Easy Access control panel, but in System 6, it's a separate INIT. Either way, it lets you type keys one by one that normally all have to be pressed at the same time. For example, to press Command-S for Save with Sticky Keys on, you press Command and then press S.

To activate Sticky Keys, you'll need to press the Shift key five times *without moving the mouse.* If you move the mouse, you'll have to start pressing Shift over again.

It's not likely that you'll turn on Sticky Keys by mistake (pressing Shift five times in a row is rare in normal typing), but if you're messing with the keyboard, it might happen. If you hear a weird siren and beeps while you're using the keyboard, you've probably turned on Sticky Keys by mistake.

When Sticky Keys is activated, you'll hear a rising siren sound and you'll see a U-shaped icon in the upper-right corner of the menu bar. Type the first key you want to press, such as Command. You'll hear a beep, and the menu bar icon will change to show you a tiny down arrow. Press the key again to lock it, and the arrow on the icon will move down. Now press the rest of the keys that complete the key combination you want to use. For example, if you're in the Finder, typing **n** if you've pressed Command first will create a new folder, just as though you pressed Command-N.

Press a modifier key (like Command, Option, Shift or Control) twice to lock the key. You'll need to do this if you want to Shift-click without a mouse so you can select more than one item at a time.

You can use Sticky Keys in combination with Mouse Keys. For example, here's how to Shift-click with Sticky Keys and Mouse Keys to select items that aren't next to each other in a list. With both Mouse Keys and Sticky Keys active, press Shift twice to lock the key; then press 5 on the numeric keypad to select your first item. To select the next item, move to it by using the arrow keys and press the 5 on the numeric keypad again.

To turn off Sticky Keys, press Shift five times again or press any two of the modifier keys (Option, Shift, Command or Control) at once. It's off when the icon disappears. You'll hear a falling tone. You can also turn Sticky Keys on and off via the Easy Access control panel in System 7, but if you can use that control panel with the mouse, why do you need Sticky Keys? Silly question, I guess.

In short, Sticky Keys and Mouse Keys are excellent tools for allowing anyone to use every aspect of a Mac without touching a mouse, but they're also handy for times when mouse users need precise control over the cursor or want to use only the keyboard.

Installing desk accessories in applications. With System 7, you can install desk accessories directly into applications, instead of putting them in the Apple menu. For example, a Thesaurus desk accessory that only worked within Microsoft Word came with version 4 of the program. (Version 5 has a new Thesaurus, but you may not have upgraded yet.) Unless you were running Word, you couldn't use it, so that Thesaurus DA usually just sat there taking up space in your Apple menu. But with a little magic, you can put that DA into Word or MacWrite so that it won't be on the Apple menu unless you're running Word or MacWrite. The trick is to use Font/ DA mover (yes, even with System 7).

First, use the Font/DA Mover to open the suitcase that holds the desk accessory you want to install. Make sure the Desk Accessory button is checked, or Option-double-click on the Font/DA mover icon so that it will open with the Desk Accessory button checked.

Then press and hold Option and click the Open button to see the applications listed. Open the program you want to install the DA into and click Copy. Now you'll only see that DA in the Apple menu when the selected program is running, instead of having it in the Apple menu all the time, taking up space or confusing beginners.

Switching startup monitors. Some folks have two monitors—maybe a big monochrome monitor for doing desktop publishing and a regular color monitor for the rest of the time. What's not immediately obvious is how to designate one of them as the startup monitor (with the happy Mac face). Open the Monitors control panel (see Figure 6-3) and press the Option key. You'll see a Mac face. Just drag it to the monitor you want to use as your startup monitor. It doesn't appear in Figure 6-3 because I haven't pressed Option yet—when I do, I can't take a screen shot. Try it on your own Mac.

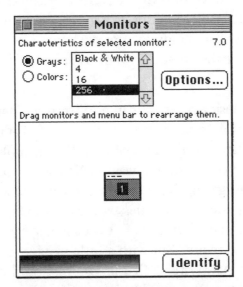

Figure 6-3: To switch startup monitors, go to the Monitors control panel, press Option and drag the Mac face that appears to the monitor you want activated on startup.

Likewise, you can set which monitor will host the main menu bar (which can be different from the monitor you designate as your startup monitor) by dragging the tiny menu bar icon to the monitor you want to specify as the one with the real menu bar that appears after you restart your Mac.

What kind of mileage is on the Map? The mysterious mileage that's shown on the Map control panel (see Figure 6-4) is the distance between the last location you viewed and the location you're looking at now. Click on your home town (see "Neat Map tricks" below for how to add your home town to the Map) and click Set if you always want to see the distance between your home and the places you look at on the Map.

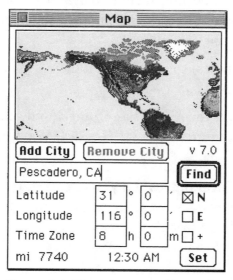

Figure 6-4: The Map control panel has lots of hidden tricks.

Neat Map tricks. The "real purpose" of the Map is probably for quickly giving you the local date and time while you're traveling, but it seems that the more straightforward a utility is, the more tricks we can find in it.

- Just put the mouse pointer at the inside edge of the Map and press and hold the mouse button. As you drag the pointer outside the Map's boundaries, it will scroll in that direction.

- To add your own city, type its name and then click on the location. *Then* click Add. If you know its latitude and longitude already (well, some people do), you can enter them instead of clicking on where you guess the city is.

- To see which cities are already on the Map, press Option and click Find repeatedly. You'll see cities appear in alphabetical order from the location where you are.

- To check the difference in time between the last location you clicked and your current location (on the Map, of course), click on the words Time Zone. They change to Time Differ., and you see the difference in hours and minutes ahead, in terms of Greenwich Mean Time.

- Click on mi (miles) to switch to kilometers (km). Click on km to switch to degrees (dg).

And don't forget the Map's Easter Eggs (and other surprises) that were discussed back in Chapter 3, "Hoodoo Voodoo."

Check the local time when you click Set. If you're choosing your home town as the set location in the Map, make sure the time showing at the bottom is the same as your local time. If it isn't, use the Alarm Clock to reset your Mac's clock.

Setting the Alarm Clock. That Alarm Clock isn't "intuitive," as they say. If you've never used it before, good luck figuring out how. Here are the secrets. To change the time or date with the Alarm Clock or set an alarm time, click on the weird thing that looks like a key. That opens up the rest of the Alarm Clock's window. Click on the clock or calendar icon to set the time or date. Click on the alarm clock icon to set an alarm time. Then make the actual changes in the middle section of the dialog box. Click the keyhole icon to set the alarm clock part of the Alarm Clock.

Mouse tricks. You *do* know the real mouse secret, yes? That you can pick it up and the pointer on the screen doesn't move? So put this trick to your advantage by setting the speed to Fast in the Mouse control panel. You won't have to move the mouse on your real desktop very far to get big results on your Mac's desktop; you can just pick it up, put it down, and sweep it in small, rapid motions, while keeping your wrist on the desktop. I've saved many a cup of caffeine from getting knocked over this way.

POWERBOOK TRICKS

PowerBooks are hot! Apple sold 300,000 of them in 1992, and that number will skyrocket in the future. Meanwhile, new PowerBooks are being introduced every time you turn around, and prices are slowly but steadily dropping, too. Many first-time Mac users are starting off with a PowerBook, while hordes of long-time Mac fans are investing in one of the neat Macintosh Duos, which give you all the portability of a super-lightweight PowerBook with the regular features of a stationary Mac (just like the saucer section separating from the *Enterprise*, Star Trek fans). Either way, you'll find plenty of great Power-Book tricks in this section.

The PowerBook has trouble reading some floppies. Disks that are commercially duplicated often seem to cause trouble in PowerBooks. If you get a disk like this, take it over to a regular Mac (not a PowerBook) and copy it to another floppy disk, preferably a brand-name one. Apple knows about this problem and is offering a swap for disk drives. If the problem occurs often enough, it might be worth your while to take them up on the offer. (Call 800/767-2775 for the PowerBook repair hotline.)

Also, be aware that the PowerBook floppy drives are exceptionally prone to problems caused by dust—as are all the FDHD SuperDrives.

Selectively pick the programs you're going to use when your PowerBook is running off its battery. Some programs, especially ones that have to work with lots of information but run on relatively little RAM, access the hard disk a lot more than others.

Databases are notorious for lots of disk access; so is HyperCard. QuickTime is another application that needs lots of disk access. And since Virtual Memory uses your hard drive as makeshift RAM, it is also heavy on disk access. Since working with the hard disk is one of the main draws on your battery, try to avoid using those kinds of programs when you know you'll be running your PowerBook off its battery—say, on a plane trip. Save that work for when you've got a power outlet handy.

On a PowerBook 170, use the Power-Saver option. The 170s have a Power-Saver option in the Battery DA. Click on that weird-looking flag (some folks think it looks like a keyhole) at the far right to get at it. When the Power-Saver is activated, your processor runs at 16 Mhz instead of 25 Mhz, and you can run your PowerBook about half an hour longer than usual at the slower speed. Of course, this will hamstring your PowerBook's performance, but for most things you're likely to be doing (like telecommunications or word processing) the slower speed will scarcely be noticeable, if at all.

Backlighting eats batteries. The one biggest power-eater on your PowerBook is the backlighting. It's more power-hungry than disk accessing. To conserve energy, use the Backlight control panel and pick a very small amount of idle time before the backlighting goes off. Set it to 15 seconds or so; your PowerBook lights up again very quickly when you touch the keyboard or the trackball.

Keep your PowerBook in Sleep mode when you're not using it. Use the Portable control panel and set Minutes until Automatic Sleep at one or two minutes to conserve on power. You can also use the Special menu or the Battery desk accessory to put the PowerBook to sleep immediately when you know you're going to stop for a bit.

Get the PB Sleep FKEY. You can download a really useful FKEY named PB Sleep that puts your PowerBook to sleep, bypassing the dialog box that you normally get when you go through the Finder with AppleTalk active.

There's also another useful set of utilities (freeware) called PB Tools, by Bill Steinberg. It includes SafeSleep, which prompts you for a password before it wakes your PowerBook.

Use keyboard alternatives until you can get used to that trackball. If you're having trouble getting accustomed to the PowerBook's trackball, consider spending a few minutes with ResEdit (see Chapter 4, "Customizing Your Desktop") and create Command-key equivalents for often-used commands, like Shut Down and Restart. Also, use built-in keyboard shortcuts like Command-W to close windows, Command-F to find things instead of clicking and scrolling and Command-Y to eject disks. No matter what kind of keyboard shortcuts you devise, you'll still have to train one finger to stay down on the click button when you're dragging.

Set up a RAM disk on a PowerBook. If you have at least 6-8 Mb of RAM, you'll benefit from setting up a RAM disk on your PowerBook. With a RAM disk, you'll save battery life, because you aren't accessing the hard disk and consuming as much power. See Chapter 9, "Memory Demystified," for more details on how to set up a RAM disk. Here's the short and sweet version.

First, set up a 4 Mb or so RAM disk by using the Memory control panel (you won't see that option in the control panel if your Mac doesn't support it). Then restart your Mac. Then install a System Folder on the RAM disk (use the System disks that came with the PowerBook). Set the RAM disk as your startup disk by using the Startup Disk control panel.

Powering down erases a RAM disk (unless you've got a non-volatile RAM disk like Maxima from Connectix; see Chapter 9), so use Sleep instead of Shut Down to turn off your PowerBook when you're not using it. (Yes, you can carry a sleeping PowerBook around, despite what the manual says.)

Get At Ease to save about 200k of RAM. Apple's At Ease application is designed to let you restrict access to your computer (from prying neighborhood kids and co-workers, too), but it has a secret appeal to PowerBook users: you can run At Ease under System 7 and free up about 200k of RAM, which you can then make available to the programs you use most often. Another At Ease attribute that some PowerBook users appreciate is its oversized buttons and generally more forgiving interface—pointing and clicking while riding in the back of a station wagon or wedged in the middle seat of a long flight can be harder than you might think. So if you have a PowerBook, you may want to opt for the At Ease desktop.

Checking your PowerBook's power. Put an alias of the Battery control panel in your Startup Items folder if you're using a PowerBook. Then you can glance at the desktop to see how much juice is left in the battery. Don't constantly recharge the battery, or you won't get as much use out of it before it'll need another charge. About once a month, use the computer until it goes to Sleep after the *third* low-power warning, which says it will go to sleep within 10 seconds and so Good Night. Take out the battery and recharge it.

Turn down that symphonic boot bong! If you have a PowerBook or a Quadra, you know that the startup sound is rather like the older Mac's, but *more so.* If you're hauling your PowerBook to a press briefing or lecture, you've probably found that it's embarrassingly loud when you turn it on and everybody turns around to look at you. Even if you set the volume to zero, it's still pretty loud. Here's the secret: set the volume to one or two instead of zero. If you set it at zero, it resets to a midrange sound.

You can stick a standard 1/8-inch stereo or mono connector in the sound jack at the back to disable the external speaker, too. See your friendly Radio Shack if you don't have one handy.

The newer PowerBooks (160, 180 and beyond) come with a simple beep in the PowerBook Sound control panel that takes care of this problem. Just switch to it.

Fast file transfer to a PowerBook and back again. If you need to transfer files between your main Mac and a non-Duo Power-Book, try this trick: set up a two-Mac AppleTalk network. Don't let the sound of that scare you; it's actually really easy. You can connect the two computers to each other through their printer ports with an Apple system cable or with a less expensive set of third-party cables, like Farallon PhoneNET connectors. Then just turn on file sharing and zip files from one computer to the other really quickly. The PhoneNET connectors come with a standard Mac printer port plug on one end and a modular telephone jack on the other. To connect the two computers, put the plugs in each Mac's printer port; at the other end of the connectors, use a standard modular phone cord like those found with every new phone or modem sold (known to techno-philes as an RJ-11 patch cord).

Here's how to do it, even if you've never used networking before. On one computer (it doesn't matter which), go to the Chooser and turn AppleTalk on (click Active). Then, in the Finder, highlight the hard disk icon and choose Sharing from the File menu. Click Share this item and its contents.

On the other computer, go to the Chooser and turn on Apple-Talk; click AppleShare and pick the other computer as the file server. Log on as a guest. You should now be connected to the first computer and its icon should appear on the second computer's desktop. Select the hard disk as the item you want to use. In the Finder, double-click on the icon of the shared hard disk. It will open in its own window; just drag items from window to window to exchange files. If you're copying a lot of files, put them in folders for fast copying.

Get a disk compression program. If you're using a Power-Book, a disk compression program like AutoDoubler, Super-Disk or SpaceSaver is really useful. They'll compress your files to about half their normal size so you can keep more stuff on your hard disk. Keep in mind, though, that these types of programs often work in the background—while your Mac is otherwise idle—to continually com-press files in an effort to free up more hard drive space. This could be counterproductive if you think your PowerBook is sleeping when it's really furiously working the hard drive to compress files. Check the compression program's manual to make sure it won't be keeping your PowerBook awake when you want it to be asleep.

Clean all the extra stuff off your PowerBook's hard disk. Do you really need all the control panels and extensions that are on your PowerBook? Nuke a few. The less extensions you run, the more RAM you'll have free to devote to applications or a RAM disk. Also, get rid of Help files and tutorial files, templates you don't need, and so forth. Take a hard look at your fonts and get rid of most of them. If your PowerBook has a floppy drive, Make aliases of programs you don't use very often and remove the originals from the hard disk, putting them on floppies with meaningful names. The Mac will ask you to insert the correct floppy when you double-click on an alias of a removed program (so don't back 'em all up to a set of "Untitled" disks).

More tricks for saving battery power: don't run a spell-checker till you get back to the office. Spell-checking requires lots of disk access and will drain your power quickly. Don't change fonts, either, until you're at an electrical outlet. Saving requires disk access, too, and that takes power, so save only as often as you finish a block of work you want to save. Turn off backlighting if you can see without it, or try 50 percent intensity as a compromise between readability and battery conservation.

Swap the Esc and tilde (~) keys. Arrgh!! They moved the Esc key on the PowerBook keyboard so it isn't where God intended, in the upper-left corner. See "Swapping Keys Around" later in this chapter for how to swap the Esc and tilde keys.

Install the Caps Lock extension. Unlike separate Apple keyboards, the PowerBook's keyboard doesn't have a light or a locking button to tell you when Caps Lock is on. If you're running System 7.1, there's a PowerBook extension called Caps Lock on the Tidbits installation floppy that may save your sanity. Drag it to your System Folder so that your PowerBook will display an icon on the menu bar whenever Caps Lock is on. If you can't find Caps Lock, get this extension from a friend, or check with online services and user groups.

⚡**TRAP** **Be careful at the airport.** When you get to the airport metal detector, you'll probably be asked to demonstrate that the PowerBook is really a computer, so keep a charged battery inside it and always ask the guards to hand-search it rather than sending it through the X-ray machine—the motors that drive conveyor belts can often cause problems with floppies, hard disks and delicate circuitry. Don't walk through the metal detector with your PowerBook, either—some metal detectors use magnetism to sense metal objects, which isn't a lot of fun for the files on your hard drive. The absolutely safest way to get your PowerBook onto a plane is to demonstrate that it's really a computer and let the guard take it around.

QUICKTIME TIPS

Drawing almost as much buzz and attention as the PowerBooks has been QuickTime, Apple's multimedia extension for the Macintosh. With Apple's QuickTime Starter Kit, you'll get the QuickTime extension and a few utilities for QuickTime (SimplePlayer for playing and editing movies; Convert-to-Movie for changing animations into movies and using sounds in movies; and PICT Compressor, which compresses huge movie files). You'll also get a sample movie or two to see what QuickTime can do. And you'll get a catalog of third-party applications: be aware that you may need to spend money (probably at least $1000) if you want to get further into QuickTime. If all you want to do is play a movie or two and see what QuickTime is all about, all you need is the QuickTime extension—it comes with several applications, such as Word-Perfect for the Macintosh—and you can download it from services like America Online.

QuickTime makes video into data that can be included within documents and copied and pasted, so you don't have to be a technology freak or gear-head to use it. You can add movies to presentations, create training films and HyperCard stacks that play movies, play a movie on startup, put a movie in a letter...you get the idea.

What you need for QuickTime. First, you need to be running system 6.0.8 and up. A popular myth says that QuickTime is only for System 7, but that's not right. You *will* need at least 4 Mb to 5 Mb of RAM, though. Then you need a program that supports QuickTime, like WordPerfect 2.1, which comes with the QuickTime extension. Or you can get the QuickTime extension from Apple or from a user group like BMUG (see Appendix B for phone numbers).

You'll also need a *lot* of hard disk space or a cartridge or removable hard drive, because QuickTime movies eat up a lot of real estate: a 4.5-minute movie can easily occupy a 44-Mb removable cartridge.

If you want to use video clips or make movies, you'll need a video board, a video recorder and a video tape deck, or at least a TV. You'll also need a third-party video editing program, like Adobe's Premiere, especially if you want to do special effects. For the following tricks, though, all you need is the QuickTime extension and the SimplePlayer. To simply play QuickTime movies, you can get EasyPlay, a shareware movie player, from user groups and online services.

Use the hidden slider bar to control a movie's playing speed. In a QuickTime movie using the standard movie controller, hold down the Control key and click one of the single-step buttons at the right end of the controller. A tiny slider bar appears; drag it to play the movie at variable speeds, either forward or backward.

Thanks to Mike O'Connor, Huntington, New York. Mike is the author of the EasyPlay movie cataloger; download as EZPLAY.SEA in MacFun Library 1 on CompuServe.

Undocumented QuickTime tricks! If you're into QuickTime, check out these hot tips. For playing movies, try these:

- You can double-click on an image to play the movie. If you click once, you pause the movie.

- Shift-double-click to play an image *backward*.

- Use the Left and Right Arrow keys to play the movie one step at a time.

• Press the Space bar and Return to toggle between play and pause.

Here are a few hidden shortcuts for controlling QuickTime sound, too:

• Use the Up and Down Arrow keys to turn the volume up and down.

• Option-click on the Speaker icon to toggle sound and muting.

Thanks to Eric Apgar, Apple Worldwide Technical Assistance, and Mike O'Connor, too.

Selecting parts of QuickTime movies. Here are two good, little-known ways to select a section of a QuickTime movie. First, go to the first frame of the section you want to select. Then hold down the Shift key and press the Space bar or the Return key to start the movie playing. The portion that plays will be selected as it goes. To stop the selection, release the Shift key.

Or you can also simply Shift-drag the play bar to select a section of the movie. Remember, once you've selected a portion of a Quick-Time movie, you can cut, copy and paste it into documents created by any QuickTime-compatible application, just like moving text between word processors.

Thanks to Eric Apgar, Apple Worldwide Technical Assistance, and Mike O'Connor.

A startup movie. Recall from Chapter 4 that if you put a movie file in your System Folder and name it Startup Movie, QuickTime will play it as the QuickTime extension loads. And don't forget that you can also drop a QuickTime movie in your Startup Items folder and it will play first thing after your desktop appears.

Two quick QuickTime Easter Eggs. First, open Simple Player and choose About Simple Player with the Option key down. To continue the egg hunt, turn on Balloon Help and point at the QuickTime extension.

SOUND ADVICE

The advice in these sound tips is described in System 7 terms. If you're running System 6, sounds work just a little bit differently, but not so differently that you won't be able to follow along.

These sound tips depend a little more than most on your acquiring additional software or hardware, such as SoundMaster (shareware) or a microphone if your Mac isn't one with a built-in mike. Also, in the area of sound, there doesn't seem to be any one shareware program that takes care of everything—sound editing, conversion, assigning sounds to events, and so forth—so you may need to acquire a couple or more shareware programs, depending on how much you want to do with sound and your Mac.[1]

All you can you do with sounds, with no extra acquisitions, is record sounds (if you've got a built-in mike), play them (by double-clicking on them in System 7), assign them to beeps, and put them in your Startup Items folder to use as the startup sound. You can also edit them a bit in HyperCard. These are the basic sound functions that Macs come with. If you've got ResEdit or a similar program for working with sound resources, you can steal sounds from other programs, and if you get a program like SoundMaster, you can assign shutdown sounds, bad disk sounds, and so forth.

Like most of the tip collections in this book, these tricks are an eclectic assortment. They won't take you through a whole tutorial of how to use sound, how sounds are created, and all that, but you'll undoubtedly find a tip or two here that you can use.

TRAP **System 7 sounds are a little different.** System 7 sounds use a new format that lets you simply double-click on their icons to play them. Older sounds that you may have acquired aren't in this format. The latest versions of SoundMaster, MasterJuggler and

---

[1]Strange that Apple doesn't provide a comprehensive sound utility with Macs that have built-in microphones, but they don't. (Some of the other things they do, like suddenly charging for system software, are a little inexplicable, too...)

Get Ruffin Prevost's and Rob Terrell's *Mac Shareware 500 Book/Disk Set*, also from Ventana Press, for an excellent guide to available shareware, sound and otherwise.

similar programs let you use either type of sound. But if you don't have one of these programs, you'll need to get a program that converts the older formats for sounds to System 7 sounds (which sport the loudspeaker icon). SoundExtractor and sndConverter are shareware programs that let you do this.

Creating your own system beep. If you have a microphone built into your Mac, all you need to do to create your own system beep is record your sound and save it (use the Sound control panel). It'll be stored in the System file. Use the Sound control panel to assign it as your beep.

If you don't have a Mac with a built-in mike, you can get Mac Recorder (from MacroMedia/Paracomp, which you may remember as MacroMind).

Your own startup sound. Once you've recorded a sound, you can make it your startup sound just by dragging it to your Startup Items folder. In fact, you can do this with any System 7-type sound, not just one you've recorded.

Get SoundMaster if you want to play with sounds. Sound-Master is a shareware utility that lets you assign sounds to events like pressing the Tab key, ejecting a disk, restarting and about every other Mac event you can imagine. You can download Sound-Master from the Mac Shareware 500 Library on America Online or get it from most user groups, online services (like CompuServe) and bulletin boards.

Get the commercial program MasterJuggler (AL Soft) and use its HotSounds feature if you can't lay hands on SoundMaster.

There's a difference between HyperCard sounds and Mac II sounds. When the Mac II first came out, lots of folks were very confused (me among them) about why there were HyperCard sounds and Mac II sounds and why you had to get a sound conversion program to convert them from one format to another. I still don't know exactly *why* Apple did this, but there are format 1 snd resources and format 2 snd resources out there. Format 2 could only be played in HyperCard, and format 1 could only be played on a Mac II. If you run across any of these, get Riccardo Ettore's Sound Mover application (shareware), which will let you extract a sound no matter what type of resource it is (see the trap, "All those different kinds of sounds!"), or try to find another of the shareware sound conversion programs, or purchase SoundEdit or SoundEdit Pro from Farallon.

You can convert sounds to System 7 with sndConverter 1.2.1 or greater. If you download sounds from an online service or bulletin board and they appear on your System 7 desktop as documents, go back online and find a program named sndConverter 1.2.1 or greater, and download it, too. It'll convert those sounds to the format System 7 uses.

Sound Mover will convert them, too, if you have it. The difference is that sndConverter converts non-System 7 resource sounds and changes them only to sounds that can be played in System 7. Sound Mover converts to all sorts of other sound formats.

All those different kinds of sounds! The Mac uses several different types of sounds, and you can't always use them interchangeably without conversion. First, there's a sound type that's just data—its icon looks like one of those old RCA ads, where the little dog is listening to the loudspeaker (technically, they're FSSD sounds because of their file type). These are SoundEdit files (Sound-Edit, from Paracomp, is a commercial sound editing program).

Then there's a second sound type: a resource file that can be stored *inside* other files. For example, the sounds that show up in the Sound control panel are sounds that are stored in your System file (technically, they're type snd). If you're running System 7, you probably already know that you can play these kinds of sounds just by double-clicking on them, and you can move them around the desktop just like any other kind of sound. These types of sound files have icons that look like loudspeakers. If they're inside another file, though, the file's icon looks like whatever type the file is.

Now, to use the first kind of sounds (the ones with the dog icon, which you may also see called sound wave files) in System 7 or in HyperCard, you'll need SoundEdit, Sound Mover or some other sound conversion/extraction utility (there are quite a few that will do this; see the preceding tip).

To further confuse you, sounds you download from bulletin boards are usually compressed using StuffIt, Compact Pro or some other compression utility. If you see .sit at the end of the icon's name, that's a StuffIt archive. An icon name ending in .sea indicates a self-extracting archive, and .cpt is a Compact Pro archive. You may find sounds in any of these compressed formats.

So look at the icons of the sounds to see which kind you have if you can't get them to work for you. You may need to convert them to snd resources. In Figure 6-5, going from left to right, there's a sound suitcase, a System 7 sound file, a sound in a document and a StuffIt sound archive file. Remember, you can also find sounds in some HyperCard stacks, in applications such as games that have sounds and in resource files that contain sounds.

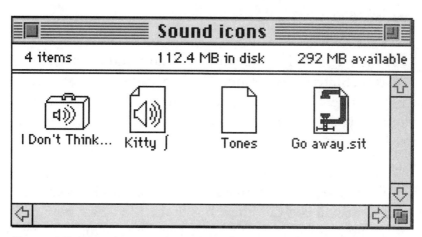

Figure 6-5: Sounds come in various formats and sport different icons accordingly.

By the way, QuickTime movies use a different type of sound—AIFF (Audio Interchange File Format)—but the QuickTime Starter Kit comes with a Convert-to-Movie utility for converting sounds to movie sounds.

Got a lot of sounds? Use a suitcase. If you install all your sounds in your System file, you run the risk of losing them because your System file is easily corrupted, and you'll have to replace it from time to time (see Chapter 10, "In Trouble?" for why and how). You can keep a duplicate System file handy, but a better idea is to store sounds in suitcases that are easy to manipulate all at once, instead of working with each individual sound. Suitcase II and Master-Juggler both handle sound suitcases; on a more affordable level, so does the shareware program Carpetbagger. And SoundMaster, although it doesn't handle suitcases, lets you store sounds in folders separate from your System Folder.

One other benefit of storing sounds in a suitcase is that you won't need to convert them to System 7 sounds; they'll work just fine.

Finally, if you're looking for the cheapest solution to the sound storage dilemmas, you might consider creating a single separate Scrapbook file just for all your sounds. You can copy each sound individually into the Scrapbook, where you can store and even play them. Also, you can copy and paste sounds directly from the Scrapbook into the Sound control panel.

How to create a sound suitcase. Can't find MasterJuggler's Create Suitcase command? That's because there isn't one (Suitcase has one, though). To get around this, locate a sound suitcase elsewhere on your hard drive or another disk, duplicate it, empty it and use it to store your new sounds.

Adding a new system beep (System 7). This is about the easiest thing you can do with sounds: add a new system beep to your Sound control panel. The only trick to remember is that you must first quit all the programs you've got running. Then drag a sound icon to your System Folder or directly to the System file. That's it. The next time you open the Sound control panel, you'll see the new sound listed (see Figure 6-6).

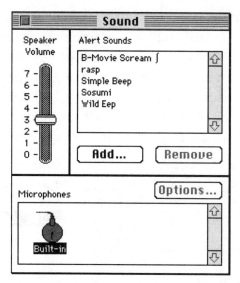

Figure 6-6: When you install a new system beep, that sound appears in the Alert Sounds list in your Sound control panel.

By the way, there's a new system beep in the System 7 Scrapbook. Go hunting for it and remember that you can simply copy it, open the Sound control panel and paste it, regardless of what programs are running at the time.

Getting neat sounds. You can download prerecorded sounds from most online services and bulletin boards, or you can record your own if you have a Mac with a built-in microphone. If you have a model before the IIsi and LC or a PowerBook 100, you won't have a built-in mike, but you can purchase a MacRecorder or another sound input device and use it.

Sources for downloading sounds: on America Online, check out the Macintosh Music and Sound Forum (keyword: Mac Music). On CompuServe, look in the MACFUN forum libraries. Sound Source Unlimited has Star Trek sounds that you can buy (800/877-4778), and large user groups like BMUG sell floppy and CD-ROM collections of sound files. See Appendix B for details.

Editing sounds. You can edit sounds by using several different applications. SoundEdit is a commercial program that you can purchase if you get serious about sounds—it has functions for adding special effects like an echo chamber or a flanger. For the rest of us, Sound Mover has sound editing features that will probably fit our needs. Look at Figure 6-7 to see how editing sounds with Sound Mover works; it's similar to most other sound-editing programs.

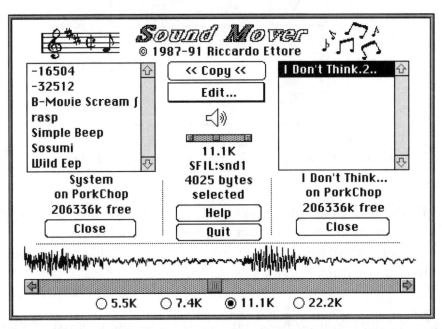

Figure 6-7: Sound Mover has an interface like Apple's Font/DA Mover, but it lets you edit sounds as well as copy or move them.

Click on the sound you want to edit in the box on the left. You'll see a waveform display of the sound at the bottom of the dialog box. You can click to put the cursor at any point in the sound and drag it to select just that part of the sound. This is a handy technique for lifting certain phrases or words from a sentence. For example, you can take "I don't think" from the sound clip "I don't think there's anybody back there."

Once you've selected part of a sound, click the speaker icon to play it. To cut, copy or paste the selected sound portion, click Edit, or use Command-X, Command-C or Command-V. You can copy selected sound samples to combine several into one sound file.

To copy the selected part of the sound into a new sound file, press the Option key while you click on the Copy button at the top center of the Sound Mover dialog box. You'll be asked for a new name for the snd resource.

Drag the scroll bar to change the playback rate. You can save your sound file with the new playback rate to get some truly strange effects.

Rustling sounds. You saw a lot about using ResEdit for rustling icons back in Chapter 4. Now you get a chance to steal sounds from applications like games, which come with lots of weird sounds, and use them for your everyday sounds. Get SoundMaster if you really want to make use of this trick, because it lets you assign sounds to all sorts of events. Otherwise you'll probably only be able to use your borrowed sounds as system beeps.

Use ResEdit to open a copy of the application that has the neat sounds. (For more on what ResEdit is and how to use it, see the sidebar in Chapter 4.) Then double-click on the snd resource and select and copy the snd resources you want from the list (see Figure 6-8). You can choose Try Sound from ResEdit's snd menu (or type Command-T) to hear each sound. Choose Select all from the Edit menu or press Command-A to select all the sounds; then copy them—although you may not have enough memory to copy all the sounds in a particular application.

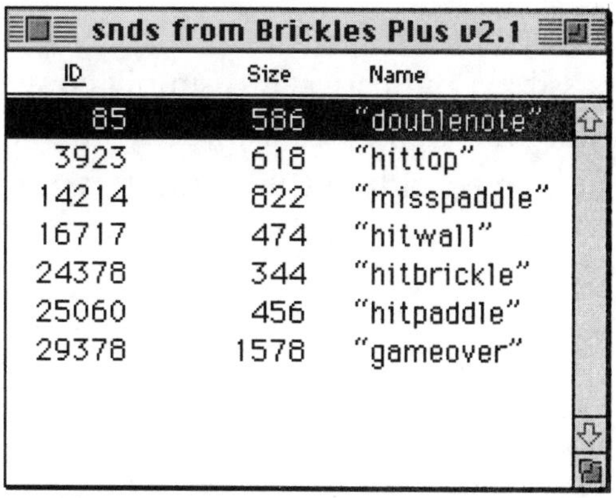

ID	Size	Name
85	586	"doublenote"
3923	618	"hittop"
14214	822	"misspaddle"
16717	474	"hitwall"
24378	344	"hitbrickle"
25060	456	"hitpaddle"
29378	1578	"gameover"

snds from Brickles Plus v2.1

Figure 6-8: Copy the sound IDs that you want to use elsewhere.

After you've copied the sounds you want, open a copy of the System file in ResEdit. Double-click on the snd resource and paste with Command-V. You'll see the sounds you copied appear in the list (see Figure 6-9). Now you can use that sound via SoundMaster or the Sound control panel.

ID	Size	Name
-32512	194	
-16504	4080	
1	228	"Simple Beep"
8	1566	"Wild Eep"
9	2040	"Sosumi"
128	29122	"B-Movie Scream ʃ"
12980	3930	"rasp"
26169	16938	"I Don't Think..."
29378	1578	"gameover"

snds from System copy, working

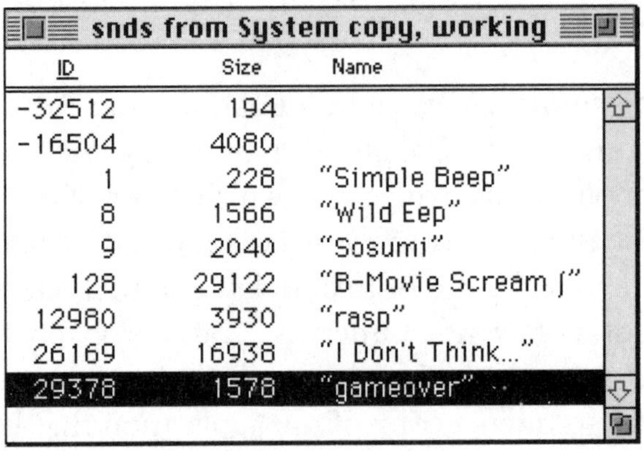

Figure 6-9: The swiped sounds as they appear pasted into the copy of the System file.

Another way to shuffle sounds around is to do it through the Scrapbook. Paste them in the Scrapbook (see Figure 6-10) and then copy and paste them into the Sound control panel. You'll be asked to give each sound a name (see Figure 6-11). This method will give you a Scrapbook record of all the sounds that are in your Sounds control panel.

But it's also possible (and easiest) to simply copy the sound resource from ResEdit and then paste it directly into the Sound control panel, skipping the step of adding the sound to your Scrapbook.

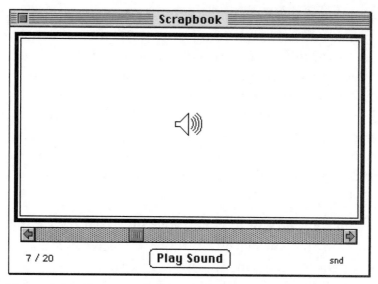

Figure 6-10: You can paste sounds from ResEdit into the Scrapbook.

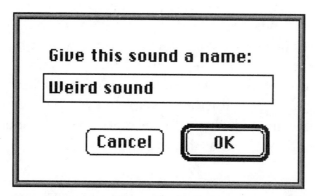

Figure 6-11: You'll be asked to give your sound a unique name when you paste it into the Sound control panel.

Thanks to Eric Apgar, Apple Worldwide Technical Assistance.

Stealing the "Ta-Dah!" sound from the Puzzle. If you've ever successfully solved the Puzzle DA in the Apple menu, you've heard the "Ta-Dah!" sound it makes when you reach the solution. For a little hands-on sound rustling, let's steal it.

With ResEdit, open a copy of the Puzzle (it's in the Apple Menu Items folder in your System Folder). Double-click on the snd resource and select ID -16000. Press Command-C for copy and quit ResEdit. Now open the Sound control panel and paste your copied sound with Command-V.

There's a rude sound in Disinfectant. If you're a whoopie cushion fan, you may want to rustle a secret you-know-what sound from Disinfectant, the shareware anti-virus utility. Open Disinfectant in ResEdit and open the snd resource. The flatulence is ID 191. Choose Try Sound from the snd menu in ResEdit to hear it.

SoundMaster sounds take precedence over Sound control panel sounds. If you're using SoundMaster to assign a sound to your system beep, that sound will preempt any alert beep you assign with the Sound control panel. To add your system sounds (such as your newly added Ta-Dah!) to your SoundMaster setup, Option-drag (to copy, rather than simply move) the sounds out of your System file into whichever folder is holding your SoundMaster sounds. Then they'll be available in SoundMaster.

More easy ways to rustle sounds. Get a shareware program called SoundExtractor. To use it, all you do is drag and drop onto it any file that contains sound resources. It automatically extracts the sounds as separate files, and you can drag them to your System Folder (in System 7) or to your System file (in System 6).

Another overlooked trick for swiping sounds: use SoundEdit or Sound Mover. With SoundEdit, open the suitcase as a resource file by clicking the Resource button at the bottom of the window. Once it's open, you can save an individual sound. In fact, you can save it directly into the System file so that it appears in your Alert Sounds list in the Sound control panel.

With Sound Mover, the process is a little different: press the Option key as you click Open. This lets you open just about any kind of file that has a sound in it. Once you locate the sound you want, copy it into a new file or into your System file to use as a beep.

Voice annotations in documents? No, it's not yet the twenty-first century, but you can create voice annotations right now, if you have Word 5.0 or greater (KidPix from Broderbund lets you do it, too, and a host of other programs are sure to soon offer this capability). Think of voice annotations as very personal Post-It notes.

In Word 5.0, there's a Voice Annotation choice on the Insert menu. All you need to do is select it and record your notes. Of course, you'll need a Mac with a microphone to be able to have fun with this feature in Word.

The catch: voice annotations take up *a lot* of space. Just a sentence or two can swell a document's size to the point where it's difficult to manage on your hard disk and extremely slow to send over a network (and don't even think about sending the file over a modem). The good news: with voice annotations, you don't need the best sound quality, so record at the lowest possible quality to save space. Better sounds require more space than low-quality sounds.

Hijacking voice annotations from Word. If you've recorded voice annotations in a Microsoft Word 5 document (or someone sends you one that you want to swipe), here's the voodoo way to get them out of the document so you can use them as startup sounds, or whatever you'd like. First, select the sound icon in the Word document (click once). The Edit Voice Annotation command appears on the Edit menu. Choose it, and a dialog box will appear (see Figure 6-12). Now you can select Save As from the Voice Record dialog box's File menu and save that sound as a file, changing its format to a Resource, an Audio IFF (AIFF file for use in Quick-Time), or whatever you want. In fact, you can save it directly into your System file.

Figure 6-12: Swiping a voice annotation from a Word document.

Trouble with sound on a IIsi. If the sound on your IIsi frequently cuts out on you (a common problem), slide the volume control up to 7 in the Sound control panel and then slide it back down to the level you want.

Better yet, get an FKEY called IIsi SoundFix via America Online, CompuServe or your friendly local user group. SoundFix is much faster than adjusting the Sound control panel every time the sound cuts out.

Or, even better, get a pair of external amplified speakers and bypass the Mac's internal speaker. You'll get better sound quality, that way. You can get inexpensive ones at Radio Shack, or relatively expensive ones like MacSpeakers from Monster Cable.

SWAPPING KEYS AROUND

Rustling icons and sounds aren't the only things you can use ResEdit for, but they do happen to be fun. On the more practical side, you can use ResEdit to modify KCHR resources so a particular key you press on the keyboard generates a different character on the screen. This is a neat trick for getting Caps Lock turned off or for assigning special characters to keys you rarely use. I used this trick to bypass and reassign my p key after one of the cats (Pusser) expressed his displeasure on my keyboard and shorted out a couple of keys—for a while, I found myself typing things like "usser eed on my keyboard."

There are two safe ways to try out these keyboard tricks. The safest thing to do is duplicate your System file and edit that copy; then, when you've finished your resource editing, drag the original System file out of the System Folder and store it in a different folder, name the copy "System" and restart. (You can't trash the original System file until after you restart, because it's active.) But if you're careful, you can make a copy of the KCHR resource (which controls what characters are applied to which keys) and edit it instead, or edit the original KCHR resource knowing that you can switch to the copy if things aren't working as you planned. (To switch between KCHRs—keyboard layouts—you've created or installed, you use the Keyboard control panel.)

Remapping your Mac's keys. Using ResEdit, you can remap your Mac's keyboard so that when you press a key, it generates a completely different character than the one printed on its physical keycap. I've seen this trick described for remapping the shifted comma and period keys, which normally produce less-than and greater-than symbols (< >), responsible for all those P>O> Boxes you type by mistake. But you can also use it to map special symbols—like the trademark or copyright sign—to keys you seldom use, such as @ or |.

First, we'll look at how to get rid of those pesky greater-than signs on the shifted comma and period keys. If you feel confident using ResEdit, you can work on the real System file, but you should first make a copy of the KCHR resource so you can get it back the way it was—just in case.

Start ResEdit and locate the KCHR resource in your System file. (Yes, ResEdit will complain about your editing the System file, but it's OK because you're going to copy a resource and work on it.) Select the KCHR resource and press Command-C to copy it. Then press Command-V to paste it. In the dialog box that appears, click Unique ID to give it a unique ID number. Then double-click on the KCHR resource. You'll see a dialog box listing all your KCHR resources (see Figure 6-13).

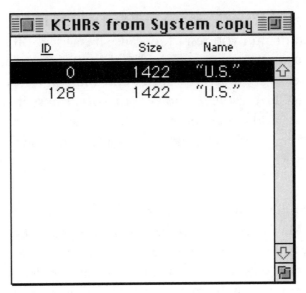

Figure 6-13: You can use ResEdit to edit a KCHR resource.

Double-click on ID 0, and you'll see the KCHR editor (see Figure 6-14).

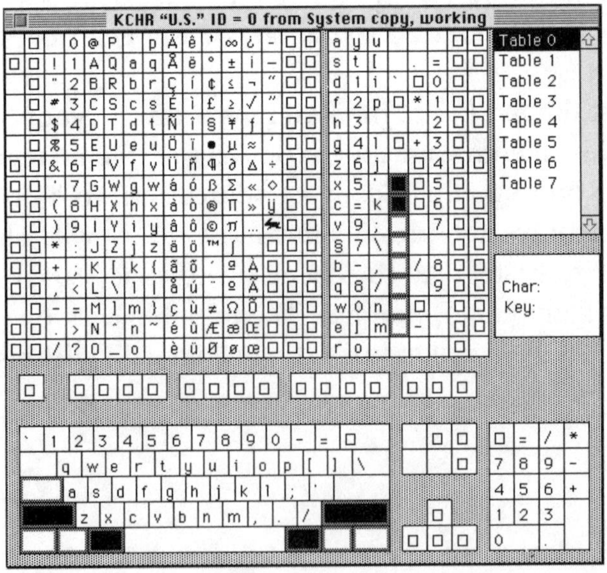

Figure 6-14: The KCHR editor shows the keyboard layout and its corresponding characters.

Now, to make the shifted period key stop producing >, locate the period key in the upper-left array of characters (if you can't find it quickly, press the period key on your real keyboard to make it highlight.) Press the Shift key and drag the period box to the greater-than symbol on the keyboard diagram at the bottom of the dialog box. You've just remapped the key, and now when you press Shift-period, you'll get a period instead of a greater-than sign.

Repeat for Shift-comma to remap that one, too, if you like. Then save your changes and quit ResEdit and restart. (Swap System files if you worked on a copy of the System.) Now, when you press Shift-<, you'll get a comma, and Shift-> generates a period. If you want a greater-than or less-than symbol now, use KeyCaps.

Mapping a special symbol to a key. If you do a lot of specialized typing, such as legal documents that use copyright symbols, paragraph and section symbols or registration marks, you might want to create a special keyboard layout that will type those symbols when you press certain keys instead of reassigning keys that are on your regular keyboard. Use the same general steps as above to assign the symbols, but instead of working on the KCHR with ID 0, edit the copy you've made that has a unique ID number (just double-click on that number instead of on the line that shows 0).

Remember: the symbols you remap over won't be available any more unless you move them to other keys or key combinations, such as Option-Shift-*key*.

When you're done, all you need to do to access your new alternative keyboard layout is switch to that keyboard in the Keyboard control panel (see Figure 6-15). See the next trick for how to give it a unique icon.

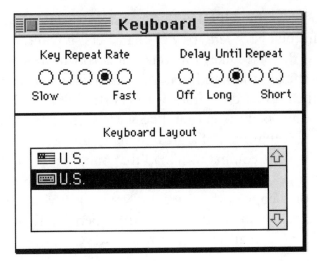

Figure 6-15: Use the Keyboard control panel to switch to a different keyboard layout.

Here's another way to switch keyboards. If you're using the International version of System 7.1, you can switch keyboards by using the International menu, which appears on the menu bar over by the Applications menu. But if you recall from Chapter 2, there's a way to get that icon to display in System 6 and 7.0, too (see "Bring up the International menu" in Chapter 2).

All you need to do is edit the itlc resource in the System file and click the Always show icon button. Restart, and you'll see the new International menu icon. Click on it to see all the keyboards available to you. This is a quicker method of switching keyboard layouts than using the normal control panel route.

If you want to create a unique icon for your custom keyboard, open the System file again in ResEdit. Then open the KCHR resource and check the ID number of your new keyboard resource. Write it down and close the KCHR resource.

Open the SICN (small icon) resource from the System file and choose Create New Resource from the Resource menu. You'll be taken to a pixel editor where you can create a custom icon (see Figure 6-16). Here, a paragraph symbol indicates a special-symbol keyboard.

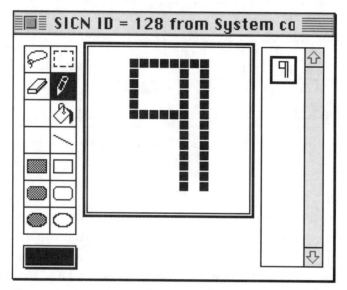

Figure 6-16: Use ResEdit to create a new small icon for your custom keyboard layout.

When you're done, give your new SICN resource the same ID number as the KCHR resource you want it to indicate. Now, when you choose the International menu, you'll see your new icon next to the modified keyboard resource.

You don't have to remap the keyboard to use special characters. If you only use special characters from time to time, an easier way to access them is to use the Key Caps desk accessory (see Figure 6-17). It's preset to show the symbols in the Chicago font, but you can choose a different font from the Key Caps menu. Then, to see a font's special characters, press Shift, Caps Lock, Option or Control, and combinations of those keys, like Shift-Option.

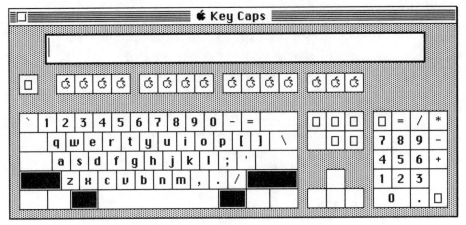

Figure 6-17: Use Apple's Key Caps DA to view and type special symbols.

Click on a symbol to "type" it. You can then copy it from Key Caps and paste it in a document. If the symbol you want doesn't appear in the document, you've forgotten to switch to that font in the program you're using. If you find KeyCaps lacking, there are a host of commercial and shareware alternatives available that do essentially the same thing, only with more bells and whistles.

Chapter 7 has more information on special symbols.

A GRAB BAG OF TRICKS

Want to get screen dumps? Change a file's type so that you can open it in a different program? Bypass TeachText? This section's full of neat tricks that defy categorization.

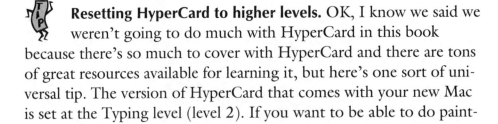

Resetting HyperCard to higher levels. OK, I know we said we weren't going to do much with HyperCard in this book because there's so much to cover with HyperCard and there are tons of great resources available for learning it, but here's one sort of universal tip. The version of HyperCard that comes with your new Mac is set at the Typing level (level 2). If you want to be able to do painting, authoring and scripting, you'll need to use a little voodoo on it.

Start HyperCard and go to the last card. Press Command-M for Message. In the Message box at the bottom of the screen, type **magic** and press Return. Then click level 5, Scripting, and you'll have access to all five levels. Magic!

If you do a lot with HyperCard, though, you'll want to purchase the complete package from Claris so you get Help and the extra stacks that come with it.

Screen dumps, and printing them. Screen shots don't work the same in System 6 and System 7. In System 7, screen shots that you take with Command-Shift-3 become PICT files named Picture 1, Picture 2, and so forth. Just double-click on any of these Picture files to open it in TeachText. You can print it from there.

To open one of those Picture files in a program like Photoshop, just drag its icon over the Photoshop icon (or the icon of whatever program you're using).

Instead of having TeachText open your screen dumps, direct them to your drawing program. You can use ResEdit to change the creator code that TeachText assigns to your screen shots. Rather than the normal ttxt creator tag, you can assign any program's creator tag to the PICTs you get when you take a screen shot. That way, when you double-click on a screen-shot PICT, the drawing program will open it.

Let's use MacPaint as an example. First, as always, duplicate your System file and work on that copy with ResEdit. Pull the System file out to the desktop where you can find it easily.

Start ResEdit, and if you don't know the creator type of your drawing program, check it first. Close the Open dialog box and choose Get File/Folder Info from ResEdit's File menu; then select your drawing program. You'll see a dialog box listing the Creator (see Figure 6-18).

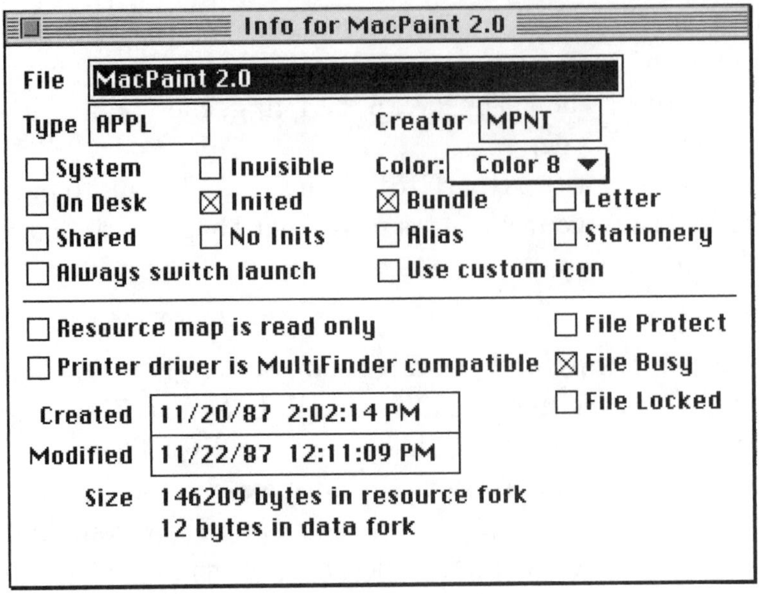

Figure 6-18: Check your drawing program's creator code with ResEdit.

Make a note of the creator code exactly as it appears, including capitalization and spacing. Then close the dialog box and choose Open from the File menu. Open the copy of the System file and double-click on the FKEY resource (click Yes when you get that message about saving the uncompressed version). Press Command-G for a Find ASCII shortcut; enter **PICT** to find and press Return.

When the Find command locates PICT, close the dialog box to get it out of the way. Then scroll to see TeachText's creator type (ttext). It should be the next entry after the PICT entry. Highlight ttext and replace it with the creator type of your drawing program— **MPNT** for MacPaint. Be sure to type it just as it appeared when you looked it up; capitalization counts here. Now save and quit ResEdit, replace your old System file with the new one, and restart your Mac.

Now, whenever you take a screen snapshot with Command-Shift-3, you can edit it in MacPaint (or whatever drawing program you chose) by double-clicking on it.

TeachText can't open large documents. Have you ever gotten a message saying a file was too big to be opened by Teach-Text? This often happens when you're saving the log of a communications session from CompuServe, for instance, and you've designated TeachText as the application to use for opening your text files.

TeachText is a freebie program designed by Apple to let users have a standard way of creating and reading those Read Me files. It can't handle anything bigger than 32k.

TeachText is designed to handle short, simple documents. All too often you'll try double-clicking on a mysterious-looking document only to be told that the application that created it isn't present. You'll have the option to try opening the document with TeachText, but then you might get a message saying a document is too big for Teach-Text to open. To get around this, get a neat DA named Quill (it's freeware). Quill will open just about any text document of any size—text files, MacWrite, MacWrite II, Word, Microsoft Write, WriteNow and Nisus. The only catch is that you can't print with Quill (but see the next tip).

Another way to get around the message that a file's too big for TeachText: use ResEdit to open the file. Choose Get Info from the File menu and change the file's creator to something else—such as your big word processing program. Use WORD if you have Microsoft Word, MWII for MacWrite II, SSIW for WordPerfect, and so forth. See Table 6.1 for details on applications and their creator codes.

You can also redirect TeachText documents so that when you double-click on them, they launch a full-featured word processing program like MacWrite or Word (see the tip "You can 'permanently' switch which programs open which documents" below). Or you can try first launching Word or MacWrite and then opening the Teach-Text document from within the program. You can also try dragging and dropping the stubborn document icon onto the icon of a word processing program. Either of these tricks can sometimes open a document you can't open otherwise.

Can't print a document? Cheat—take screen shots. I've found more than once that an offending PostScript error stops a document from printing after a page or two. First, I try to find the PostScript code and delete it, but that doesn't always work. I've always found that the brute-force screen dump will work, though.

Obviously, this isn't an elegant solution—it won't be acceptable if high-quality type and graphics were the whole purpose of trying to print the document—but if all you're after is a way to get a hard copy of what's on your screen, this method works. Display the document and then press Command-Shift-3 to take snapshots of successive pages. Then print those snapshots from TeachText (or whatever program you now use to open your screen shots).

You can "permanently" switch which programs open which documents. If you've been following along with these Teach-Text-replacement tricks, you may have discovered that you'd like to be able to fix things up more or less permanently through the Finder, so that any time you try to open a certain type of document and the Mac can't find its creator, a different program will launch and try to open it. If you edit the Finder (a copy of it), you can do this.

Using ResEdit, open the fmap resource. Then open ID 17010. The first line specifies that TEXT is the file type and ttxt (TeachText) is the application that is to try to open files of that type. Say that you own a copy of Microsoft Word, but not WordPerfect, and you want Word to open any WordPerfect files you double-click on. (If you have Word, you know that it will usually open WordPerfect files seamlessly from within the program, but you want it to open them when you double-click on them.)

First, you have to know Word's file type code and WordPerfect's creator code. They're WDBN and SSIW, respectively; see Table 6.1, which shows the creator codes for several popular word processing programs. With that knowledge in hand, you can add a fourth line to ID 17010 that says, in effect, "If you can't find WordPerfect, open this document with Microsoft Word." Click at the end of the line that reads "PICTttxt" and, with no extra spaces or other characters, type **WDBNSSIW**. Make sure that the last row is still all zeroes; then save, quit, rename the Finder copy, and so forth.

Code	Program
MACA	MacWrite
MWII	MacWrite II
MSWD	Microsoft Word
ttxt	TeachText
SSIW[2]	WordPerfect
nX^n[3]	WriteNow

Table 6.1: Many popular programs have obscure file type codes.

Figuring out a file's type and creator. Maybe your word processor isn't listed in Table 6.1. No matter. You can use the Get Info command in ResEdit to look up a file's type and creator any time you like. When you choose Get Info for a file, you'll see a screen like the one in Figure 6-18, listing the Type and Creator.

Make Scrapbooks to transfer art files from one program to another. This may be a perfectly obvious tip to most of you, but it wasn't to me until a translator asked for the art files from one of my books, and I hadn't saved them separately from the PageMaker files. Just copy your art to the Scrapbook, name the Scrapbook file something to identify what it is, and you've got a handy utility for transporting art from one desktop publishing program to another as PICT files.

A PageMaker tip. OK, I said no program-specific tips, but this one doesn't really count because it applies to any program (like PageMaker) that makes temporary saves as you work. Whenever

---

[2]This is WordPerfect's code because WordPerfect Corporation's original name was Satellite Software International.

[3]I have no idea why this is WriteNow's code.

you save, PageMaker writes only the changes you've made since your last save (unless you've set its preferences to do otherwise), rather than recompiling and resaving the entire file. This makes for faster saves but larger file sizes.

If you want to save your document under a new name but don't want to wait for PageMaker to perform a time-consuming Save As, just save it the normal way, then exit to the Finder and Duplicate the file (Command-D) and then rename it. It's a lot faster than Saving As within the program. Try it and see.

A hidden puzzle. You may not be aware of it, but there are two Puzzles in System 7. The first is an Apple logo, and the second is a number puzzle. To switch from one to the other, select Clear from the Puzzle's Edit menu.

You can create your own custom Puzzle by copying a graphic image and pasting it in the Puzzle, too.

Invisible files and folders. Recall from Chapter 1 that making a file invisible is a sneaky way to protect it from being deleted. After all, if you (or anybody else) can't see it, how will you know it's there? This trick works equally well whether you're protecting your stuff from six-year-olds at home or sixty-year-olds at work.

You can use ResEdit (or a program like DiskTop) to make files and folders mysteriously disappear from your desktop. Just open the item in ResEdit and choose Get Info from the File menu. You'll see a dialog box where you can click Invisible.

Hint: keep your invisible files in one folder so that you can easily find and access them again by simply launching ResEdit and navigating to that single folder from ResEdit's Open dialog.

Dastardly things you can do with this trick:

• Make your System Folder invisible, and nobody will be able to mess with your Mac.

• Make a program invisible, and launch it by double-clicking on its documents.

• Make invisible all the important document files that you want to keep unchanged and away from prying eyes (like last quarter's budget or your list of complaints about your boss).

If you're running System 6 using MultiFinder and the file is on the desktop, it won't disappear until you restart your Mac. If the file's in a Finder window, just close the window to make it disappear.

Protecting a file's name from being changed. If you just want to protect a file from getting its name changed, don't make it invisible, as in the previous tip. Check the System box instead of the Invisible box. This is an even sneakier trick than locking a file with its Get Info box in the Finder. Would-be name-changers go to the Get Info box and see the file isn't locked...but they still can't rename it!

A System file can be deleted, though. One thing can happen to a file you've turned the System bit on for: it can be deleted by dragging it to the Trash. If you really, sincerely want to protect a file, make it invisible.

By the way, a duplicate of a System file can have its name changed. The System bit isn't copied when you copy a file.

A wicked, wicked trick. Is today the first of April? No matter. Make a screen shot (Option-Shift-3) of your office mate's screen when the person goes to get coffee. Double-click on the Picture file that's created to open it in TeachText (System 7) or MacPaint (System 6); then enlarge it to fill the screen. When your soon-to-be enemy gets back, there'll be a picture of the screen on the monitor. Drives them nuts!

Thanks to Robin Williams, who is usually such a nice person.

Making read-only Read Me files. Remember those TeachText files with the newspaper icons? They indicate that a file is read-only, so other folks can read it but can't change it. You can make your own read-only TeachText files.

First, create the document in TeachText and save it. Then open ResEdit and cancel the Open dialog box that first appears. Choose Get File/Folder Info from the File menu and select the TeachText file you just created. Change the type from TEXT to ttro (for Teach-Text read only). Don't change the creator. Save and quit to see the "EXTRA" newspaper icon, indicating a read-only file. (If you don't see the newspaper icon, you may have an old or damaged version of TeachText, or you may need to rebuild your Desktop.)

Using stationery. With System 7, you can turn a document you've worked on for a long time into a stationery pad, so you can reuse its formatting and text without changing the original. (A lot of programs—like Word and WordPerfect—let you do this too, without using the system software.) Stationery pads, also called templates, are great for creating boilerplate text, forms, labels, envelopes, invoices and all the rest of the documents you use often.

All you need to do to turn a document into a stationery pad is choose the document's icon in the Finder and then get info on it (Command-I). Click the stationery pad box (see Figure 6-19) and close the window.

```
┌────────────────────────────────────────┐
│ ▣  ════ Chapter 4 Info ════            │
├────────────────────────────────────────┤
│  ┌───┐   Chapter 4                      │
│  │   │   Created with WordPerfect™ 2.1  │
│  └───┘                                  │
│   Kind: WordPerfect stationery pad      │
│   Size: 20K on disk (13,148 bytes used) │
│                                         │
│  Where: PorkChop: Extra chapters:       │
│                                         │
│                                         │
│ Created: Wed, Aug 19, 1992, 4:04 PM     │
│ Modified: Thu, Aug 20, 1992, 10:33 AM   │
│ Version: 2.1, Copyright © 1987-1992     │
│          WordPerfect Corporation        │
│ Comments:                               │
│  ┌──────────────────────────────────┐   │
│  │                                  │   │
│  │                                  │   │
│  │                                  │   │
│  └──────────────────────────────────┘   │
│  ☐ Locked         ☒ Stationery pad      │
└────────────────────────────────────────┘
```

Figure 6-19: Click the stationery pad box to make a document into stationery that can be read but not changed.

The document's icon then looks like a stationery pad. If you'd rather use the icon of the program that created it, copy an icon from one of that program's documents and paste it in the stationery pad's Get Info box. Then name the stationery something that helps you remember it's stationery, like "office labels pad" or "home labels pad." When you double-click on stationery to open it, you'll be asked to give the new document a name. (If you've created stationery through a program, the pad will open and you'll name it when you save it, instead of naming it as soon as it opens.) Either way you name it, you won't run the risk of hitting Command-S by mistake and overwriting the original.

MOVING ON

Had enough magic? While this chapter has been an eclectic trip, covering tips ranging from the pointless to the priceless, Chapter 7, "Printing Mysteries," will bring you back to earth with all sorts of tips and tricks for printing, using fonts and pondering PostScript and TrueType alike.

PRINTING MYSTERIES

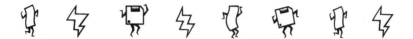

It's still a paper world out there, despite all the talk you hear of the paperless office. Sooner or later, you're going to want to print—and frankly, printing can be a chore. Try a little of the magic in this chapter.

GENERAL PRINTING TIPS

No matter what kind of printer you have, there will probably be a tip or two in this section that you can use. Rather than spend a lot of time and space covering the eccentric details of every brand and model of printer, I've focused mainly on general tricks that most anyone with a Mac and a printer can use.

The easiest printer tip of all. If everything's stuck, or nothing is working the way you expected, turn off your Mac and printer. Wait a minute for the printer's memory to clear completely; then turn both of them back on again.

Sometimes, the problem is that there are just too many fonts or other information going in and out of the printer's memory. Also, if you're on a mixed Mac-PC network, like me, and you're alternating printing from Windows and DOS while also printing from a Mac, the dinner just gets indigestible at the printer's end and the green light (on a LaserWriter) blinks and blinks. Restarting resets everything, and then you can usually print again.

Printing on networked printers. On a network with a mix of System 6 and System 7 Macs, you can easily go nuts when you try to print to the network printer and it keeps reinitializing itself because you're using a different version of the printer driver. Instead of suffering through this, install the System 7 printer drivers on all your machines, even the System 6 Macs. *It will work.* Use the System 7 Printing Tools disk and run the Installer that's on it to create updated printer drivers on your System 6 Macs. Then copy the Laser Prep file from the Printing disk, too. System 7 doesn't use the Laser Prep file, so the Installer doesn't copy it, but System 6 needs it. Make sure you've got the LaserWriter driver (or the driver for your printer) in your Extensions folder. Laser Prep, Backgrounder and PrintMonitor go "loose" in your System Folder.

If you want to switch back to the System 6 driver temporarily for printing a few jobs on a locally connected printer, keep a copy of it in a separate folder outside your System Folder. Then drag the System 7 driver out of the System Folder and replace it with the System 6 driver icon.

Batch-print to save time. Instead of individually opening all the documents you want to print in the application that created them and then choosing Print from the File menu over and over, simply select the icons of all the documents you want to print in the *Finder*. Then choose Print from the Finder's File menu. The program that created the documents will start, and you'll see the Print dialog box. Click the Print button, and your document will go to the printer; the next document's Print dialog box will come up for you to choose Print or Cancel, select a number of copies, and so forth.

Lost printer? Try this trick. Sometimes your printer may not show up in the Chooser. AppleTalk may get confused about which printer is where. If this happens, turn off AppleTalk in the Chooser (click Inactive) and close the Chooser (see Figure 7-1). Then open it again and click Active; if everything is working correctly, you should see your printer appear again.

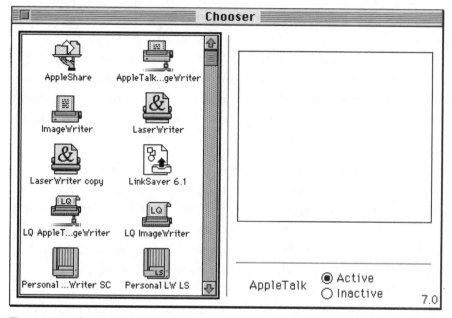

Figure 7-1: Sometimes turning AppleTalk off and then back on will find a lost printer.

Of course, a much simpler solution to this problem is that you (or somebody else) may have switched your printer off, and that's why it's not showing up in the Chooser. Also, your AppleTalk cabling may have come unplugged from your Mac, the printer or one of the Macs along the network chain, so be sure to check your cables if all else fails.

Set up your print queue with the printer off. I hate to hear the LaserWriter grinding away as I work. Instead, I use Print-Monitor's File menu and tell it to Stop Printing; then I switch off my LaserWriter to give it a rest. Then I continue working and hitting

Command-P whenever a document's ready to print. When it's time for a break, I turn on the LaserWriter, choose Resume Printing from PrintMonitor's File menu, and get out of Dodge.

This trick has its limitations, of course. If you send too many jobs to the printer and leave it unattended, you're likely to run out of paper. You may also bog down the printer's memory with too many fonts of graphics at once. But since LaserWriters produce small amounts of ozone that can conceivably build up in enclosed spaces (which can be hazardous to your health) printing files using this method is a good way to set things up to run while you're away. (For more health information, look at one of the newer LaserWriter manuals. I didn't know about this ozone stuff, either, until I upgraded to a LaserWriter IIf. But I probably glow in the dark by now anyway.)

Turning on the print spooler. If you've got both PrintMonitor and Backgrounder (in System 6) installed, but you still have to wait and wait for a document to print, you probably haven't turned on background printing in the Chooser. Remember, you have to have your printer selected in the Chooser before the background printing option appears. This happens to me frequently, so even though it's an "easy" tip, I mention it here.

If you're running System 6, be aware that print spooling (also called background printing) works only when MultiFinder is on. And print spooling only works with laser printers and StyleWriters (ink-jet), not with dot-matrix printers.

Put an alias of PrintMonitor in your Apple menu. Drag an alias of the PrintMonitor icon to your Apple Menu Items folder so you can get at it easily even when it's not running (see the next trick). This is a neat trick to use if you're working in an office where several desktop publishers always hog the laser printer and the order of priority for your documents may change as the day wears on. This way, when you finally get your chance to print and you need quick and easy access to PrintMonitor, it's right there under the Apple menu.

Flashing PrintMonitor icon? If the PrintMonitor icon in the upper-right corner of the screen flashes, it means that Print-Monitor needs your attention. This is a basic tip but one that can drive you to the manual if you don't know what's going on.

Switching printers? Be sure to open the Page Setup dialog box. This is another "easy" tip, but one that's also easy to forget. If you switch to a different printer in the Chooser, be sure to choose Page Setup from the File menu in your program to open the Page Setup dialog box. You don't have to change anything; just opening the box and closing it again is enough to let your program know which printer to format the document for. Otherwise your formatting may not be what you're expecting.

Want a printed list of all the files in a folder? Use the often-overlooked Print Window... command in the Finder's File menu to get a list of all the files in a folder. This is a handy trick if you're archiving files to floppy disks and you want to keep a printout of what's on them.

Can't print? Try this trick. If your program isn't finding your printer and you're running System 7, there may be an easy fix for you. Some older applications look only in the System Folder for the printer driver, but, as you know, System 7 puts printer drivers in the Extensions folder. Try putting an alias of the driver in the Extensions folder and keeping the original in the System Folder.
Thanks to Gene Garbutt, Apple Computer.

Application menu icon blinking? You don't have enough memory to print. If you see System 7's Application menu icon (in the upper-right corner of the screen) blinking, you'll need to quit a program (or perhaps two) to free up enough memory for printing. If you don't have an open window in a program, the Finder will politely ask if you'd like to quit that program. If you do have a window open, save your work and quit. Then you should be able to print.

LaserWriter on a SCSI port? Turn it on before you switch on your Mac. In most cases, any attached SCSI devices should be up and running before you turn on your Mac. This includes any LaserWriters, hard drives connected to them, or anything else you've got connected to a SCSI port. So don't forget to turn on your SCSI-connected LaserWriter before turning on the Mac.

Nuking the LaserWriter startup page. The newer LaserWriter installation disks come with a LaserWriter Utility program (on the Installation disk, in the Printing Tools folder) that lets you easily turn the startup page on or off (choose Set Startup Page from the Utilities menu). But if you don't have this new LaserWriter Utility program, here's how to nuke the startup page.

Create two text files (use any word processing program and save the files as text only), one named Startup Page On and the other named Startup Page Off (or whatever you like). Each should consist of these two lines.

The "Off" one:

```
serverdict begin 0 exitserver
statusdict begin false setdostartpage
```

The "On" one:

```
serverdict begin 0 exitserver
statusdict begin true setdostartpage
```

Use a font downloading utility program (like Font Downloader) to download to your laser printer the file you want to be in effect.

Of course, there's the brute-force way to suppress the startup page, too: pull out the paper tray as your printer's warming up and shove it back in when the green light's a steady glow. But that method is a bit of a hassle and you have to remember to do it, while the other ways are relatively foolproof.

Naming your LaserWriter. The newer LaserWriter Utility program (version 7.1) also lets you name your LaserWriter easily (just choose Name Printer from the Utilities menu). But if you don't have the new version, you can cheat and name your LaserWriter in System 7 with the utility called the Namer that came with your System 6 disks.

First, drag your LaserWriter icon out of the Extensions folder and put it "loose" in the System Folder, where the Namer can find it. Then open the Namer and name your LaserWriter. Now quit it and put the LaserWriter icon (or an alias of it) back in the Extensions folder. Select the new printer in the Chooser; you're ready to print.

Fast draft ImageWriter printing. If you're using an Image-Writer to print a quick draft copy for proofing only, try this trick. First, select all the text in the document and change it to 9-point Monaco. Now print it, choosing Draft in the Print dialog box. Make sure you've pressed the ImageWriter's Draft button, too.

Avoid automatic self-pasting envelopes. The heat from a laser printer often (usually) makes an envelope's flap seal itself to the envelope, and you have to force it open, thus messing up the neatly printed envelope. There are a couple of things you can do to try to avoid this situation.

First, try sticking the flap inside the envelope before you put it in the printer. However, what this often does is seal the flap inside the envelope, making it even harder to get the censored thing unstuck and open.

What usually works for me is putting a small piece of paper between the flap and the envelope. Keep handy a supply of these slips of paper, cut to fit.

You don't have to have a printer connected to format a document for it. Say you're working at home on a document that's going to be printed on a LaserWriter at work, but the printer you have at home is an ImageWriter. Put the LaserWriter driver icon in your System Folder on the Mac at home, too. Then you can choose that LaserWriter with the Chooser and open the Page Setup

dialog box in your application so that your document will be formatted for it. Go ahead and work on the document; the next day, take
your disk to work and print it.

If you format the document for the ImageWriter, some programs
may truncate its page width by as much as half an inch off what you'll
get if you format it for a LaserWriter. But you'll need to take an extra
step to fool the Mac into thinking you have a LaserWriter attached
when you really don't: unplug the ImageWriter from your printer
port and turn on AppleTalk in the Chooser.

The converse of this works, too: if a document's going to be
printed on an ImageWriter or other printer, choose that driver before
you format the document.

Printing via fax with a PowerBook. If you have a PowerBook
with a built-in fax modem, you can get a quick printout when
there's no laser printer to be found. Just hook the modem up, dial a
fax machine and fax your document. You probably thought of this
already, and I've seen this tip in many places, but it's a great one.

Pondering laser printer problems. If you've got a laser printer, you may occasionally be puzzled by the strange patterns of
toner (blotches) you sometimes get in your printed documents. The
problem's not always that you need a new, expensive toner cartridge.
Use these tricks to make a diagnosis:

- If you're getting a regular pattern of blobs running down the
  page, you've probably got dirty rollers. Find those Q-Tips that
  came with your printer, or buy new ones, and clean the rollers.

- If you get a thin line running down the page, there may be dirt
  on the cleaning pad. If cleaning the pad doesn't work, your drum
  or rollers may be scratched, which means a trip to the shop.

- If you're getting blacks that look too black, use the print density
  wheel to make them lighter.

- If you're getting blacks that look too light, use the print density wheel to make them darker. If that doesn't produce darker blacks, you may be low on toner.

- If blacks are printing instead as grays in odd places, you're probably running out of toner. Taker the toner cartridge out and rock it sideways (lengthwise, from side to side, not rolling it back and forth). That will usually revitalize a cartridge that's low on toner so you can squeeze out a few more pages until you can get a new cartridge.

FONT MAGIC

TrueType? PostScript Type 1 fonts? Adobe Type Manager? And where are the mysterious secret symbols? The tips in this section are all about font mysteries.

Fonts demystified. There are several different types of fonts, and like a lot of people, I have trouble figuring out which is which. Let's look at the simplest first.

TrueType fonts have icons with multiple letters on them (see Figure 7-2). They don't show any point size, because TrueType fonts can be scaled to any size. To install a TrueType font, just drag it to your System Folder in System 7. You don't need a printer font with a TrueType font—one size fits and prints all.

PostScript (Type 1) fonts have two icons (again, look at Figure 7-2). One is for the screen font and the other is the printer font. Different printer font vendors have different printer icons, as you can also see in Figure 7-2. Going clockwise from the upper left, there is a TrueType font (Symbol), a PostScript screen font (18-point Palatino; note that the size is given as part of the font file's name), a PostScript printer font (Futura Bold), a printer font from another manufacturer (Schneider Bold from Bitstream) and a font suitcase (holding screen fonts; in System 7.1 font suitcases can hold TrueType fonts also).

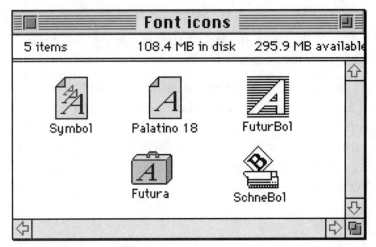

Figure 7-2: You can often tell what kind of format a font file is in by viewing by icon.

TrueType versus bitmapped fonts. Which is faster? Purists will note that bitmaps display a little faster on your screen. But especially at small sizes, TrueType fonts will match your printed output better.

If you have a dot-matrix or QuickDraw printer such as an Image-Writer II or LaserWriter SC, by all means use TrueType fonts. You'll get lots of fonts to choose from and excellent printed results, because your Mac will create the fonts and send them to the printer.

Got a LaserWriter with less than 2 Mb RAM? If your laser printer is an older LaserWriter Plus or if it doesn't have at least 2 Mb of RAM, you may have trouble printing TrueType fonts. (The original LaserWriters came with only 1.5 Mb.) If your older laser printer isn't printing the TrueType fonts you called for, you may be able to manually download one TrueType font at a time by using System 7's LaserWriter Utility program.

Mixing TrueType and PostScript fonts. If there's a TrueType font file and a PostScript font file for the same typeface in the System file (for instance, both a PostScript and TrueType version of

Palatino), the Mac will use the PostScript version. And if you have TrueType fonts that match your printer's built-in fonts, you'll see the TrueType fonts on the screen, but the printer will print its built-in fonts (which are most likely PostScript). If this causes a problem for you (such as screen images not exactly matching printed output), get FontMonger (Ares Software) or Metamorphosis Professional (Altsys) and convert all your fonts to one format or another. Or you can just get rid of one set or the other (see the next tip).

Switching to a PostScript-only system. If you decide to go the PostScript route and avoid TrueType, take the duplicate TrueType versions of your PostScript fonts out of your System file. In System 7, open the System file and drag out any duplicated fonts that have three As on their icons (see Figure 7-3). In System 7.1, you'll find fonts in font suitcases inside a Fonts folder in the System Folder, and you'll need to double-click on a suitcase to open it.

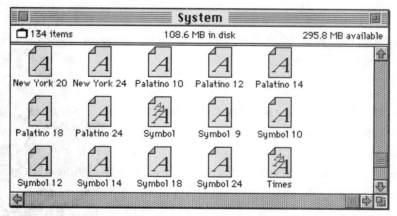

Figure 7-3: TrueType fonts in the System file are recognizable by their multi-letter icons.

Don't remove the TrueType versions of Chicago, Geneva, Monaco and New York. These fonts don't have Postscript counterparts, and you may want to use them some day, especially in on-screen presentations.

Switching to a TrueType-only system. If you decide that you want to go the TrueType-only route (probably because you have a dot-matrix or QuickDraw printer), you can delete all the screen fonts (bitmaps) from your System file or Fonts folder. They're left there because Apple assumes you may have a few pre-System 7 documents lying around that rely on these screen fonts.

When the Mac uses what type of font. For any given font, if you have a fixed-size (bitmap) version, a TrueType version and a PostScript version, the Mac will show you the fixed-size version on the screen. If you go to print on a PostScript printer, the Mac will use the PostScript version; on another type of printer, it will use the TrueType version. If this is likely to produce output using a font format that isn't what you intended, delete the offending font version.

If you delete the fixed-size version of a screen font, the Mac will display the TrueType version. If you delete *that*, it will display the Adobe Type Manager (ATM) version of the PostScript font (assuming ATM's installed).

Keep backups of all these fonts you're deleting in case you want any of them back someday.

Wrong font? Or no "font" at all? If your laser printer can't find the PostScript font you're calling for, it uses Courier. You probably don't want that, because it makes your printed documents look like you did them on a typewriter. (The only people I know who use Courier are, for some inexplicable reason, book publishers.) If you're getting Courier, check your System Folder to make sure the right font is there. With System 7, PostScript printer fonts should be in the Extensions folder and bitmapped fonts should be in the System file (or, with System 7.1, in the Fonts file). If you're using Master-Juggler or Suitcase II, make sure both the bitmapped font and printer font are in the same folder.

If you get a really ugly unreadable font, the problem is that the printer located the screen font but couldn't find the printer font and instead used the screen font to create a bitmapped version for the printer. Check as above, but you only have to look for the printer (outline) font.

 Do you need a font manager? Easy answers: with System 6, yes. With System 7, maybe.

If you use a lot of fonts with either system, a font manager such as MasterJuggler (ALSoft) or Suitcase II (Fifth Generation Systems) is probably a worthwhile investment. Although it's certainly easier to install fonts in System 7, they do take up a lot of space on your disk, and some font managers compress fonts. A font manager also lets you arrange fonts in folders according to your own organizing scheme, so that your System file doesn't become whale-sized. (With System 7.1, which lets you store fonts in a Fonts folder, you don't have the problem of fonts swelling your System file.)

Programs like MasterJuggler and Suitcase II also let you store your font suitcases and outline fonts outside your System Folder. If you need to reconstruct your System after a crash, you won't have to reinstall all those fonts.

Another great benefit of these suitcasing programs is that they let you store sets of fonts that you use for specific tasks in suitcases. If you keep all your fonts in your System file or Fonts folder, they have to be opened each time you start your Mac, even if you're only going to play a game. In your word processing program, your Font menu can take a long time to open, too, if you have a lot of fonts on it. So create specialty suitcases and open *them* for projects as needed.

If you don't have Apple's Font/DA Mover, which lets you use font suitcases in the absence of MasterJuggler or Suitcase II, you can get it from your System 6 disks or from a user group or information utility. Use version 4.1 or greater if you're running System 7; that version works in System 7, but earlier versions may not.

Damaged suitcases? Check this out. If you have several fonts with the same names and the same point sizes in the same suitcase, you can easily get a "suitcase damaged" message when you try to open it by double-clicking. This often happens to very large or complex suitcase files, even though there's nothing really wrong. Use Font/DA Mover 4.1 or greater and delete the duplicate fonts and sizes. After that, you should be able to get into the suitcase by double-clicking on it. If not, simply use Font/DA Mover to create a new suitcase and move all the old fonts from the "damaged" suitcase into the new one.

With System 7.1, you can combine suitcases. System 7.1 lets you merge the contents of two (or more) font suitcases. Just drag one suitcase onto another and drop it. This is a neat trick for assembling sets of fonts for specialized jobs.

System 7.1 magically reroutes fonts to a Fonts folder. With System 7,1, just drag fonts or font suitcases to the System Folder and drop them. They'll be put in a Fonts folder inside the System Folder, where you can easily find and work with them, instead of hunting through a big System file. (In previous systems, fonts were stored inside the System file.)

Freebie bitmapped fonts with System 7.1! There's an Apple Classic Fonts folder on System 7.1's Fonts disk that holds the original bitmapped "weird" fonts—San Francisco, London, Athens, Cairo, Mobile, Los Angles and Venice. If you have fond memories of these funny faces or you'd just like to try these fonts, they're there.

Fonts that you add to the System Folder don't show up in your applications until you restart. If you've added a font or two to your System Folder (to the System file in versions before System 7.1) and you don't see them listed on the Font menus in your applications, you haven't restarted after adding the fonts. They won't show up until you restart.

You can install fonts in an application—if you have System 7.
With System 7 and version 4.1 or greater of Font/DA Mover, you can install fonts in an application instead of in your system, which frees up memory when you're running other programs that don't need those fonts. Printer fonts remain in the Extensions folder, or wherever you normally store them, depending on how you have your system set up.

Open Font/DA Mover, hold down the Option key and click Open. Option-Open lets you open applications and install fonts and desk accessories in them. You might want to put those special but odd fonts in PageMaker or Microsoft Word only, or put your Calculator DA in Excel.

Don't have a laser printer? Get ATM. The wonderful thing about ATM (well, one of the wonderful things) is that it lets non-PostScript printers (like an ImageWriter) print using the bit-mapped fonts from the Type 1 PostScript versions of fonts like Helvetica, Times, Courier and Symbol—or any other Type 1 PostScript font, for that matter. So if you've got an ImageWriter or similar printer, get ATM.

Got ATM? Use its font cache. ATM stores screen fonts in a font cache. If scrolling or zooming seems to be taking longer than usual in a document that has lots of fonts, try resetting the cache's size to 256k or even greater. Use the ATM control panel (see Figure 7-4). I have 8 Mb of RAM on my system, and I've found that a 1 Mb font cache is about right.

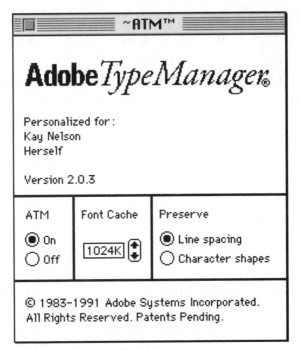

Figure 7-4: Adjust the font cache in ATM's control panel for greater font display speed.

If you've got ATM, you can get rid of a lot of screen fonts.
The more fonts you acquire, the less space is left on your hard disk. You can save disk real estate by trashing screen fonts; if you have ATM, you won't need (most of) them any more. Keep a couple of sizes for each font—I keep the 10- and 12-point sizes. You may want to keep the 9-point size of Courier, Helvetica, Symbol (if you use it) and Times, too, as this size is more readable on the screen than the ATM version. Otherwise, you can trash most other sizes of bitmapped fonts unless there's one in particular you use most often. ATM creates italics for you, too, so you can trash the italic bitmaps to save space.

Bitmapped fonts look better than ATM fonts in some sizes.
ATM fonts look great on the screen in 14-point and larger sizes, but you may want to keep the bitmapped screen fonts in 10- and 12-point sizes. It's also faster to print with bitmaps than with

ATM fonts, so for fastest printing, keep the bitmaps of the text sizes you use most often.

Secret Chicago symbols. You probably already know that the Command key cloverleaf symbol can be generated by pressing Control-Q in the original Chicago bitmap font.

Other secret symbols lurk in TrueType Chicago, too. For example, Control-S is a solid diamond, Control-P is an open Apple logo, Control-R is a check mark and Control-T is a solid Apple logo. There are quite a few other secret symbols, too; Control-A is the Option key symbol, Control-E is the Caps Lock symbol and Control-D is the Shift key symbol, for example. There are no secret symbols for H, I, M, Y or Z, but there are for the rest. The real secret? You can't see most of them on the screen. To see what these symbols are, use Key Caps; in Key Caps, switch to the Chicago font and press the Control key. Then "type" out the keyboard line by line by clicking on each key that's represented by a square. Copy each line and paste it in a document, making sure the document's font is Chicago, too. You still won't see anything, but print the document, and you'll see the secret symbols. Mark it up with the keys you used to generate the symbols. If you "typed" line by line as the keys are arranged on your keyboard, you should be able to figure out which key generates which symbol. These symbols are used to represent keys.

Secret Symbols

Keystroke	Symbol
Control-A	Option
Control-B	Control
Control-C	Enter
Control-D	Shift
Control-E	Caps Lock
Control-F	Rotate
Control-J	Left tab
Control-K	Switch right
Control-L	Page Down
Control-N	Return (right)

Keystroke	Symbol
Control-O	Fixed space
Control-P	Open Apple
Control-R	Check mark
Control-S	Diamond bullet
Control-T	Solid Apple
Control-U	Delete
Control-V	Right tab
Control-W	Return (left)
Control-X	Switch left

 Other neat symbols. You can create other symbols in almost any font by using these key combinations. Here are a few.[1]

Everyday Symbols

Keystroke	Symbol	Example
Option-8	Bullet	•
Option-g	Copyright symbol	©
Option-2	Trademark	™
Option-r	Registration mark	®
Option-t	Dagger	†
Option-v	Check mark	√
Option-Shift-V	Diamond bullet	◊
Option-$	Cents	¢
Option-3	Pound sterling (Brit.)	£
Option-;	Ellipsis	…
Option-hyphen	En dash	–
Option-Shift-hyphen	Em dash	—
Option-[	Opening double quote	"
Option-Shift-[	Closing double quote	"
Option-]	Opening single quote	'
Option-Shift-]	Closing single quote	'

---

[1]In System 7, most of these can be generated with an Option-Caps Lock combination, too. For example, the copyright symbol will appear with Option-g or Option-Caps Lock-g.

Math Symbols

Keystroke	Symbol	Example
Option-w	Summation	Σ
Option-z	Omega	Ω
Option-Shift-1	Solidus (schilling) fraction bar	/
Option-Shift-8	Degree sign	°

Accented Characters

To get accent marks over letters, type the Option-combination (you won't see anything on the screen) and then type the letter you want to have accented. For instance, to get an e with an acute accent, type Option-e and then another e. You'll get an é. Here are some other examples:

Keystroke	Symbol	Example
Option-e	Acute accent	á
Option-~	Grave accent	à
Option-u	Umlaut	ä
Option-i	caret	â
Option-n	tilde	ñ

And don't forget Zapf Dingbats, which is full of neat symbols like arrowheads, all sorts of bullets, and round bullets with numbers (try Option plus a character in Zapf Dingbats to see a sample of these).

LaserWriter ligatures. The LaserWriter's built-in fonts provide two ligatures—fi and fl. For a professional look, use them in your printed documents. Go ahead and type the document as you normally would in your word processing program; then search for fi and replace it with Option-Shift-5 (fi). The fl ligature is Option-Shift-6 (fl).

Em dashes and en dashes. You probably have heard by now that it looks really ugly to keep on typing dashes the way you did on a typewriter (or on a PC, snicker), with two dashes for a long dash (an em dash). Use the Mac's elegant em and en dashes instead. What's the difference? An em dash is a long dash, the kind you used to indicate by typing two dashes--like this. You get an em dash—a longer dash like this, by typing Shift-Option-hyphen.

An en dash is a short dash that's longer than a hyphen. It's used in ranges of dates and page numbers—"page 45–54" or "the years 1941–45," for example. You get an en dash with Option-hyphen. You can map these symbols to little-used characters on your keyboard if you use them a lot. See the "Swapping Keys Around" section in Chapter 6, "Miscellaneous Voodoo Tricks."

You may need that Symbol font, so don't delete it. You may think you can delete the Symbol font because you'll never type equations and such. But there's an undocumented trap: some symbols in Helvetica, Courier and Times rely on Symbol to produce their characters. If Symbol's missing, you get a bitmapped, jagged character for these symbols on screen and when you print. So if you think you'll ever need any of those characters (you probably will), keep Symbol installed.

Spaces have sizes, too, so use tabs for precise alignment. In any given font, the space character produced by pressing the space bar is a specific size, related to that font and point size. So use tabs instead of the space bar to align text. If you line items up using the space bar and later switch fonts, text that you've carefully aligned will become misaligned. This can happen when you take text from a word processing program into a page layout program, too.

Do you get a bomb when you pick a different font? This unusual occurrence usually indicates the bitmapped version of the font has gotten corrupted, not that there's something wrong with your Mac. Reinstall the font from the original disk.

MORE PRINTING TRICKS

If you send output to a service bureau, print to PostScript files, print complicated graphics, or need to get printouts of the screen, you'll find useful tricks in this section.

Service bureau hints. If you use a service bureau for high-resolution output (typesetting), try to get a copy of the driver they use with their output device. With that driver selected as your printer, you'll be able to see just how your document is being formatted, and you won't get any unpleasant line-break surprises when you get your final output.

If you're using a service bureau for printing, you don't need to buy expensive PostScript fonts. You can often purchase sets of screen-only PostScript fonts much cheaper than buying the whole set, which includes the printer fonts. If you're doing work that will ultimately be taken to a service bureau for printing, the service bureau will supply the printer fonts anyway. So you might want to investigate saving a little money by getting just the screen font set, which will allow you to set the document up on the screen just fine. Of course, things will look jagged if you proof them on a laser printer, but they should come out fine at the service bureau.

The most common source of mistakes: mismatched fonts. If you're taking a document to a service bureau, be sure to tell them exactly which fonts you're using, or you may get weird-looking output. And include *all* the fonts, too! It's easy to overlook a graphic image that has a couple of callouts in a special font. Send with your document a list of the fonts that are in the document—with the font's name, the manufacturer, as well as the version number. If you find that you have to do this a lot, get one of the programs like Else-Ware's CheckList (for PageMaker documents that are going to a service bureau) or QuarkPrint that peek in a document to see which fonts it uses.

Proofing a document on a LaserWriter? It's lighter than you think. If you're proofing a document on a LaserWriter before taking it to a service bureau for Linotronic output, be warned that because a laser printer isn't capable of the subtle imaging of an image-setter, it will look a lot darker in laser proofs than it will when the Linotronic gets through with it. If you're using 10% screens, for example, they'll be much lighter in the final Linotronic output. Bold type will be less bold, too.

Printing paint graphics. For best results when you're printing a bitmapped graphic on a laser printer, reduce it first. Why? Because your laser printer is going to print at 300 dots per inch, and a 100%-scale bitmapped graphic consists of 72 dots per inch. You can't divide 72 into 300 evenly, so the proportions won't match and you may get ugly patterns in the image. Reduce the graphic to 96% (or 72% or 48%) for better results.

To do this reduction automatically, select Precision Bitmap Alignment from the Page Setup dialog box before you print. That will get you the 96% reduction. If you want more reduction, scale the graphic down in the painting program that created it, or resize it in the program you're printing it from.

Ugly graphics? Check out this trap. If you get a really ugly PostScript graphic image, the problem may well be that the printer couldn't find it and printed it as a bitmapped PICT instead of as an encapsulated PostScript (EPS) image. To fix this problem, go back to the original document and place the EPS image again, or re-establish the link to the placed document from within the program.

Change the default number of copies to print. If you always have to print two copies of everything, why not use this trick to make 2 the default number of copies for your printer? First, make a copy of your printer driver icon in your System Folder. In System 7, it'll be in the Extensions Folder inside the System Folder. Then open it in ResEdit and double-click on the DITL resource. (For more information on what ResEdit is and how to use it, check out Chapter 4, "Customizing Your Desktop.")

Assuming your printer is a LaserWriter (or is controlled by the LaserWriter driver), find ID -8191 and double-click on it. You'll see what looks like the usual Print dialog box (see Figure 7-5). Double-click on the number next to Copies, and you'll get another dialog box (see Figure 7-6). Just change the number to the number of copies you want that LaserWriter to print most of the time.

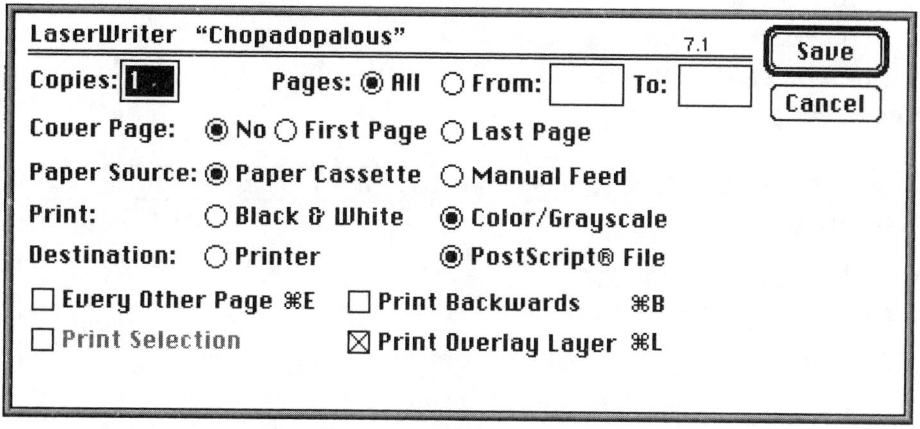

```
┌─────────────────────────────────────────────────────────────┐
│ LaserWriter  "Chopadopalous"                    7.1   ╭──────╮│
│                                                       │ Save ││
│ Copies:[1 ]        Pages: ◉ All  ○ From:[    ] To:[  ]╰──────╯│
│                                                       ┌──────┐│
│ Cover Page:  ◉ No ○ First Page ○ Last Page           │Cancel││
│                                                       └──────┘│
│ Paper Source: ◉ Paper Cassette ○ Manual Feed                 │
│ Print:        ○ Black & White  ◉ Color/Grayscale             │
│ Destination:  ○ Printer        ◉ PostScript® File            │
│ ☐ Every Other Page ⌘E   ☐ Print Backwards    ⌘B              │
│ ☐ Print Selection       ☒ Print Overlay Layer ⌘L            │
└─────────────────────────────────────────────────────────────┘
```

Figure 7-5: With ResEdit, you can edit the printer driver's DITL resource.

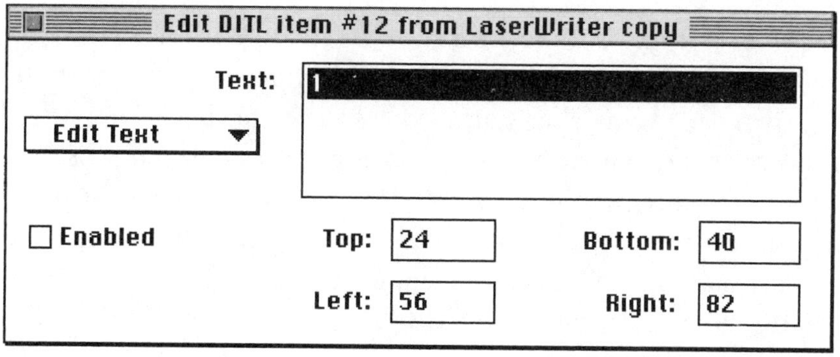

```
┌─────────────────────────────────────────────────────┐
│ ▤      ═══ Edit DITL item #12 from LaserWriter copy ═══│
│                                                       │
│               Text: [1                              ] │
│       ┌──────────────┐ │                            │ │
│       │ Edit Text  ▼ │ │                            │ │
│       └──────────────┘ └────────────────────────────┘ │
│                                                       │
│  ☐ Enabled      Top: [24  ]     Bottom: [40  ]        │
│                                                       │
│                Left: [56  ]      Right: [82  ]        │
└─────────────────────────────────────────────────────┘
```

Figure 7-6: Change the default number of copies to whatever you like.

Other things you might want to do include unchecking Font Substitution and Graphics Smoothing (or both) to change their defaults.

Saving a PostScript file. If you're running System 6, you can save a file as a PostScript file (for sending to a service bureau, for instance) by turning off background printing and pressing Option-F or Option-K right after printing. You need to press that key combination as soon as the Print dialog box disappears, within a couple of seconds. If you get a "looking for LaserWriter" message, you were too late.

This feature is built into System 7.0's LaserWriter driver as an option you can control from the Print dialog box using a radio button (see Figure 7-7).

DITL ID = -8191 from LaserWriter copy		
LaserWriter ""		**Print**
Copies: 1 Pages: ○ All ○ From: To:		**Cancel**
Cover Page: ○ No ○ First Page ○ Last Page		**Help**
Paper Source: ○ Paper Cassette ○ Manual Feed		
Print: ○ Black & White ○ Color/Grayscale		
Destination: ○ Printer ○ PostScript® File		**Feeder**

Figure 7-7: You can easily print to a PostScript file in System 7.

When everything's done, you should see a file named Postscript0 in the current folder. That's your PostScript file. You can create 0 to 9 files; then the numbering starts over, so use another folder after 9 (or renumber the first ten) if you're doing more than ten jobs. However, if you're planning to take that file to a service bureau for Linotronic output, be aware that the header is included in that file, so you'll have a *big* file. You can make it smaller by not using TrueType fonts (they all go into the header). With System 6, use Option-K to exclude the header.

Thanks to Eric Apgar, Apple Worldwide Technical Assistance.

Making print to disk the default (System 7). If you always want output that would normally be sent to the LaserWriter to be prepared instead as a disk (PostScript) file, you can use ResEdit to make printing to disk the default. For example, you may not have a laser printer and always use a service bureau for laser output, or you may always upload PostScript files to a remote computer.

First, duplicate your LaserWriter icon. Open it in ResEdit (see Chapter 4 for more on ResEdit); then double-click on the PDEF resource and ID 4. Press Command-H for Find Offset and enter 195E. The string 00 will be highlighted (you may have to move the dialog box to see it). Change the 001A to 001B and close the PDEF windows.

Now, double-click on the DITL resource and open ID -8191. Double-click on the Print button in the upper-right corner and change the button text from Print to Save. Save and quit Res-Edit.

You can do this in System 6, too, but it's much more complicated in ResEdit.

Change the default print color to black and white. OK, here's one you System 6 users can use, too. Printing in black-and-white mode speeds up the vast majority of printing jobs, and you can easily make that the default.

Duplicate your LaserWriter icon and open it in ResEdit. Double-click on the PDEF resource and open ID 4. Then locate 18F3 and change 0017 to 0018. Save and quit, and black-and-white is now your default printing mode.

Getting screen dumps. If you have System 6, you can press Command-Shift-4 to get a printout of the screen. If you try this in System 7, though, it doesn't work. The secret is that screen dumps in System 7 are directed to TeachText and you must use Command-Shift-3 instead. Open the file named Picture 0 (they're numbered starting with 0) in TeachText and print it from there.[2]

If your screen dump prints out chopped up across two pages, change the orientation from portrait to landscape in the Page Setup dialog box under the File menu.

---

[2]For a wicked, nasty trick to pull on somebody using the built-in screen shot feature, see Chapter 6 and blame Robin Williams.

Also, be aware that some screen shots can be too big for Teach-Text to handle. Try opening those in Photoshop or some similar graphics program; Photoshop is limited only by the amount of RAM you have available, and you can even get around that problem by using Photoshop's built-in feature that substitutes disk space for RAM. (Also see Chapter 3's trap "You can't edit System 7 dumps in MacPaint" for additional tips about getting screen dumps.)

MOVING ON

That's a pretty full grab bag of printing tips, but it's only a random collection. Send me your favorite printing tricks (see the introduction for details) and contribute to the second edition.

And while connecting your Mac to a printer is (usually) easy enough, that's just one of the many things you can plug your Mac into. The next chapter takes a look at the mysterious area called connectivity, which encompasses everything from SCSI drives to downloading freeware and shareware to networking hints and tips.

CHAPTER EIGHT

CONNECTIVITY SECRETS

Connectivity is one of the hottest Macintosh buzz-words around. It covers everything from hooking two Macs together for exchanging files to downloading shareware from bulletin boards and online services to using System 7's fancy networking and file sharing capabilities. You'll find tricks for all of these in this chapter.

NETWORKING MAGIC

If you have two Macs, or a Mac and a laser printer, you've got a network. System 7 comes with built-in networking software that doesn't cost you another dime. All you need to do to hook up another Mac to it is plug a LocalTalk connector into your Mac's printer port. You can get a LocalTalk Connector Kit or its cheaper third-party equivalent from your local software-o-rama or by mail order (see Appendix B for a couple of reliable mail order houses).

Once you get the kit, you'll see that it's a cable with two round 8-pin plugs plus a connector box. Plug one of the plugs into one Mac's printer port and plug the other one into the other Mac's printer port. (The printer port has a printer icon on it.) Now you have a network.

By the way, if all you have is one Mac and one laser printer, don't bother getting any network connectors or special cables. You can get an inexpensive null modem cable for about $10, or use the one from your old ImageWriter II (see the tip "Lightning-fast data transfer").

You can have a mixed System 6 and 7 network. Your System 6 users on the network won't be able to share folders that are on their Macs, but they can access all the shared folders that are on the Macs running System 7. They'll have to install AppleShare, but it comes with System 6. Then all they do is access the AppleShare server.

Without AppleShare, a System 7 machine on a mixed network can access System 6 machines; but you can't access System 7 machines from System 6 Macs without third-party software (or AppleShare).

System 7's file sharing has its limitations. If you need to do heavy-duty file sharing, be aware of System 7's built-in file sharing limitations. For example, you can share only ten folders at once, and only ten users can access a shared volume at the same time. It's designed for a few Macs and moderate traffic. For larger networks, use AppleShare (or third-party networking software like Novell Net-Ware) and a dedicated file server.

System 7's file sharing is also designed to be used without a system administrator. Each individual decides what to share, sets his or her own passwords, and so forth. There's no way to do regular system-wide backups and all the other housekeeping that comes with a good-sized network. And if the guy with the file you need didn't turn on his Mac or open it up to outside access, there's no way to get at that file on the network. But a problem like that is usually easily solved, and System 7's built-in file sharing is great if you have only a few Macs and a few folks using them.

Networking demystified. There are several different control panels that deal with networking, and it can get confusing as to which does what and what you have to do, and in what order. Here's the streamlined, no-tutorial version of how to do it:

- Go to the Chooser and click the Active button to make Apple-Talk active.

- Use the Sharing Setup control panel first to set up your access to the network, including your password. Click Start to turn on file sharing.

- Select a folder to share (or, if you don't mind sharing everything, select your whole hard disk icon) and choose Sharing from the File menu. Click Share this item and its contents. (You can't use the Sharing command unless you select something first.)

Now you've shared that folder (or whatever you selected), and other network users can access it.

To access somebody else's folder, the procedure's a little different:

- Use the Chooser to turn on AppleShare.

- In the Chooser, pick the computer you want to access (assuming that it's turned on and sharing has been activated at its end). That's the file server. Then click OK.

- You'll be asked for your user name and password. You can sign on as a guest if you haven't been registered or if you've forgotten your password.

- After you click OK, you'll see a list of the items that are being shared by that server. Pick the folder or folders you want to get into and click OK.

If all is working properly, you'll see a shared icon of the computer you're accessing on your desktop. If you're using a custom icon for that drive, you'll see that icon; otherwise, you'll see the generic file server icon—the hand holding a tray with documents on it.

If you don't want everybody who's on the network to be able to get into your folders, use the Users & Groups control panel. To register a user, choose New User from the File menu. You can assign that guy a password, too. (Be sure to tell him what it is.)

Don't allow guests if you want to keep track of who gets to peek in your folders. If you want to restrict access to just a few folks on the net, double-click the Guest icon in the Users & Groups control panel and uncheck the Allow Guests to Connect box.

You can then register just the people you want to have access to what's on your Mac.

Sharing your whole drive means sharing your whole drive. Lots of beginning file sharing users mistakenly assume that their Mac is still relatively secure even when they've chosen to share their whole hard drive. Sharing an entire volume is often the most convenient way to allow others access to files they need, but you should remember that doing so gives any user on the network, even one who logs on as a guest, access to everything on your hard drive.

Worried about sharing? Here's the secret. There may be things on your Mac, like next quarter's budgets and projected salary raises, that you don't want everybody on the net to see. But don't get bogged down in the details of setting up users and groups and giving everybody secret passwords and magic decoder rings. Nobody can see what's on your computer unless you select a folder and choose Sharing from the File menu. So just share folders that have stuff in them that you don't mind having everybody see. Make a folder called Shared Stuff (or whatever) and share that. Believe me, it's easier than restricting different types of access and trying to figure out what to put where.

If you really need to let certain folks see some information and other folks get at other information, set up folders with those items (one for Tom and Dick and another for Harry) and restrict access to them. Then drag the icons of what you want to share for each set of people into the proper folder.

Really sneaky trick: Make the Sharing Setup control panel invisible. If you're serious about not letting casual users get access to your sharing setup, where they could give themselves access privileges and so on, make your Sharing Setup control panel invisible with ResEdit. To make it invisible, all you need to do is open a copy of the Sharing Setup control panel in ResEdit and choose Get Info from the File menu. In the dialog box that appears, click Invisible. Replace the original control panel with the copy, but save the original as a backup for a while, just in case you need it. For more details on using ResEdit, see Chapter 4, "Customizing Your Desktop."

Make a bulletin board folder where people can read messages. If you'd like to set up a drop folder where people can leave and read message files but not change them or take them out once they're there, use the Sharing command. In the dialog box (see Figure 8-1), uncheck the Make Changes boxes for User/Group and Everyone, and make sure the Can't be moved, renamed or deleted box is checked.

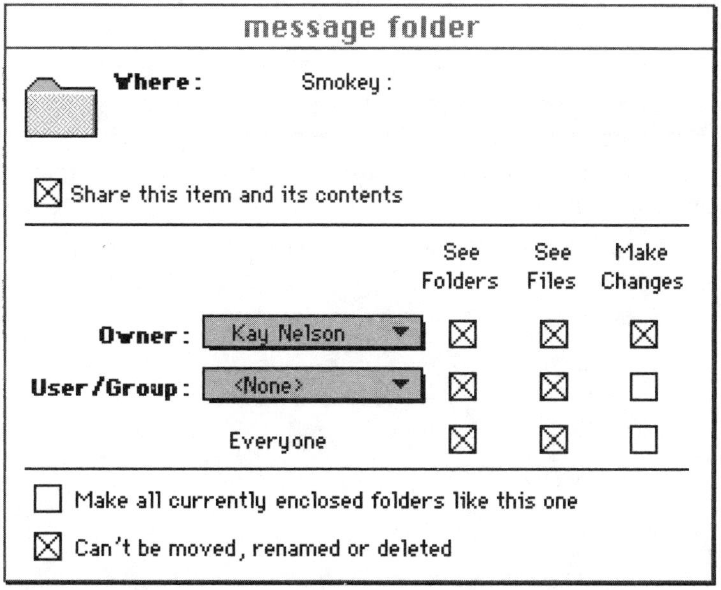

Figure 8-1: You can use System 7's file sharing features for setting up a message center folder.

The icon with the strap and the arrow (see Figure 8-2) indicates this type of In Box folder. A folder icon with a strap is locked—it can't be used at all. You should never see this icon on your own desktop, only displayed from someone else's shared disk. A folder icon with a darkened tab indicates you own it, and one without a darkened tab indicates that you can read what's inside the folder and use it, but you aren't the owner. This last type of folder is also useful as a bulletin board because others (everyone, including a group named Readers) can see into its files and folders, but they can't add or delete anything. Figure 8-3 shows how I set it up on my other Macintosh so that it's displayed this way on my Quadra—where I'm viewing the setup as a guest. Figure 8-3 shows which options I chose in setting it up.

Figure 8-2: You can tell the different types of shared folders by their icons.

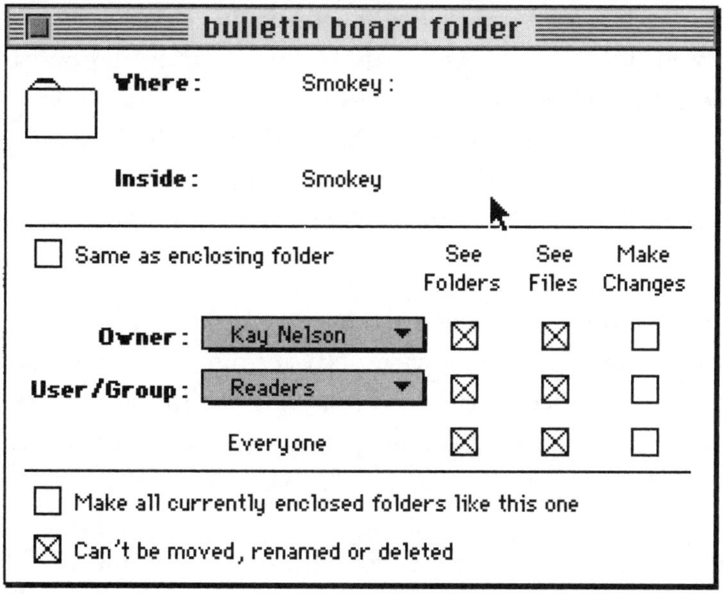

Figure 8-3: Here's how to set up a bulletin board folder that other folks can see into.

Make yourself a private mailbox. If you want a folder to hold your private mail, which only you can read and no one else can open, uncheck the See Files and See Folders boxes for User/ Group and Everyone in the Sharing dialog box. Anyone accessing your Mac will see a folder with a strap and arrow on it like the message folder in Figure 8-2; they can put documents (and other folders) into this folder, but they can't get a peek at what it contains.

Protecting files on a network. Since you can protect a folder from being accessed by unauthorized persons, all you need to do to protect a file is drag it to a restricted folder. Give users read-only access to that folder by checking See Folders and See Files but by leaving the Make Changes boxes unchecked.

Uppercase and lowercase matter in passwords. The Mac is a little quirky about passwords and user names. Uppercase and lowercase are meaningful in passwords (that is, "duck" won't work if "DuCK" is the original password) but they don't make a difference in owner or user names. If your Mac isn't accepting your password, check to see that Caps Lock hasn't been pressed by mistake.

Prevent password loss with this trick. The Mac really wants you to use a password with networking, and it complains mightily when you don't. If you think you may forget your password, register yourself as a user. Because you get to see the passwords of the users you've registered, you can check to see what your own password is.

Now you can get wild and crazy with passwords and use all sorts of sneaky tricks, such as making up words that aren't in the dictionary, using alphanumeric combinations, deliberately misspelling a word, and so forth.

Connecting to a shared disk each time you turn on your Mac. If there's a shared disk or a folder on a shared disk that you want to connect with every time you switch on your computer, set things up in the Chooser. Click AppleShare and Active; then pick the file server you want to connect to. Log on as a registered user and supply your password. Then check the box next to the hard disk or folder you want to access (see Figure 8-4). Click Save My Name and Password if you don't want to have to enter your password when you start up your Mac.

Of course, the other computer needs to be on before you can access it.

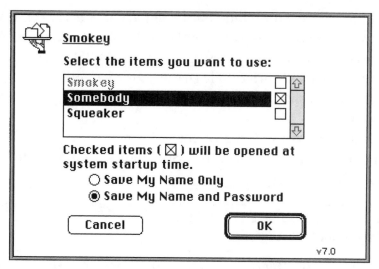

Figure 8-4: You can set up automatic sharing for easy
network access.

Copying shared programs. Once you have access to a shared
folder, you can copy the things that are in it onto your own
hard disk. Just drag the item to your hard disk icon.

To copy a program, though, put it in a folder and then copy the
folder, so that the Mac will know you want to make a copy of the
program, not just share it.

Copying items to share. To copy items into a shared folder
instead of moving them there, press the Option key while you
drag them to the shared folder. Or consider putting aliases in the
shared folder; they take up lots less room on your disk.

Share aliases instead of the real things. If you share aliases,
you'll save disk space, as you saw in the preceding tip. But
sharing aliases has another sneaky advantage: the folks at the other
end can't throw the item away—the worst they can do is erase the
alias, which is no monumental loss since you can easily create a new
one from your safely stored original.

Can't share your whole hard disk? Try this trick. If the Mac won't let you share your whole hard disk, you're probably already sharing one or two items on it. Check the File Sharing Monitor control panel and turn off file sharing for each folder that's being shared. Now you should be able to select your entire hard disk icon and share it.

Use the File Sharing Monitor control panel (see Figure 8-5) to find out which item is being shared. Sometimes it's a pesky folder several levels down.

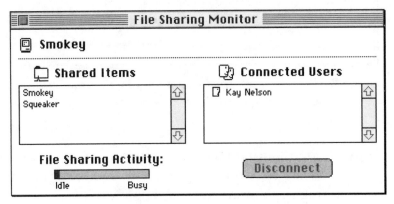

Figure 8-5: For the fastest way to find out what's being shared, use the File Sharing Monitor control panel.

Slowdown on a network. Your Macs can really slow down if you're sharing a lot of folders. If you get a slowdown, unshare as many folders as possible, or put the things you want to share into one folder and share *it* instead of sharing your whole hard disk.

Magic disconnecting. The fastest way to disconnect from the network is to drag the icons of the items you're sharing to the Trash. (Selecting the item or items and pressing Command-Y for Put

Away is another way to disconnect.) Of course, shutting your Mac down works, too, but you may want to just disconnect from the net and continue working.

If you drag a shared item to the Trash, it's not actually in the Trash—you've unmounted it from your desktop, not thrown it away like a normal file—so you can't re-access the network by going to the Trash and retrieving any shared items you unmounted.

A more polite way of saying goodbye to the network is to use the Sharing Setup control panel, click Stop, and enter a particular number of minutes before your Mac closes down. The other users on the network will get a message warning them that you're about to go off the air, so to speak, so they'll have a chance (however long you specified) to save any work that involves the items you're sharing.

You can disconnect individual users by using the File Sharing Monitor control panel. Click on the names of the guys you want to disconnect; then click Disconnect.

MORE SYSTEM 7 CONNECTIVITY TRICKS

System 7 brought lots of networking features to the Mac. I'll admit it's a little clunky getting file sharing started, but once you figure it out, you can do amazing things—like connect to the Mac in your office by using a floppy disk in your pocket (of course, you have to take it out and put it in another Mac first). Here, then, is the famous office-on-a-disk trick (and a few more advanced tricks, too).

 The office-on-a-disk trick. You may have heard of this one. But here it is again, because it's such a great trick.

If you're on a network running System 7, you can access your Mac from any other Mac on the network via a simple floppy disk. First, make an alias of your hard disk and copy it onto a floppy. Then, turn on file sharing in the Sharing Setup control panel. Now make your hard disk available on the net by selecting it and choosing Sharing from the File menu.

Now all you need to do is put the floppy in your pocket and walk away. When you're in another office, put the floppy in the drive of any Mac connected to the same network and just double-click on the alias of your hard disk to connect to it. Magic.

Make an alias of your file server for easy connecting, too. If there's another Mac or a file server on the network that you routinely connect to, make an alias of it and keep it out on your desktop. That way, you can access it without going through all the normal steps and multiple mouse clicks that it takes to go through the Chooser.

Instead of letting the icon take up real estate on your desktop, try putting the alias in your Apple Menu Items folder. That way, you'll be able to choose the server directly from your Apple menu.

Even more magic: make aliases of all the shared items on other people's Macs that you frequently work with, put them in a folder, and leave it on the desktop. It's easy to access anything that's in that folder from any Open dialog box by clicking on the Desktop button.

Thanks to Mike Chow, Apple Computer, for some tips on this one.

Easy copying to your file server. Dragging a file to an alias of a file server will do two things: mount the file server, if it isn't already mounted, and copy the file to the file server. Magic.

Thanks to Eric Apgar, Apple Worldwide Technical Assistance.

An easy way to set up network users. If there are a few folks who need to get on your network from time to time but really don't want to learn all this networking mumbo jumbo, just set up a shared folder for each of them. Inside that folder, store anything that you want them to be able to share. Give them a floppy disk with an alias of that folder on it. They can access their own shared folder by inserting the floppy and double-clicking on the folder's alias. Since they own the folder, there's no special procedure to remember.

This trick is too cool. I read about it on America Online. *Thanks, DMorton.*

Securing your password with AppleTalk Remote Access. If you use AppleTalk Remote Access and you (or your users) are worried about inadvertently checking that suspicious Save my password dialog box, use ResEdit to remove the dialog so that it will never appear. Open AppleTalk Remote Access in ResEdit (see Chapter 4 for more on ResEdit); then open the view resource, Open ID 2000 and find offset 3b4 (Command-H is a shortcut for Find Offset). Change the B7 at position 3b4 to 00 (zero zero). Now quit and save changes, and you won't see that dialog box again.

Thanks to Eric Apgar, Apple Worldwide Technical Assistance.

SCSI SECRETS

A SCSI (small computer systems interface, or "scuzzy") device is one that's connected to a high-speed parallel port—called, appropriately, the SCSI port—on the back of your Mac. SCSI devices are things like printers, external hard disks, scanners, CD-ROM drives and so forth. If you look at the back of your Mac, you can find the SCSI port easily, because it's the biggest one. You can connect as many as six SCSI devices to your Macintosh, as long as you connect them in an unbroken chain and connect the first one to the computer. Unfortunately, the process is rarely as simple as that. There are a few more tricks that you'd be well advised to use when working with SCSI devices, and we'll look at them in this section.

Don't have a twenty-foot SCSI chain. According to the experts, a SCSI cable network shouldn't be longer than 19.6 feet (6 meters). Each device takes up about a foot of internal wiring, so figure in an extra foot per device, too, when you calculate how long a chain you've got.

Don't break a SCSI connection with the power on. You probably know that one already, but you can cause damage to the other devices that are cabled together (including your internal hard drive, which is part of the SCSI chain) if you disconnect a cable with the power on. Likewise, it's usually best to start up your SCSI devices *before* you start your Mac. Shut them down after you turn your Mac off.

Use a power strip if you've got SCSI devices. It's a pain in the neck to switch on all your SCSI devices one by one and then switch on your Mac. Instead, plug all your SCSI boxes into a power strip, switch it on, count to ten (to give them a chance to start up and kick in), and then switch on your Mac.

SCSI ID numbers. Each device in a SCSI chain must have a unique ID number ranging from zero to seven. In theory, you can assign SCSI devices any number between 0 and 7 but in practice, you're limited to 1 through 6. There are a few rules to follow about assigning ID numbers to SCSI devices.

- All Apple (and nearly every third-party brand) internal hard drives are assigned the ID number 0, so be sure not to assign 0 to any external hard drive you buy.

- The Mac itself is always ID 7.

- If you have an external hard drive (and no internal drive), the Mac will use the SCSI drive with the highest ID number as the startup disk, so assign ID 6 to the external drive you want to boot from.

You can use the Startup Disk control panel to designate which device to start up with, no matter what the SCSI ID numbers are, unless you're running a Mac Plus. If you're on a Plus, you'll have to renumber SCSI devices to change the startup disk.

How to renumber SCSI devices? Depends on the device. Some come with special software for renumbering; others make you locate and set tiny switches or push buttons to change counters, like my external Cutting Edge hard drive.

Duplicate termination can cause crashes. A SCSI chain has to be terminated at both ends. Most internal hard drives are self-terminating, and you can usually terminate the last device in a chain with a little connector that doesn't have a cable attached to it (called, appropriately enough, a terminator). All you need to do is find the last device in the chain and plug up its empty cable connector with a terminator so that the Mac knows this is the end of the chain. If you're having difficulties with SCSI devices, make sure that the last connector is terminated.

If you have an internal hard SCSI disk that begins acting up after you add SCSI devices to your Mac, check to see that you don't have duplicate termination on the internal hard drive and the motherboard. How to do it: take the drive out and look at the terminators. There should be three DIP resistor packs next to the connector. If you're uncomfortable poking around on your internal hard drive or you don't want to crack open your Mac's case[1]—especially if it's a compact Mac—take it to your dealer or friendly computer repair place for a check-up.

SCSI troubles? Try these tips. The most common cause of SCSI problems is that you simply forgot to turn the device on. As outlined in a previous tip, put all your SCSI boxes on a power strip and turn it on; that way you won't forget to switch on a device or two.

The next most common cause is a conflict in SCSI addresses—that is, you've given two (or more) SCSI devices the same ID number. If you add a new device to your system, check all the numbers and make sure each device has its own unique number from 1 to 6. Unless you're working out a special boot sequence with external hard drives, it doesn't matter which device receives which ID, as long as it's the only one with that ID. Check out Robert Polic's excellent shareware program SCSI Probe. Not only does it help you determine a device's SCSI ID without breaking your neck looking at the backs

---

[1] I hate telling anybody to crack open their compact Mac's case. Although I've seen it done, and it's not that hard, I don't want to get cards and letters and e-mail saying, "Dear Kay, I opened my Mac up like you said and now it won't work. What should I do?"

of all your SCSI devices, but it also helps you locate problems in your SCSI chain and mount (during and after startup) those stubborn drives that don't seem to want to work properly.

If you still have problems, take the SCSI chain apart and put it back together, one device at a time, restarting after each one. That way, you can isolate which device is causing the problem. As you try this, make sure the last device in the chain is either internally terminated or has an external terminator.

Use aliases for SCSI drives, too. If you have more than one SCSI drive, you should probably also have SCSI Probe, mentioned in the preceding tip. In addition to helping you locate problems in a SCSI chain, it also lets you mount SCSI drives that you've dismounted (by dragging them to the Trash) without restarting your Mac. But if you don't have SCSI Probe, you can use this trick to do the same thing.

Make an alias of the SCSI drive. Now, even if you trash the original drive icon to dismount it, you can double-click on the alias to quickly get it back again without restarting.

Be sure to secure your SCSI cables. As I mentioned earlier, unplugging SCSI cables while something else is turned on can cause a lot of damage, including frying your hard drive. The same goes for plugging the cables *in*. You should only make or break a SCSI connection when everything is turned off. That's why SCSI cables come with screw-in connectors and locking cable tabs.

Sometimes the cable is the culprit. Just as electrical cords develop shorts or other problems, SCSI cables are prone to wear and tear, too. If you've tried everything else you can think of, try swapping cables around between different devices (or borrow a friend's cable if you have only one device). Try using a particularly long or short cable, as this can sometimes affect termination. Finally, check to make sure all the cables in the SCSI chain are plugged in all the way and locked down (you might actually consider this step early on in the SCSI diagnostic process). If just one cable on one device is only halfway connected (a common problem), it can spoil the whole show for every other device in the chain.

Be careful, though. What might seem like a cable problem could also be a problem with the device's SCSI port itself. Port contacts can work loose or develop shorts over time, especially if you're constantly connecting and disconnecting cables.

Dealing with indeterminate termination. While it's clear that the last device in a SCSI chain should usually be terminated, it's not always clear how or where to terminate it. Since some devices have built-in termination, you may have to *remove* that termination if the device is in the middle of the SCSI chain (or make sure that device falls at the end of the chain). Likewise, some devices have a complex set of switches that have to be set a certain way, depending on the number and nature of other devices in the chain.

Where you install the external terminator can even sometimes play a role. Some devices work better if you plug the second, open port (every SCSI box has two) with the terminator; others seem to work best if you plug the cable into the terminator and then plug the terminator into one of the ports, leaving the other one open. And you can sometimes get away with not at all terminating some devices, such as a single external hard drive hooked straight into your Mac's SCSI port.

The mysterious black terminator. Apple makes some devices, namely the Mac IIfx and the LaserWriter IIf and IIg, that require a special terminator rated for different operating specifications. While most external terminators are gray or platinum (like the color of the Mac's case), the special terminator used by the IIfx and the LaserWriters IIf and IIg is made with black plastic and is therefore commonly referred to as "the black terminator." Unfortunately, Apple tends to bury this information deep in its product documentation, so it's easy to miss. If you've been trying to terminate one of these devices with a regular platinum terminator, you may never succeed. Call your Apple dealer for details on buying and using a black terminator.

Be sure to get a cable, and the right kind, too. Most SCSI devices are sold by the manufacturer or retailer with their own SCSI cable included (you'll sometimes see the cable sold separately for a lot of money, cleverly packaged as a "SCSI interface kit"). If you're paying several hundred dollars for the SCSI device, you deserve the cable (or "interface kit") as part of the bargain. The SCSI port on your Mac has 25 tiny holes, which 25 matching pins on the SCSI cable go into. But the ports on SCSI devices themselves all have 50 contact points. So to connect a SCSI device to your Mac, you'll need a 50-pin to 25-pin cable. But to connect a second SCSI device to the first one, you'll need a 50-pin to 50-pin cable. When you're buying a second SCSI device, be sure to specify that you need a 50-pin to 50-pin cable; otherwise, you'll get stuck with a second (and relatively useless, at this point) 25-pin to 50-pin cable.

PowerBooks require special SCSI connections. You've no doubt noticed how large the SCSI port on the back of a normal Mac is. When the folks who designed Apple's PowerBooks were faced with integrating this huge port into the new notebook's sleek design, they cheated by changing the shape of the port. Consequently, you'll need special cabling to hook your PowerBook up to a SCSI device, so be sure to mention that you're using a PowerBook when you're buying a SCSI cable for it.

MODEM MAGIC

Mac owners fall into three categories when it comes to modems. There are those who have them, use them and love them; there are those who have them but never seem to use them because they think it's all too complicated; and there are those who want a modem but won't buy one because they are afraid of all the stuff they think they have to know to use one. Rely on the tips in this section for help in connecting to electronic bulletin boards and online services.

If you're just starting out with an information utility, I recommend you get yourself an account on America Online—the interface is very similar to the Mac's, and you won't have to wrestle with a bunch of cryptic uncertitudes, like figuring your stop bits, parity or which protocol to use. Even picking the phone number to dial is easy. You won't need to use very many of these tips with America Online. Or, for an additional fee when you join CompuServe, you can get CompuServe's Information Manager or Navigator, which greatly simplifies working with and navigating CompuServe.

The (almost) universal settings. Just about all the bulletin boards and online services you'll communicate with use 8 data bits, no parity and 1 stop bit. If you don't know which modem settings to use when configuring your telecommunications software, try those first.

X-, Y- or ZMODEM? Unlike ASCII format, which is used only for straight text, you can use any of the XMODEM, YMODEM or ZMODEM protocols to send and receive programs.

XMODEM is the most widely supported transfer protocol, so using it is a safe bet. YMODEM allows you to send several files as a batch. ZMODEM has the advantage of built-in error correction, so it's the safest of the three to use, and much faster than the other two. Another huge advantage that the ZMODEM protocol has is it can resume an aborted or interrupted file transfer where it left off. In other words, if you're downloading a file that takes 45 minutes to transfer and you get cut off after 40 minutes, you can simply log back on and download the last five minutes of the file. Not all bulletin boards and telecom software support ZMODEM, though, but use it if you can.

Compressed files, and how to identify them. Most of the files you download or transfer over the modem will be compressed. Look at the end of the file's name. If it ends in .sea, you can decompress it just by double-clicking on it. (That *sea* means *self-extracting archive*.) Files ending in .sit need to be decompressed by using one of the StuffIt family of programs. You can download a free "unstuffer" utility from most any place that features files compressed by StuffIt.

Files ending in other cryptic extensions require the original compression program to decompress them. So go back and download the right utility if you wind up with a file you can't decompress.

If you do a lot of downloading, uploading or file transfer via modem, you should definitely invest in a reliable file compression program. There are a number of different versions of the popular StuffIt program—distributed both as shareware and commercial software—to fit your needs and budget. Figure 8-6 shows StuffIt Classic in use. Bill Goodman's Compact Pro is a fine shareware compression utility, and Fifth Generation System's DiskDoubler is an excellent commercial product. Whatever you spend on any one of these utilities will more than be recouped in reduced online time and telecommunication charges.

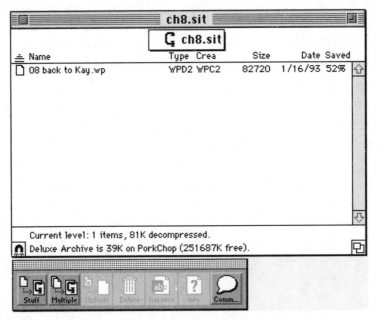

Figure 8-6: StuffIt Classic has become a standard for telecommunications compression.

Taking PC files through your Mac. If you need to upload or download compressed PC files using your Mac, don't despair. For example, I prefer using Navigator on my Mac to access Compu-Serve, even if I'm sending someone else a PC file. Just use PKZIP on the PC and take the .ZIP archive over to the Mac via Apple File Exchange, Macintosh to PC Exchange, DOS Mounter, a TOPS network or what have you. Then upload them as usual on the Mac side.

If the opposite is the case, and you're using a PC to download files that you want to be able to use on your Mac, rest assured that Stuffit Classic or Compact Pro archives will go through the PC. Just download them to your PC and transfer them to the Mac. Don't, however, try to do this with self-extracting archives (they end in .sea). It won't work.

If you have difficulty opening a stuffed (.sit) archive on the Mac, use ResEdit (or a utility like DiskTop) to make sure the file's type and creator are SIT! (for StuffIt Deluxe). See the tips in Chapter 6, "Miscellaneous Voodoo Tricks," about changing a file's type and creator for how to do this.

If you download a Mac file via a PC and it doesn't work when you get it to the Mac, try using a MacBinary to Mac translator on the file. You can get a translator like this as shareware from most bulletin boards and user groups.

Finally, if you'd like to download TIFF or EPS files for use on your Mac but the files are zipped (compressed using the PC utility PKZip) but you don't have a PC, don't despair. Get a copy of Un-Zip, a shareware Mac decompression utility that unzips PKZip files.

How long is the download going to take? Many communications programs will figure this out for you and show you a little thermometer indicating how long the download (or upload) will take. But if you don't have one of these programs, you can figure it out for yourself.

I used to fret about spending big bucks downloading files until I hit upon the secret formula for figuring out (roughly) how long a file will take to download. Say that you're using a 2400 bps modem, so you can receive around 240 bytes/second. (Eight bits plus one start and one stop bit equals 10 bits/byte—divide that into 2400.) Figure that the transfer is going to take a little more time for checking bits, correcting transmissions, and other housekeeping, and say that you can receive around 200 bytes/second. Divide the size of the file (in bytes) by your reception speed, and you've got a rough idea of how long the download will take. For example, say that the file you want to download is 300,000 bytes. It will take about 150 seconds (two and a half minutes) at 2400 baud.

Thanks to Elise Hannah of Brunswick, Georgia.

The Call Waiting trap, and its solution. If you have Call Waiting on your telephone service, you probably know how it can interrupt a download (or any file transfer over the modem) when someone calls you. To disable Call Waiting for the duration of your modem session, add *70 just before the number your modem is supposed to dial to access the service. On a pulse phone, add 1170. If your telecommunications software allows you to enter pre-dialing strings, such as the number 9 to reach an outside line, you should add *70 so that Call Waiting will always be disabled before every call. This trick may not work everywhere. Contact your local phone service if it doesn't work for you—there may be other options.

If you have several phones in the house, the same thing (losing your connection) can happen if somebody picks up an extension. To prevent this, get a little device called a Teleprotector from Radio Shack ($7.95) for each of your phones.

Your modem is only as good as your software. You can spend several hundred dollars on a top-of-the-line modem with all sorts of fancy high-speed protocols and built-in features, but if the telecommunications software you use to run the modem isn't up to snuff, it doesn't matter how much you paid. Likewise, if the software is so complex that you have no idea where to begin, you're not likely to spend a lot of time online. Many modems come bundled with great software, but if you're unhappy with yours, you might try the popular commercial product Microphone II. If cost is a factor, you can try ZTerm, Dave Alverson's shareware offering, for free, and it's only $35 if you decide to keep it.

Buy the fastest modem you can afford. If you haven't bought a modem, but you're considering picking one up, buy the fastest one—within reason—that you can afford. If you end up using it very much at all, you'll more than make up the higher modem cost in lower phone bills and online charges. There are, of course, limits to the practicality of this advice. There are still relatively few services that support the high-end warp speeds that the latest modems offer. Don't spend $600 on a modem if you don't expect to be online at super-fast speeds on a regular basis. You can get a reliable 2400 baud modem (which is the minimum speed you should consider working with) for around $100. Get a 9600 baud model if you can, but for now, forget about the other models. The average phone line isn't built for communication above about 9600 baud.

Watch out for noisy phone lines. Often, you'll experience problems transferring files reliably; sometimes you might even have difficulty just staying connected to a BBS or online service. While the first temptation is to blame the modem or whatever online service you're calling, the culprit is often a faulty phone connection. Make a call to a friend and listen for static or noise on the phone line (ask your friend to hush for a second while you listen). Sometimes there's noise or interference that you may not even be able to hear. So if you're consistently having trouble making reliable calls over your modem to *any* service or individual, odds are your phone line may be the problem. Have the phone company (or a telephonically inclined pal) check it out.

Those mysterious abbreviations. If you're online a lot, you'll see all sorts of abbreviations folks use to save typing time when they're communicating via electronic mail, bulletin board postings and chat sessions. I had trouble figuring out what some of them meant, so I pass these along for those of you who are just getting started with telecommunications:

Abbreviation	Definition
LOL	Laughing Out Loud
AFK	Away From Keyboard
BAK	Back At Keyboard
RSN	Real Soon Now
ADN	Any Day Now
IMO	In My Opinion
IMHO	In My Humble Opinion
OTOH	On The Other Hand
IOW	In Other Words
FWIW	For What It's Worth
FYI	For Your Information
GD&R	Grinning, Ducking, & Running
BTW	By The Way
ROFL	Rolling On the Floor Laughing
RTM	Read The Manual
RTFM	Read the Funny Manual
DSPSG	Drooling Slobbering Patrick Stewart Groupie—seen frequently in the STTNG ("Star Trek: The Next Generation") forum

You'll see emoticons, too. Emoticons—or "emotion icons"—can be pretty mystifying until you get the secret of *turning your head sideways*. Tilt it counter-clockwise 90 degrees, and you'll see the little smiling or sardonic faces. There are *lots* more of these, but here's just a sampling:

Icon	Meaning
:-)	Smile
:-(	Sad
:-}	Ironic smile
;-)	Wink and smile
:-{	Too bad
:+<	Hard night last night
:-Q	Neener, neener

Lightning-fast data transfer. If you've got two Macs, it's easy to connect them so that you have an instant network (see the tip "Networking demystified") for transferring files. If you have a PC and a Mac, you can use Macintosh to PC Exchange or Apple File Exchange (see Figure 8-7) to transfer files via your SuperDrive (also called a FDHD, for floppy drive high density). But copying and transferring files via floppy disk can be slow.

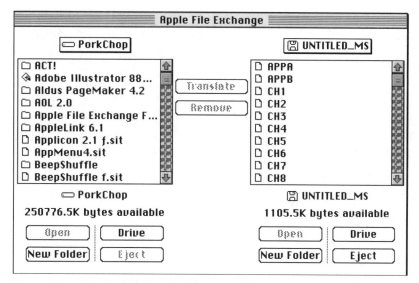

Figure 8-7: You can use Apple File Exchange to transfer DOS files onto your Mac.

There are a couple of other solutions. One is to get a network like Sitka/TOPS and hook up your PC(s) and your Mac(s). But you'll need an AppleTalk card in your PC, and you know what that means (down two days while you futz with the PC). A simpler solution is to get a null modem cable (use the one from the ImageWriter II, if you have one) and run a communications program on both computers. They'll act as though they had already called each other. You can set up both communications programs for the highest speeds they'll provide, since nothing's going out over the phone lines and everything's directly connected via the cable. The result: lightning-fast data transfer. You can do the same thing by purchasing MacLink/Plus; it comes with a cable, a manual and file transfer software on both the Mac and PC ends. But if you already have communications programs on both your PC and your Mac and you know how to use them, you can do the same thing by just getting a cable (and it's cheaper than buying MacLink/Plus).

Macintosh PC Exchange doesn't always recognize DOS disks. Sad, but true. I tried several disks that were originally formatted on my DOS machine, and got that "Do you want to initialize?" message every time. It reliably recognizes floppies that *it* formats as DOS disks, though, and my DOS machine recognizes them as DOS disks, too (they have a directory on them called RESOURCE.FRK that the Mac creates). So, although Mac PC Exchange has a few advantages—it lets you specify which application on your Mac is supposed to open which DOS files—so you can say that documents created in Ami Pro for Windows will automatically be opened in MacWrite, for example—I think you're probably better off sticking to Apple File Exchange (or DOS Mounter from Dayna Communications, if you're willing to spend a little money). Or perhaps Apple has improved PC File Exchange's performance by the time you read this.

Turn off any "mount a DOS disk" utilities before you try to use Apple File Exchange. If you try to translate files from your Mac to a PC format, or vice versa, and they're not being recognized by the other machine when you're done, the problem may be that you have an application such as DOS Mounter running. If one of these types of utilities is on, Apple File Exchange may not be able to translate properly. Turn it off, and then you'll be able to use Apple File Exchange.

Launch Apple File Exchange *before* you put a DOS disk in your drive. If you want to transfer files on a DOS disk to your Mac, the trick is to start Apple File Exchange *before* you put the disk in the drive. Otherwise you get that "Do you want to initialize this disk?" message.

What are those weird boxes in files from a PC? DOS computers need to see a line feed character at the end of each line (some even need a carriage return character, too); Macs don't. If you're getting weird boxes in text files that you got from a PC, they're prob-ably DOS line feeds or carriage returns. You can use a special program like MacSink or a similar shareware utility to strip out the line feeds, or you can use your word processing program. (Search for Control-Js and replace them with nothing; Control-J is the line feed character[2]).

Some files can be transferred without any filters. Graphics files in EPS and TIFF (Tagged Image File Format) format can normally be used on both the Mac and PC without any conversion. However, you may sometimes run across TIFFs captured on a PC that can't be placed in your desktop publishing program, or they may place but appear reversed—as a negative image of the original. The Capture screen shot utility program (from Mainstay) has a TIFF converter that may be able to convert those files, and there are similar commercial and shareware utilities (Such as FlipTIFF or Imagery) that do much the same thing.

---

[2]I know you can do this in Mac WordPerfect 2.1 and Microsoft Word 5.0, but I don't know about other word processors, which may not have such sophisticated Search features.

Faxing small type. Noise on the phone line, poor-quality fax machines and even misaligned paper can all cause characters in small type sizes (9 points and less) and detailed artwork to become broken or blurred. To avoid broken, unreadable type, use larger point sizes in documents that are going to be faxed. Also, stick with bold serif faces and clean sans-serif faces, or at least avoid using heavily ornamented or delicate serif faces in your faxes—those details are almost always lost or corrupted in transmission.

Keep generous margins on documents that are going to be faxed, too, so that type doesn't get chopped off. And don't put type too near the bottom of the page, for the same reason.

Faxing PostScript graphics. If you've tried to send PostScript graphics in documents over your fax modem, you've probably found that the resulting images are, in a word, ugly—at least compared to their PostScript representations. What's happening is that your fax modem is converting the PostScript information to a PICT screen image and sending that instead. To get around this problem, print your PostScript graphics on a laser printer and then scan them back in. But don't get carried away with trying to produce perfect graphics via a fax transmission. Faxes are still faxes, after all; there's a limit to their resolution, and your results are still going to look like a fax at the other end.

MOVING ON

Well, even if you don't have a SCSI device, a modem or your own network, there were probably a few tricks in this chapter you could use, because it covered so many different areas. If you're not equipped with these things now, expect that to change in the near future as the prices of such peripherals continue to drop dramatically.

The cost of RAM continues to fall as well, and since you can never seem to have enough of the stuff, in the next chapter we'll look at memory.

CHAPTER NINE

MEMORY DEMYSTIFIED

There are lots of different kinds of memory. There is RAM and ROM, and even the mysterious virtual memory—which is there, but then again it isn't. The voodoo Mac tricks of the future—the ones that will deal with image processing, multimedia, voice recording and animation—will all eat up lots of memory. If you're going to delve into those areas, you'll want to cram as much memory as you can into your Mac. Let's run through a quick review of memory essentials before we get into the tricks.

RAM is, of course, random-access memory—the temporary memory that holds all the extensions that load on startup, plus a fair chunk of whatever utilities or applications you're working in. Your Mac's RAM also stores your system software and any unsaved documents or recently changed documents you're working on. With System 6, you can have 8 Mb of RAM; with System 7, you can have as much as 256 Mb of RAM on a Quadra 900 or 950. That seems like an awful lot of RAM, but before much longer, we probably won't think it's much at all. My first Mac had a whopping 128k of memory, and that was only in 1984. If you add to the current limit of 256 Mb of RAM what you can squeeze from virtual memory, you're talking about 1,000 Mb— that's a gigabyte—of "RAM." Now, that *is* an awful lot of RAM. You can run a lot of extensions and open a lot of huge documents with that much RAM.

To get more RAM, you buy it in the form of SIMMs (Single Inline Memory Modules), which you or a technician can install in your computer.[1] The first tip in this chapter: don't buy SIMMs from Apple (unless they suddenly drop their prices). As of this writing, it's cheaper to buy SIMMs from just about any source other than Apple—from your favorite mail-order house or software-o-rama, for example.

There's also *ROM*, or read-only memory. This is permanent, nonvolatile memory that contains the root commands that control your Mac's most basic functions, and, luckily, it isn't lost when the lights go out. ROM stays on a chip inside your Mac, and you don't (usually) want to mess with it, although the Quadras have a mysterious empty slot for a future ROM upgrade.

Virtual memory is a fixed allocation of space on your Mac's hard drive that is used to store information that would normally be held in RAM. It works by moving information from RAM onto your hard disk and accessing the data from the hard disk when it's needed. Before you get too excited about virtual memory, remember that it's *disk* memory, and so it's a lot slower than real RAM. Only Macs running System 7 *and* equipped with a 68030 (or later model) chip can use it—see the tip "Which Macs can use virtual memory and 32-bit addressing?" for a list of them. (Mac IIs equipped with a PMMU—page memory management unit chip—can use virtual memory, too.) Virtual memory is a temporary solution to the long-term problem of not having enough real RAM. It's a way to "get by" or "fake it" on particularly large or complex documents that you wouldn't ordinarily be able work on without going out and buying more RAM. Don't expect it to solve any chronic RAM shortage you might have.

There's *32-bit addressing*, too, which is a memory feature that lets you access chunks of RAM bigger than 8 Mb. In fact, if you have more than 8 Mb of physical RAM, you'll need to turn on 32-bit addressing to use it. For more on that matter, see the tip "To work with over 8 Mb of RAM, you have to turn on 32-bit addressing" later in this chapter. While you're at it, see all the tips about 32-bit

---

[1] The Mac Portable and PowerBook don't use SIMMs. They require special boards to expand their RAM capabilities.

addressing, since it can cause problems when you're running some older programs. Again, not all Macs can use 32-bit addressing, and only System 7 can do it, unless you get a utility such as Optima from Connectix (800/950-5880) that lets you run 32-bit applications under System 6.

What else is mysterious about memory? Well, there are *RAM disks* and *disk caches*, both of which you'll see tricks for in this chapter. A RAM disk is a part of RAM that's set aside to work just like a real hard disk—except much, much faster. A disk cache (called a RAM cache in System 6) is a part of RAM that holds a fixed amount of data that has most recently been accessed.

If you're really looking for an in-depth tutorial on memory (and how to install more of it), reach for the phone and call 800/950-5880 to get the free *Macintosh Memory Guide* from Connectix in Menlo Park, California, or you can pick up the excellent companion Hyper-Card stack of the same name from online services or user groups.

MYSTERIES OF FINDER & APPLICATION MEMORY

We'll start out by looking at a few basic tricks that just about anyone can use, no matter how much memory you have.

Increasing the Finder's memory size. Sometimes you may get messages that say "out of Finder memory." Since you can manually allocate more memory to nearly any application, you can usually solve insufficient memory problems with any particular application by giving it more memory to run on. Well, the same is true of the Finder, so the obvious thing to do when you see an "out of Finder memory" message is increase the amount of application memory allotted to the Finder. In System 6, this is easy to do: select the Finder icon in the System Folder, press Command-I (or choose Get Info from the Finder's File menu), and enter a bigger memory size. Just remember that the more memory you give the Finder, the less you'll have left for your programs to use. Don't give it more than about 320k under most circumstances.

Under System 7, you shouldn't usually get these messages. If you do, you'll find that you're not allowed to change the application memory size in the Finder with System 7 running. But you can adjust the Finder's memory size the way you did in System 6. Here's the trick: start up with a System 6 floppy (for more on how to create a startup floppy, see Chapter 10), select the Finder icon on your hard drive, press Command-I, and reset the memory size. The setting you specified will be in effect when you restart with your hard disk as the startup disk.

If, for some reason, you don't have a System 6 startup disk, you can also allocate more memory to the Finder by using ResEdit. Open a copy of the Finder in ResEdit; then open the SIZE resource (see Figure 9-1). Double-click on ID = 1 and scroll to the bottom of the dialog box that appears (see Figure 9-2). You'll see the size and the minimum size in bytes, and you can increase them. For example, to increase the size by 50k, add 51200 bytes (1k = 1024 bytes).

Figure 9-1: Use ResEdit to allocate more memory to System 7's Finder.

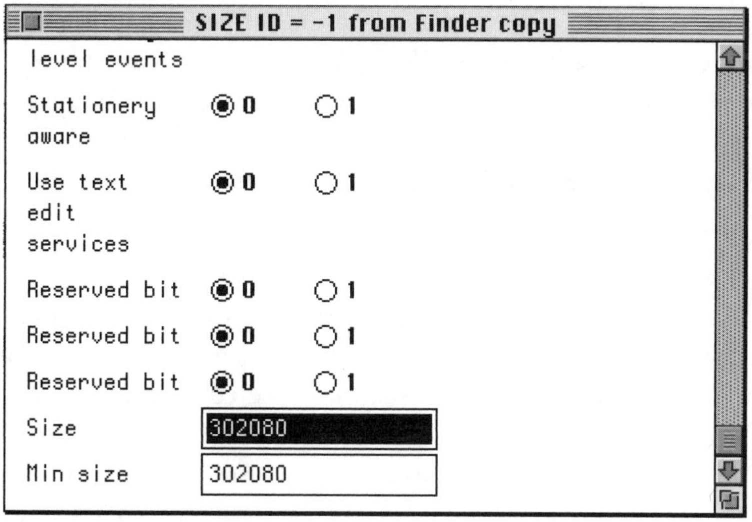

Figure 9-2: Edit the SIZE resource to increase the Finder's memory partition.

When you're finished, save your changes, quit ResEdit, replace your old Finder file with the newly edited copy, and restart. Be sure to keep the old, unedited Finder in a safe place outside the System Folder for a few days, just in case something went wrong and you need to reinstall it.

More system memory voodoo. There are a couple of things that take up RAM, so you may want to consider them when you check memory allocation:

- The amount of memory that you see the system using when you choose About This Macintosh (under the Apple menu in the Finder) depends on the extensions (INITs) you're using. If you want to see the bare-bones system size, start up with the Shift key down (under System 7) to disable all extensions.

- Files and folders that are shared also take up RAM, even if you're not using them right now. Turn off file sharing for an accurate RAM reading.

Increase the Finder's memory allocation (System 6) if you have suitcase troubles. With System 6, you can sometimes run into problems when you move desk accessories in and out of suitcases and fonts and sounds in and out of the System file. To get around these troubles, increase the Finder's memory allocation by, say, 100k, and see if that doesn't help.

You can increase a program's memory allocation, too. You can also adjust the amount of memory allotted to a program like Microsoft Word or Adobe Illustrator. Select the program's icon in the Finder and press Command-I to bring up the Get Info dialog box. Then type a new (larger) size in the Current Size box (see Figure 9-3). The program will request the new amount of RAM the next time you launch it.

Increasing a program's memory allocation by only a small amount usually won't result in any significant performance increase, so if you're going to the trouble of allocating more memory, you might as well add a significant amount to be sure you'll see worthwhile results—usually about 200k or 300k—perhaps a little more or less, depending on the size and needs of the program.

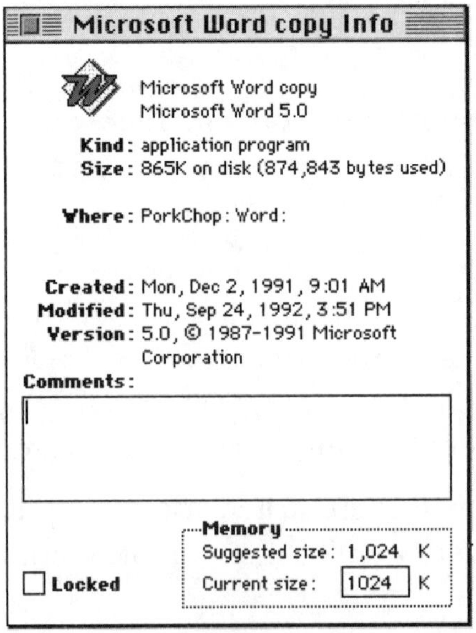

```
┌──────────────────────────────────────────┐
│ ▦▦ ▤ Microsoft Word copy Info ▤ ▦▦         │
│                                            │
│      W     Microsoft Word copy             │
│            Microsoft Word 5.0              │
│                                            │
│      Kind: application program             │
│      Size: 865K on disk (874,843 bytes used)│
│                                            │
│     Where: PorkChop: Word:                 │
│                                            │
│                                            │
│   Created: Mon, Dec 2, 1991, 9:01 AM       │
│  Modified: Thu, Sep 24, 1992, 3:51 PM      │
│   Version: 5.0, © 1987-1991 Microsoft      │
│            Corporation                     │
│  Comments:                                 │
│  ┌──────────────────────────────────────┐ │
│  ││                                      │ │
│  │                                       │ │
│  │                                       │ │
│  │                                       │ │
│  └──────────────────────────────────────┘ │
│              ┌─Memory────────────────┐     │
│              │ Suggested size: 1,024 K│    │
│  ☐ Locked    │ Current size: │1024│ K │    │
│              └───────────────────────┘     │
└──────────────────────────────────────────┘
```

Figure 9-3: You can increase an application's
memory allocation via the Get Info box.

Increasing a program's memory size is really useful if you're working on a large publication in a program like PageMaker. Increasing the memory allotted to the application lets more of the program stay in RAM, so the disk doesn't have to be accessed as often. PageMaker, for example, runs very nicely with 2048k of memory allotted to it.

Other programs, like Photoshop, simply can't get enough RAM. Since Photoshop actually prefers to store the entire document you're working on (and even a copy of that document) in RAM, the more you can allocate to it, the better. And the same is also true of other programs that work with very large documents. So if you've got RAM to spare, allocate it to your advanced programs for faster performance.

You can't change a program's memory allocation while it's running. You can't allocate more (or less) RAM to an application if it's open. You must first quit the application, then reallocate RAM, and then re-launch the program.

Some programs work fine with less memory. If you're constantly running low on memory, you might consider trying to run your applications with slightly less RAM. While you can't allocate less than the suggested amount of RAM (which is a fixed minimum amount that's set by the application's programmers), you can cut memory allocation back to that minimum level. WordPerfect, for instance, will usually run fairly well on 800k of RAM, but depending on which installation routine you run, it may be using twice that amount by default. Experiment with running programs on less RAM, when possible. If you find they seem buggy or unreliable, simply raise the current size back to a level that better suits the program.

How can you tell when you're getting low on memory? If you're really low on memory, your application won't start at all, and you'll get a message telling you that it can't be opened. Or you may get a message warning you that the application needs more memory, but that only a certain amount is available. If that's the case, you'll have to quit an open application (or two) to free up more RAM. See the next tip on how to squeeze more RAM out of your

Mac. Although I've never seen this phenomenon, I've heard that some applications warn you of low-memory conditions by reversing from black to white on the screen. Remember from the previous tip that you can increase the amount of memory allocated to a program. That often does the trick, so try it before you buy more RAM.

Out of memory? Free up RAM. If you run out of memory, there are several things you can do to free up RAM. Most of them are obvious, but it's easy to overlook one or two of them when you're faced with the situation, so here they are:

• Close as many open windows as you can.

• Quit any programs you're not using.

• Stop all print jobs that are going on.

• Turn off your RAM disk, if you're using one. (See "Removing a RAM disk" later in this chapter.)

• Turn off file sharing (use the Sharing Setup control panel).

• Disable extensions (INITs and control panels) by holding down the Shift key on startup (under System 7), or by using the Extensions Manager to disable the extensions you don't really need right now (this, of course, involves restarting your Mac).

Lowering RAM usage on 2-3 Mb Macs. If you're struggling along with System 7 and only a couple or three megabytes of RAM, you really ought to get more (see the tips in the next section). But until you do, try these tricks to lower RAM usage:

• Run System 7 TuneUp or get System 7.1.

• Turn off AppleTalk if it's on in the Chooser.

• While you're in the Chooser, turn off background printing.

• Disable any extensions you don't need (use the Extensions Manager or start up with the Shift key down).

• Run At Ease, which uses about 200k less RAM than System 7.

Thanks to Eric Apgar, Apple Worldwide Technical Assistance.

GETTING MORE RAM

If you think it's tough doing your normal, everyday work with the RAM you've got, then don't count on things getting any easier in the near future. If you're planning to do any of the real "power user" work, such as color image processing, sound input or desktop video production, you'll undoubtedly want to get more RAM than your Mac came with. This section gives you some tips for doing that.

Adding more RAM to your Mac. To add more RAM to a Mac (unless it's a PowerBook or Portable, in which you replace a custom RAM board), you buy more SIMMs (Single Inline Memory Modules). Remember, without a third-party solution, 8 Mb is the most RAM you can have under System 6.

There are all sorts of SIMMs, ranging from 256k to 16 Mb configurations, and some Macs can use one kind but not another. They come in different speeds, all the way from 150 ns (nanosecond) to 60 ns or faster. Older Macs use the slower SIMMs, and newer Macs, starting with the IIfx, use the faster chips—rated at 80 ns or better. There are also all sorts of rules about how and where to configure SIMMs on your motherboard. And there's also the problem of static buildup that can screw up your new memory chips. Again, one of the best resources for working your way through the SIMM maze is the free *Macintosh Memory Guide* from Connectix mentioned earlier in this chapter.

While many RAM outlets tout how easy it is to install RAM, the process never winds up being as simple as it seems, especially if you own a compact Mac like a Plus or Classic. But if you own a modular Mac and you're fairly adept at managing other Mac hardware issues (especially things like installing NuBus cards or setting up elaborate SCSI chains), you can probably handle installing SIMMs. However, if you're squeamish about poking around inside your Mac, particularly if it's a compact model, my advice is to take your Mac to a friendly dealer or service technician (call first for prices) and have them install the SIMMs for you. RAM and installation prices vary from place to place; in the San Francisco area (where I live), you'll be charged about $50-60 to install the new RAM. If you're asking a dealer to install RAM you bought from a mail order house, you may be charged more. If you buy the RAM from the dealer, you may have to pay less for installation, but the actual RAM may cost you more. Call first and see what the policies are.

As with any computer equipment, it's important to know what you're buying. You should be prepared with a list of questions when you call about SIMMs.

- What kind of warranty do the SIMMs come with? A reputable RAM dealer will offer a one-year warranty against defects in the chips, and since most problems with RAM usually happen right away, you should ask for a 30-day money-back guarantee.

- What is the return policy if the chips turn out to be defective? Some of the better mail order houses will ship replacement SIMMs via overnight mail without your having to first return the defective one. This is important if a SIMM goes down during a crucial project, because losing one chip can make your entire Mac inoperable until that chip is replaced.

- How fast are the SIMMs? Different Macs can handle or require different speed SIMMs, so be sure to tell the salesperson which model Mac you have.

- Are the SIMMs new or remanufactured? (Ask that one if the price seems really low, and if they are remanufactured, don't buy them.)

- If you're buying from a mail order house, ask what kind of installation instructions are provided (some companies give away with each purchase special custom Mac tools or videos that show you exactly how to install RAM chips; other companies don't).

Finding out how RAM is being used. Now that you've installed huge amounts of RAM, perhaps you're curious about how it's being used. How much is system software gobbling up, and how much do your applications use? Normally, all your extensions and control panels are using some of that RAM, but how much? If you're running System 7, there's a fairly easy way to figure this out.

Start your Mac with the Shift key held down. Then check the About This Macintosh box in the Finder's Apple menu and see how much RAM your system is using without any extraneous extensions or control panels running. Subtract this amount from the figure you get when you start up without disabling any extensions, and you'll know how much memory your extensions and control panels are using.

If you're curious about exactly how much RAM a single extension uses, there's a way to tell that, too. First, start up with no extensions active and make a note of how much RAM the system software uses. Then drag all your extensions and control panels except the one you want to check into a new folder, outside the System Folder. Now re-start, this time without holding down the Shift key. When you check About This Macintosh, the amount of RAM used will have increased by the amount that particular extension or control panel uses.

While this method is a bit labor-intensive, it is free. If you want to pay for a little extra help in managing your extensions and control panels, Now Software's Now Utilities features a control panel called Startup Manager that, among its many powerful features, can instantly give you an accurate reading of how much RAM each item uses.

Finally, if you aren't convinced that running lots of fun extensions or control panels can eat into your available RAM, consider that running only five popular startup items—DiskDoubler, QuickTime, After Dark, Super Boomerang and Adobe Type Manager—ties up nearly 700k of RAM. And while these items are popular because they're also useful, don't forget that together they use nearly 700k you could devote to opening an entire other application if you disabled them all.

Mysterious RAM creep. Sometimes, especially under System 7, you run out of RAM when there doesn't seem to be any reason. If you choose About This Macintosh to check memory usage, you'll sometimes find that the system has swelled to whale size and there isn't any RAM left—or not very much. That's because behind the scenes, System 7 is grabbing more memory to add to the system heap as it's needed and then not letting go of that memory when it is no longer needed. (System 6 doesn't do this.)

The System 7 TuneUp extension addressed this mysterious "RAM creep" problem, but if you've installed the TuneUp on version 7.0 or if you're still having the problem with System 7.1 (which supposedly fixes it) and you're still getting RAM creep, try these easy fixes.

First, if your Mac is one that provides 32-bit addressing, check to see that 32-bit addressing is turned on. If it's not, the system is probably either allocating all the memory above 8 Mb to itself or simply ignoring it.

Even if you're not using 32-bit addressing, check to see that all the programs you're running are compatible with System 7. That might be the cause of the problem.

Another thing you can do is disable all your extensions to see if a conflict with an extension (or combination of extensions) is causing problems with RAM.

If you do all this and still have the problem, try the penultimate solution (there's always one more option): try replacing your System file with a clean backup (if you have one), or better still, trash your current System file, restart with the Install 1 disk or the Disk Tools disk (System 7.1), and reinstall the system software.

USING VIRTUAL MEMORY

Virtual memory is really voodoo. As you've seen, it lets you use disk memory as if it were RAM—although not nearly as fast, by any means. There are times, though, when virtual memory is exactly what you need to use.

There's a trade-off between speedy computing and using virtual memory. Yes, using virtual memory can slow down your Mac. But if you're using a program like Adobe Photoshop (which features its own built-in virtual memory scheme) or working on a huge publication in PageMaker, you'll probably need to sacrifice lightning-fast speed for memory and use virtual memory. See the tip "Getting more speed with virtual memory" later in this chapter for what you can do to speed things along.

Don't turn on more virtual memory than you need. Virtual memory is slower than real RAM, so if it's speed you need, consider buying more real RAM. But in any case, it's not recommended that you set virtual memory to a larger amount than the RAM you have in your system. If you do, your Mac may slow way down because it must constantly swap data back and forth between the disk and the processor, which takes much more time than using real RAM.

You use the Memory control panel (see Figure 9-4) to activate virtual memory, select the disk that's going to provide it, and specify how much of it you want to use. (If you don't see the RAM disk option in your Memory control panel, either your Mac can't handle it or you need to upgrade your system software.)

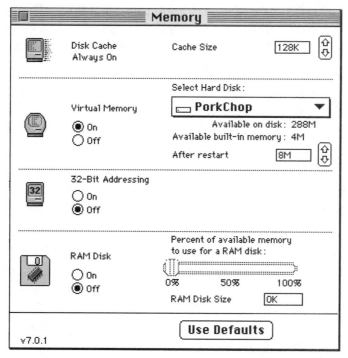

Figure 9-4: The Memory control panel lets you set the parameters for using virtual memory.

Remember to restart your Mac after altering your virtual memory settings so your changes will take effect.

Virtual memory takes up more disk space than you may think. When you set a virtual memory file size and activate virtual memory, the Mac creates an invisible file named VM Storage. This invisible storage file is not the size of virtual memory that you set—as you might expect—instead, its size matches the amount of the RAM you have plus the virtual memory size you set. For instance, if you have 4 Mb of RAM and specify 4 Mb of virtual memory, your VM Storage file is 8 Mb.

Which Macs can use virtual memory and 32-bit addressing? The question is really which of the *older* Macs can use both features, and that answer is a little harder to explain. The Classic II, SE/30, LC II, IIx, IIcx, IIci, IIfx, Quadras and PowerBooks (but not the PowerBook 100 or the Portable) can all handle virtual memory. If you have a Mac II, you can add a PMMU (paged Memory Management Unit) that will allow it to handle virtual memory. The LC doesn't have a socket for a PMMU, so if you have an LC and really need to use virtual memory, you'll need to install a 68030 or 68040 card. You can set up a Plus, Classic and SE to handle virtual memory through third-party equipment (call Connectix.)

As for 32-bit addressing, it's a function of how your Mac's ROM chips operate, and whether they are capable of using 32-bit addressing (if they are, the ROMs are considered "32-bit clean"). All new Macs made (and many of the most recent models) feature ROMs that are compatible with 32-bit addressing. If you have an SE/30 or an older modular Mac—such as the II, IIx or IIcx—you can get a free program called Mode32 that will let you use 32-bit addressing. It's available from bulletin boards, user groups and even friendly dealers. But keep in mind that you need more than 8 Mb of RAM to make use of 32-bit addressing anyway.

Getting more speed with virtual memory. If you need virtual memory to meet your occasional high-RAM demands, there are a couple of things you can do to speed up virtual memory and your Mac at the same time. First, optimize your hard disk (use Symantec's SUM, Central Point's Mac Tools or any other commercial utility package). Then set up a bigger RAM cache—but no bigger than 256k, because any cache you create that's lots larger won't do much good and will take away from the RAM available for other purposes. (See the tips in the next section for more about caches.)

Another neat trick is to divide your hard disk into several partitions—unfortunately, you'll need to back up everything before you do this, because partitioning involves reformatting, which erases everything on the disk. But if you're starting out with a new, big hard disk, partition it so you can use this trick. (The formatting software that came with your hard disk should let you partition it.)

Create a partition for virtual memory—make it as large as the amount of virtual memory you're planning on using, plus a megabyte or two for overhead. Then use the Memory control panel to tell the Mac that your newly created virtual memory partition is the "hard disk" that's supposed to hold virtual memory. The Mac won't have to search all over your hard disk to find the space allocated for virtual memory; it'll always know right where it is.

DISK CACHES & RAM DISKS

Using a disk cache or a RAM disk (if you have a lot of real RAM available) can greatly speed up your work. They're two very different things, though. Here are some tricks for both of them.

Setting a disk cache. Also known as a RAM cache, a disk cache is part of random-access memory that stores data the disk needs to access frequently. You'd think that the bigger the cache, the better, but it ain't necessarily so. If you set too big a disk cache, that memory isn't available to your programs; it's tied up caching recent information that the processor might need. So the trick is to set as *small* a disk cache as possible that will still speed up your Mac by letting it access data in RAM instead of accessing the disk.

Using System 7's Memory control panel, start out with a disk cache of 128k. If everything runs speedily, try setting it a little lower. If things don't go as fast as you'd like, bump it up a bit. Remember to restart your Mac for the new RAM cache to take effect.

In System 6, you can also set a RAM cache (it's called a disk cache under System 7, a RAM cache under System 6). Just use the General icon in the Control Panel and click in the RAM cache box.

Turning off the cache on the fly. On a Mac that has a cache control (like a Quadra), Option-click the radio buttons in the Cache Switch control panel to turn the cache on or off without having to restart your Mac.

Some programs won't start with the cache on, but they'll often run fine with caching enabled after the program has launched. Try turning the cache off, starting the troublesome program, and *then* turning the cache back on to speed up the program. (Sneaky.)

Disk caches vs. RAM disks. They're not the same! A *disk cache* is a part of RAM that stores data that's frequently accessed by the processor as a part of working with a document or a program. A *RAM disk* is just like another hard disk—except that it's not really a disk at all; information stored in the average RAM disk will disappear when the lights go out. It works much, much faster than a real hard disk, because everything that's "on" a RAM disk is actually stored in RAM, and since no disk is spinning—in fact there are no moving parts at all—everything's instantly accessible.

To get real use from a RAM disk—practically speaking—you'll need lots of memory. If you're running System 7, you'll probably need at least 8 Mb of RAM if you want to work with a RAM disk. (Remember, System 6 can normally only address 8 Mb of RAM anyway.)

The newer model Macs—including the PowerBooks and Quadras—let you create a RAM disk by using the system software. Open the Memory control panel and, in the RAM Disk portion at the bottom of the panel, click On to create the RAM disk. Drag the slider to indicate what size RAM disk you want—the slider allocates memory for a RAM disk based on how large a portion of total RAM you want to devote to a RAM disk—20 percent, 50 percent, or whatever. Close the control panel and restart your Mac. You'll see a RAM disk icon when you restart, and you can use your new RAM disk as though it were a regular external hard drive that you've mounted—except that it's much faster and requires much less power. Choosing Shut Down normally removes the contents of the RAM disk, so always copy any work you've stored on it onto a real disk (either your internal hard drive or a floppy) before you shut down. Choosing Restart doesn't remove the RAM disk's contents.

Removing a RAM disk. As you saw in the preceding tip, there's one sure way to remove everything that's on a RAM disk: shut down. A power loss will do it, too. If you don't want to power down but you're through with the RAM disk and want to free up RAM, you can remove the RAM disk as well as its contents by dragging it to the Trash and choosing Empty Trash from the Special menu. Then use the Memory control panel again and click Off under RAM Disk. Then restart your Mac. If you don't do all of these things, a new, empty RAM disk will appear when you restart, and you haven't freed up any RAM.

Despite what you might think, you won't free up RAM if you just drag the RAM disk to the Trash. Selecting the disk and choosing Erase Disk from the Special menu won't free up RAM, either.

Resizing a RAM disk. You can't change the size of a RAM disk while there are still files on it. Copy everything you want to keep onto a real disk; then trash the files that are on the RAM disk. Now you can use the Memory control panel to change the RAM disk's size.

If you don't have a newer Mac with RAM disk capabilities built into the system software but you have enough RAM, consider setting up a RAM disk (you'll need a Mac with a 68030 processor or a Mac II with a PMMU chip). You can get third-party programs—such as Maxima from Connectix —that create RAM disks. Maxima's other great benefit is that it lets you address 14 Mb of RAM without turning on 32-bit addressing (see the trap "32-bit addressing can cause flaky performance" at the end of this chapter).

Maxima also automatically copies the contents of the RAM disk to your hard disk when you shut down and reloads it into RAM when you start up—this is a blatant product plug. An alternate solution is RamDisk+, by Roger D. Bates (10899 NW Valley Vista Road, Hillsboro, Oregon, 97124, 503/645-3930), a shareware control panel utility that lets you set up a RAM disk. It's $35, but it has lots of cool features like copy back to disk on shutdown and things like that.

What to put in/on a RAM disk. There's no point putting applications onto a RAM disk, since, for the most part, they're loaded into RAM anyway. What you can best use a RAM disk for is holding big documents that you have to save often, like desktop publishing or databases files.

You can also put your System Folder on a RAM disk to really speed things up! The Mac frequently accesses resources from the system while it's working, and you'll be amazed at how fast things run if your system (the contents of your System Folder) is on a RAM disk. However, if you're like the rest of us, your system is probably bigger than the RAM disk you can create—unless you've got a lot of RAM. But to trim your System Folder down a bit, you can move unused fonts, sounds and desk accessories out of it.

To run your system in RAM, copy the System Folder to the RAM disk, set it as the startup disk, and restart.

Remember to copy the RAM disk's contents back to your hard disk when you're done. Unless you have a special RAM disk with a backup feature, you lose what's in RAM when you shut down, so remember to copy the contents of your RAM disk back to your hard disk before you power down. Just drag the RAM disk icon to your hard disk's icon. That's it. (If you have Maxima or RamDisk+ 3.16, they will copy the RAM disk's contents automatically for you.)

32-BIT ADDRESSING

If you're running System 7 *and* using a Mac with a 68030 processor or greater, you can address huge chunks of RAM—*if* your programs are "32-bit clean,"—luckily, if you're running the most current version of a program, the odds are that it's compatible with 32-bit addressing. If you need to keep several big programs in memory at the same time, or if you're doing color image processing, you'll want to turn on 32-bit addressing.

To work with more than 8 Mb of RAM, you have to turn on 32-bit addressing. On a Mac that uses the 68030 processor or greater, you need to use System 7's Memory control panel and turn on 32-bit addressing to be able to use any RAM beyond 8 Mb. Otherwise you'll think you're using all the RAM that you've bought, but if you check the About This Macintosh dialog box, you'll see that it's all going to your system files, where it's usually unused or ignored.

If you have a II, IIx, IIcx or SE/30, your ROM doesn't support 32-bit addressing, but you can get the above-mentioned free program called Mode32 that will let you use 32-bit addressing. It's available from bulletin boards, user groups and even friendly dealers.

How can you tell whether your Mac supports 32-bit addressing? Easy. Go to the Memory control panel, and if you don't see it there, you haven't got that capability (but see the preceding paragraph for a possible software solution).

If you're running System 6, you can only address 8 Mb of RAM at a time (without a third-party solution like Optima), so don't worry about 32-bit addressing.

Your extra RAM isn't showing up. If you know that you just bought and installed, say, 16 Mb of RAM but you're not getting it when you view About This Macintosh, the likely problem is that you haven't activated 32-bit addressing.

You'll see that your system has mysteriously become whale-sized, though. This is because extra memory is added to system software, even if you're not running in 32-bit mode.

Use the Memory control panel to turn on 32-bit addressing, and you should be in business with all that extra RAM.

32-bit addressing can cause flaky performance. A lot of folks report that their Macs crash frequently with 32-bit addressing active. The easiest solution to this problem is to turn it off if you don't need it—whenever you don't need to make huge amounts of RAM available to your applications. If you decide suddenly that you want to turn off 32-bit addressing, then go ahead and restart the Mac, because clicking Off in the control panel doesn't take effect until you restart.

MOVING ON

This chapter has explored some of the mysteries surrounding all sorts of memory—RAM, ROM and virtual memory—and has also shown you a few tricks for using RAM disks, disk caches and 32-bit addressing. As you may guess, there's a fine line between tweaking memory and actually solving problems memory causes—or, more accurately, problems that lack of memory causes. In the next chapter, "In Trouble?", we'll look at how to fix some of the most common problems you may run across while using your Mac. We'll look at a few uncommon ones, too.

CHAPTER TEN

IN TROUBLE?

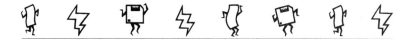

The Mac isn't perfect, and neither are we. More often than we'd like to admit, there are times when we just plain need help to get out of trouble. Unfortunately, the same friendly interface that makes the Mac so easy to use also makes it nearly impossible to diagnose when something goes wrong. The Mac's error ID numbers, for instance, sure aren't much help![1] Lofty Becker, a Mac sysop on CompuServe, summed it up beautifully when he said online, "they tell you what the car hit, but not why it ran off the road." So in this chapter we'll take a look at some of the many ways you can get in and out of trouble.

But there's more to solving problems with your Mac than memorizing system error codes. In fact, it seems like the more involved you get in customizing, personalizing and exploring your Mac, the more you seem to encounter those frustrating kinds of problems that can ruin your day (or week!). Fortunately, there are a few simple tricks and techniques you can learn that will usually help you work your way out of most any troublesome situation. The best advice, of course, is to make regular and frequent backups of your system, and if you can't (or

---

[1]If you're interested in what the system error codes mean, get a freeware application called System Errors from Dr. "Pete" Corless at Apple Computer. You can find it from your local user group and it's also available on bulletin boards and online services. Put it in your Apple Menu Items folder so that it's always handy whenever you crash (or once you restart). Get the latest, most up-to-date version, and you'll never again wonder what the difference is between a Type 1 error and a Bad F-line instruction.

don't want to) back up your entire hard drive, at least make copies of the most important stuff you're working on at any given time. Disasters never pick a convenient time to strike, so follow the advice in this chapter to make sure you're prepared for when they do.

YOUR EMERGENCY TOOLKIT

One of the most basic things you can do to make recovering from crashes as painless as possible is make an emergency toolkit. It should consist of a floppy disk you can boot from *and* disks that hold backups of your Finder and System files, because those files often become corrupted during normal use. (This advice is especially important if you've customized your Finder or System files using ResEdit or other special utilities that alter the system.) You should also back up onto floppies all of your favorite, regularly used fonts, sounds, extensions, control panels or other items that normally reside in your System Folder or the System file. All this may take up several disks, but if you have to install a new system from scratch, having all these items handy and gathered into a single collection of floppies will save you a great deal of time looking through your disk box for the original disks.

 Making an emergency startup disk. This is potentially the most valuable tip in *Voodoo Mac*, but remember it's a two-parter. First, make an emergency startup disk. Then copy all your custom items onto more floppy disks.

If you're running System 6, duplicate your System Tools disk—the one that came with your system software—to use as the emergency startup disk. If you're running System 7, the equivalent disk is named Disk Tools. It's faster to customize this disk for use as a startup disk than to create your own. System 7 is just too big to fit on a floppy and be of any use. System 6 is the system that's on both the Disk Tools and System Tools disks.

Once you've copied the Disk Tools or System Tools disk, trash everything on the copy except the System Folder, Disk First Aid (if you're running System 7) and Apple HD SC Setup (if you have an Apple brand internal hard disk). If you *don't* have an Apple hard disk inside your Mac, you're better off using the formatter that came with your third-party drive, so trash Apple HD SC Setup and copy your custom formatter onto the startup floppy instead.

If you're running System 6, copy Disk First Aid onto your custom startup floppy—you'll find it on the disk labeled Utilities. With System 7, Disk First Aid is on the Disk Tools floppy.

Now you've got a disk with a minimal System and a few repair utilities that will start your Mac whether you're running System 6 or 7. If you simply want the minimum system necessary to boot up your Mac, put a stripped-down System 6 Finder and System file into a System Folder on a floppy. This may leave you enough free space (particularly on a high-density floppy) to include a program like Norton Utilities, or at least several other smaller utilities like a drive formatter, Disk First Aid, a program like SCSI Probe, or whatever else you think you might need to solve whatever problems you encounter most often.

The trick is to always have a floppy on hand that you can use to start your Mac, no matter what's happened to your hard drive or the software on it. Then you can either find and mount your internal drive and use the software on it to fix things, or you can work directly from the utilities you've copied onto your emergency floppy.

But remember to take the second step to this tip and make copies of all your custom items (extensions, fonts, sounds) so you can easily recreate your current setup if you have to reformat your hard drive or reinstall your system software from scratch.

Thanks to many contributors for the valuable information learned the hard way and condensed into this tip.

GETTING OUT OF TROUBLE

Here's another eclectic collection of recovery tricks. They won't cover every situation you might run across, but you may find a tip or two here that helps when nothing's going right.

Follow these steps to recover lost files. Every crash has a reason (or reasons) of its own, but these guidelines can help you recover files that have mysteriously disappeared from your disk. Try these recovery tricks more or less in the order they're presented here. They're not guaranteed to work, but the files are already lost, so what have you got to lose?

First, use the Find command to search for them. If that works, copy the missing files onto another disk before they disappear again.

Then try disabling all of your extensions. If you're running System 7, restart with the Shift key down; if you're running System 6, drag all the INITs and control panel devices out of your System Folder, or use Apple's Extensions Manager control panel to selectively disable those that you think might be causing trouble. Also, take any startup items that are in your System 7 Startup Items folder out, so that they won't start.

If that doesn't bring the missing files back, try the next easiest solution: rebuild your Desktop. Start your Mac with the Command and Option keys held down. This will recreate the invisible file on your Mac's hard drive responsible for keeping track of all the other files, and, in the process, it may make the missing files available.

If the files still don't reappear, start up with your emergency startup disk. Then run Disk First Aid on the hard disk and restart. Still no missing files? Replace the System and Finder on whatever disk (presumably your internal hard drive) you're using as your startup drive; they may have gotten corrupted and may cause files that are really there to seem as if they aren't.

If that doesn't work, get out your heavy-duty diagnostic and repair utility (SUM II or Norton or Mac Tools or whatever you have) and run it on your hard disk.

Keep a list of all the ways you've customized your Mac. It's so easy to forget that you've changed things on your Mac because it's worked "that way" for so long. For example, you may have installed a font or two in an application instead of in the system.

Or you may have used ResEdit on your Finder menus to create keyboard shortcuts. Keep a list of these changes, and keep it near your Mac, because there's always a slim chance that any special customizations you've made to your Mac may conflict with something else. That way, if you have an accurate list of your changes and you have to call for technical support, you'll be able to tell the technicians what changes you've made, which will usually help them isolate the cause of the problem quicker.

Keep special "testing" folders for inactive items. There'll probably be lots of times when you'll want to remove a certain application and then reinstall it. But there are many other times when you just want to disable an application completely—say, to test for an extension conflict. To remove all traces of an application (in System 7), you'll need to check your Apple Menu Items folder, Control Panels folder, Extensions folder, Preferences folder and, of course, System Folder. If you need to test for a conflict, do yourself a favor and create these folders *inside* those particular folders so that it will be easy to temporarily move items around to disable and re-enable them and quickly find them later:

- Inactive Apple Menu Items folder
- Inactive Control Panels folder
- Inactive Extensions folder
- Inactive Preferences folder
- Inactive System Items folder

Thanks to Harry Baya, Hastings-on-Hudson, New York.

When to rebuild the Desktop? Any time you crash, there's an outside chance your System and Finder files can become corrupted in the process. In addition, System 7 stores two invisible files on every disk, and these can get corrupted, too. Usually, you can't tell that this has happened until you crash. It's a good idea to rebuild your Desktop periodically (say, monthly) by holding down the Command and Option keys during startup. You should know, though, that as a result of this process, you'll lose any comments that you've put in your files' Get Info boxes. Though this unfortunate side-effect was supposed to have been eliminated with System 7, it still persists, even with System 7.1. If keeping your Info Box comments is important, use a disk utility program to rebuild the Desktop, rather than the key combination method described above.

To rebuild a floppy's desktop, hold down Option-Command and insert the disk.

There are lots of other times you'll want to rebuild the Desktop, too, as you'll see in the following tips.

Application busy or missing? This error message often means that you're trying to open a file but you don't have available a copy of the program that created the file. This message can also mean that your invisible Desktop file has become damaged, and even though you have the right application to open a file, your Mac can't make the connection. The easy fix is to rebuild the Desktop (again, hold down Command and Option as you restart your Mac). You'll be asked if you really want to do this; click OK.

Copying files taking too long? Rebuild the Desktop. Another symptom of an invisible Desktop in need of rebuilding is that copying files seems to take longer than it used to, or opening big folders takes a while. The reason is that the Desktop maintains—for a while, anyway—information about files you've deleted, and rebuilding the Desktop erases all this extraneous information.

Save yourself some time: get Suitcase II or MasterJuggler.
Yes, I know I said there would be very few program plugs in *Voodoo Mac*. But these two utilities—which are similar but not identical—are really valuable because they let you store fonts, sounds and FKEYs outside the System Folder. This helps cut down on the huge System file size you encounter if you use a lot of fonts, and you also don't have to reinstall all these items when you replace your System. Both packages offer their own nice features, as well, like the ability to create groups or sets of fonts or temporarily open fonts until the next startup. My advice: get one or the other. And if you're on a budget, consider the shareware program Carpetbagger, which does essentially the same thing, only without the pretty interface and extra bells and whistles. Carpetbagger costs only $5 and is available online and from user groups.

Isolating the troublesome startup items. Extensions and control panels (formerly known as INITs and cdevs, respectively) are some of the most common sources of trouble on any Mac. If you're getting weird crashes, particularly if they always happen under certain circumstances or only with particular programs, it's a good bet that you're experiencing some sort of extension conflict. To test out this theory and try to isolate which extension might be the conflicting one, disable all of them (under System 7) on startup by holding down the Shift key until you see the standard desktop. Then move all of your extensions into a folder named Temporary, or something like that. You can find them easily if you view the System Folder and its subfolders by Kind. They'll be in the Extensions folder or Control Panels folder in System 7, but a few of them may be loose in the System Folder itself.

Under System 6, there's no quick and easy way—like holding down the Shift key—to disable all your startup items. You can use a program like the freeware Extensions Manger, or you can drag all of the items (which will be loose in the System Folder) into another temporary storage folder somewhere outside the System Folder.

Now that you've disabled all of your extensions, the trick is to isolate the one causing your problem. Once you've put all the extensions (or other startup items) into that Temporary folder, return them to their appropriate folders one at a time, restarting after you add each one, until the problem crops up again. Then you'll know your problem was caused by the last extension you returned to the System Folder conflicting either with an application or another extension. Keep experimenting until you find a mix of extensions that don't cause trouble (see the next tip).

Better yet, use Apple's Extensions Manager control panel (which is compatible with both System 6 and System 7) to selectively disable and enable extensions to locate the ones that cause trouble. You can also create customized sets of extensions to run under certain circumstances, which is quite handy.

Quick extension and control panel debugging. Normally, if you suspect that an extension or control panel is causing trouble, you'll need to remove all of them from your System Folder and then start up again, replacing each one at a time until you figure out which one is causing the trouble (as outlined in the tip above). There's a way to speed up this process: take *half* of them out of the System Folder and restart. If you don't have any problems, you can be sure that the offender(s) are in the half you removed. Divide that group in half and try again. Likewise, if the problem persists, then you've got at least one troublesome extension still active.

Similarly, you can use a little common sense to guess what startup item might be causing a problem. For instance, if your Mac always crashes when you try to play a sound or access a desk accessory, you may be experiencing a conflict with any extension(s) that handles sounds or desk accessories, like Suitcase II. Try disabling that extension first, since it's the most obvious suspect. These tricks can help isolate the offender in a few steps. But see the next trap.

Thanks to Holly Knight, Apple Computer.

The problem may be in the loading order, though. The previous neat trick won't do you any good if the problem is that the extensions or control panels are in conflict with *each other*. To fix that problem, you need to understand what order the pesky items are loading in, and also a little bit about how Systems 6 and 7 handle startup items differently.

- Under System 6, all startup items (INITs and cdevs) load in alphabetical order.

- Under System 7, items in the Extensions folder load first and in alphabetical order, then come the items in the Control Panels folder (alphabetically), and then any of the items lying loose in the System Folder (alphabetically).

However, some things like virus detection utilities and extension managers need to load before any other startup items. Other control panels and extensions, like ATM, must load last.

If you've got a pretty good idea of the item that's causing the problem, rename it to make it load in a different order. Begin an item's name with a blank space to make it load earlier. Use a tilde (~) to make it load last.

It's fairly straightforward to force an item to load first or last in System 6, where all items load in strict alphabetical order, but in System 7, it's a little trickier. Under System 7, to force an item to load *first*, put it in the Extensions folder and insert two or three blank spaces at the beginning of its name (use more spaces than any other item has in its name). To force an item to load *last*, put it "loose" in the System Folder and begin its name with several tildes.

Sometimes you may have a control panel that needs to be loaded before an extension, but if you drag it to the System Folder (in System 7), it will automatically be stored in the Control Panels folder and so will load after all the extensions. To get around this, open the System Folder first and then drag the item directly to the folder you want it to be in.

Renaming items may cause even more problems. While renaming an extension to force it to load earlier or later in the startup process can often solve your problems, it may make matters worse. Some extensions or control panels should never be renamed, because they work with other programs (or startup items) that identify them only by their unique name. So be careful about which items you rename (and what you rename them as). A more elegant solution is to use a commercial or shareware extension manager to control the loading order.

Zapping the PRAM. No voodoo Mac book is complete without a tip on how to zap (clear) the Mac's PRAM (Parameter Random Access Memory). Skip this one if you've seen it before.

The PRAM stores certain system software settings when your Mac isn't on. It runs off a battery, so if your clock and calendar gradually become inaccurate, it could be the PRAM. The PRAM also keeps track of your printer ports and which printers you've chosen in the Chooser. Depending on which Mac you have, there are different ways to reset the PRAM. If you still have a weird clock or calendar or a printer choice that won't "stick" after zapping the PRAM, you'll probably need to contact your dealer, because the battery's soldered to the logic board in all Macs made after the Plus.

- On a Mac Plus (or earlier models), open the battery compartment on the back, take out the battery, and wait 15 minutes or so. Then put it back in.

- On any other Mac running System 6, press Command-Option-Shift and choose the Control Panel DA. You'll be warned that you're going to zap the PRAM, so click Yes.

- In System 7, press and hold the Option, Command, P and R keys as you start up. You can release them after the second startup chord.

Any way you zap the PRAM, you'll need to restart your Mac afterward and reset all your carefully selected beep sounds, highlight color, disk cache and other customizable items, too, because zapping the PRAM returns control panels to their original factory settings.

Unexpected quits? If your application is shutting down with messages that it has "unexpectedly quit" (no kidding, Sherlock), try increasing its memory allocation. Highlight the application's icon in the finder and call up its Get Info box (Command-I) and put a larger value in the Current Size box. This will allocate more RAM to that program, which might fix the problem with it "unexpectedly quitting" on you.

Trouble with System 7? One common source of problems under System 7 is outdated disk drivers. If you've been using a third-party hard drive for a couple of years and you then install System 7, the driver (which controls how that hard drive interacts with your system) may not be updated for System 7 compatibility. It doesn't mean that you have to reinitialize (reformat) the disk—you should just update the driver. Check with the disk's manufacturer, and see the tip "Hard disks have drivers, too" in Chapter 5 for more on updating your driver.

Bus errors? If you're getting bus errors (ID code 01), the most likely culprit is a corrupted System file or an extension conflict. (Although it is less common, bus errors can also sometimes be caused by hard disk drivers that aren't compatible with System 7, as explained in the preceding tip, or by applications that aren't compatible with 32-bit addressing when it's activated.) Here are a few steps you can take to try to diagnose what might be causing bus errors on your Mac.

Try starting with the Shift key down to disable extensions. If you still get bus errors, try booting from a floppy. Then trash your old System file (remember to empty the Trash) and either run the Installer to create a new system or simply copy over a backup of your System file that you had the foresight to make (be sure to back up System and Finder files to floppies).

I know it's hard to bring yourself to trash that System file, but you really need to do it to make sure that everything gets replaced by the new, uncorrupted System. Do it.

If you haven't made copies of sounds and fonts (see "Your Emergency Toolkit" above), you'll have to reinstall them in the new System.

Bad F-line instruction? Sometimes when you try to restart, the Finder freezes and won't even let you restart, so you have to restart using the programmer's key or power down and start up again. If you find that this is constantly happening, replace the Finder (see the next tip) and restart with the Command and Option keys down to rebuild the Desktop.

Lots of crashes? Replace the Finder. The Finder can get corrupted very easily. If you've been having lots of otherwise unexplainable crashes and you're sure they aren't the result of extension conflicts or memory problems, replace the Finder, because it's probably become corrupted and you just don't know it yet.

You don't have to reinstall all the system software, just the Finder file. Copy a new, uncorrupted Finder onto your Mac. Move the old Finder from your System Folder to the Trash. Then stick the new Finder (stay tuned) into your open System Folder and restart.

Keep a clean Finder around to replace a corrupted one. Store a "clean" Finder in a folder on your hard disk, outside the System Folder. That way, if your Finder gets corrupted, you'll easily be able to find the new, unused one and replace the old one.

Keep a clean System on hand, too. Make that Duplicate command useful! Keep an uncorrupted System in a folder separate from your System Folder, just like the tip above suggests for the Finder. In fact, keep a whole set of spare parts in a folder. (Include any favorite macro keys you've laboriously set up, too.) That way, if you suspect that the System and Finder are causing errors, drag the old ones to the Trash, drag the spares to the System Folder, and

restart your Mac. You'll save a lot of time. This tip is especially important if you've customized your System or Finder files using ResEdit or
a similar utility, since reinstalling a "clean" System or Finder file will
cause you to lose all those modifications.

Thanks to Marty Silbernik, Buffalo Grove, Illinois.

Something eating memory? If you're still running System 6,
you know that you often have to reallocate Finder memory,
making changes as you get new programs and as memory require-
ments change. This isn't the case with System 7: the Finder's memory
is maintained dynamically, which means that you don't have to do
anything about changing it. Usually, you'll never have to tweak it, but
if you need to, there's a trick in Chapter 9 ("Increase the Finder's
memory allocation if you have suitcase troubles") that shows you how.

Sometimes extensions may not handle memory well, though. If you
suspect that something is eating up memory, check About This Macintosh from the Apple menu and see what's going on. If more memory's
being used than you think should be, restart your Mac with the Shift
key down to turn off extensions.

Recovering from a crash? Try the interrupt switch. Most Macs
have an interrupt switch on them that programmers can use to
enter the Mac's debugger, giving them direct access to the bowels of
the system. If your Mac crashes or freezes, you can hit the interrupt
switch and type a sequence of characters that will sometimes free up
your Mac so you can save any work still open in other programs.

First, when your Mac crashes, use the interrupt switch (it's in
different locations on different Macs; see below). You should see an
empty dialog box with a greater-than symbol used as a prompt (>). In
that box, type this (those are letter Os, not zeroes):

SM 0 A9F4 *and press Return*

G 0 *and press Return*

If you're lucky, you'll be returned to a working Finder, where you can save any work you haven't saved yet and restart as soon as possible (unfortunately, the application you were working in will almost certainly be crashed). If this trick doesn't work, what have you lost that you hadn't lost already?

Now, as to where the switch is—only some Macs have one. For example, the LC and the IIsi don't, but you can generate these signals from the keyboard on an LC or IIsi. Press Command-Control-Power (the key with the triangle) for reset, Command-Shift-Power for restart, and Command-Power for interrupt (to enter the debugger).

Suddenly, ugly icons? If you had beautiful unique icons that the Finder suddenly isn't drawing any more, or if your icons have reverted to the standard dog-eared page, try rebuilding your Desktop. If that doesn't work, install a new Finder.

Check Chapter 4 for more details about copying and pasting icon resources.

Trash folders from Hell? Sometimes—a very few sometimes—you'll get a folder stuck in the Trash that simply will not empty. What's happened is that the folder's structure has somehow gotten damaged, and the Trash just isn't reading it properly. A disk utility program (like Norton Utilities, DiskTop or even Disk First Aid) can sometimes repair the folder so the Trash will recognize it. But before you call Dr. Norton, try these magic tricks.

First, and simplest: restart the Mac and try again. If that doesn't work, reboot from a floppy disk and try again. If the item was in the Trash under System 7 and you restart from a System 6 floppy, you'll find it in the Trash folder at the top level of the desktop.

Next easiest: run Disk First Aid on your hard disk and try again. Then get out Norton or Rescue or Mac Tools (or whatever) and run one of them on your hard disk. Try again. The one you don't want to hear: reformat your hard disk, or live with that item in the Trash.

You can also sometimes move the item out of the trash and into a folder, then create a file or folder with the same name as the item that was in the trash, and then copy that same-named item into the folder where the voodoo item is. You'll be asked if you want to replace items with the same names, say yes, and you've copied a trashable item onto a stinky voodoo item. This seldom works, but it's worth a shot.

MOVING ON

We've covered a lot of tips and tricks in this book, but by no means all of the magic things you can do with your Mac. As a matter of fact, there are still a bunch of neat tricks in Appendix A, "Installation Tips," so don't stop reading yet! But if you have a tip or trick, or even a trap, that you'd like to share, send it in and I'll try to get it in the next edition of the book. See the introduction for how to get in touch. If your tip gets used, you'll get the next edition of *Voodoo Mac* free from Ventana Press.

INSTALLATION TIPS

Y ou've waited long enough. It's time to install System 7 (or 7.1, if you have a need for it). There are few programs out there that are still incompatible with System 7, and if you still haven't upgraded, you're missing all of System 7's neat new features. If you're a System 6 diehard, you can keep System 6 on one drive and System 7 on another and switch between them, depending on the programs you want to run. But, if you're like most people, once you've used 7, you'll never want to go back.

You'll also find tricks and hints in this appendix for installing most any program, not just System 7.

SAFE INSTALLATION

Before installing a completely new system (going from System 6 to System 7, say), it's a good idea (but not a necessity) to back up all the files you want to keep. At the least, though, make backups of your documents, fonts and extensions (INITs and cdevs, in System 6-speak). And if you've customized your System and Finder files with ResEdit, back them up, too. Use a compression program like StuffIt to get them onto floppy disks. (Although a really big System with dozens of fonts may be beyond StuffIt's abilities to cram on a high-density disk. Split the file across several disks, nuke a few fonts, or go to System 7.1, which stores fonts in a separate Fonts folder.)

Installing System 7 the safe way. After you've made backups of your files, if you choose to (I've never had any data loss, and I've installed System 7 many times), drag the Finder out of your System Folder and put it in another folder—an untitled folder will do. Then rename the System Folder something else, like System 6 or Old System.

Then go ahead and install System 7, using the Installer disk and program that comes with the upgrade kit. If you're installing System 7.1, start up from the Disk Tools disk and then run the Installer. After the installation is complete, you can individually drag back to the new System Folder any system enhancements, fonts, sounds and other items you want to use with System 7 from the folder you named Old System or whatever.

Creating the *smallest* possible System Folder for a PowerBook. Normally the Installer installs everything. You probably don't want every item copied if you're installing a system onto a PowerBook. Instead, choose Customize when you first launch the installer and then pick just the barebones of what you'll need; choose Min system (for a specific Mac) to create just a System and Finder file for your specific model of Mac. (See the next tip for what you won't get.) If you just want a small system, not a barebones system, choose System Software for your particular Mac. That way, you'll get control panels, desk accessories, and so forth, and you can later delete the ones you don't need.

- Don't install any printing software.

- Don't install any file sharing software.

If you install System Software for your particular Mac, go back after the installation's done and trash all the components you don't need. Get rid of Finder Help in the Extensions folder. Remove the DAL extension, if you're not using a remote database. Go to the Control Panels folder and nuke the Map and Easy Access and anything else you don't need or want. In the Apple Menu Items folder, delete the Puzzle, the Note Pad, the Calculator and all the others that aren't necessary. Finally, open the System file and trash any fonts (in System 7.1, look in the Fonts folder) and sounds you don't need. See Chapter 7, "Printing Mysteries," for some suggestions about which fonts to delete.

Getting a system on a startup floppy. System 7 is just too big to fit on a floppy disk. Even if you streamline everything and think you've got all the essentials on a floppy disk, it won't work. You can use the Installer to put a system on a floppy (it'll be a System 6 system) if you click the Customize button and choose Min system for any Macintosh or Min system (for a specific Mac). You'll get a System and Finder file, only one font, no control panels—no frills. You can also use the Disk Tools disk that comes with System 7 as a startup disk. Under System 6, use the Utilities disk as a startup disk.

The Installer disk for System 7.1 can't be used as a startup disk. If you're installing System 7.1 and you need to start from a floppy, use the Disk Tools disk, not the System 7.1 Install 1 disk. It doesn't have a system on it.

Do you really need System 7.1? The short answer: no, unless you want to be able to type in Korean or Arabic. In addition to international language support, System 7.1 also provides a Fonts folder for managing your fonts. If you've already got a font manager and just want to type in English with occasional special foreign-language characters that you can access through Key Caps, why bother buying System 7.1? (But buy my book on it, *The Little System 7.1 Book* from Peachpit Press. It covers System 7.0, too.)

Compatibility Checker doesn't really check. There's a Compatibility Checker available with System 7.0. But by now it's out of date. Be sure to get System 7.0.1 or the even newer System 7.1. If you do run the Compatibility Checker, be aware that all Compatibility Checker does is compare the names of the things you've got in your Mac with certain information in a database. Compatibility Checker doesn't really perform any kind of diagnostic test to see whether a program is truly compatible, so a new program that is compatible may not have made it into the database. Also, it doesn't check desk accessories at all. And it ignores any item that has an unknown creator code. So you still can't be completely sure that a program will work if you run Compatibility Checker and have it move all your May Not Work With System 7 items to a separate folder.

Checking the May Not Work With System 7 items. Even extensions and control panels that have been flagged as May Not Work With System 7 may work just fine. To test them, drag them one by one to your System Folder and reboot after each one. If you crash, that program doesn't work with System 7.

Call the publisher to check a program's compatibility. While it's usually fine to check out an extension the way that's described in the previous tip, unruly programs can cause you a lot more trouble and possibly even loss of some work. So if you're concerned about compatibility, don't experiment with programs. If one of your programs has been classified as Mostly compatible, Must upgrade or Not available, call its publisher and find out what the situation is.

The "incompatibility" may simply be with 32-bit addressing. Although more and more programs are coming out 32-bit clean (so they'll run beautifully on a Quadra, for example), not all are there yet. If the Compatibility Checker reports AD in the Notes column for a program, it won't work with 32-bit addressing.

Likewise, a VM indicates a program doesn't work with virtual memory. The solution: turn off 32-bit addressing or virtual memory before running the program.

How to tell whether a program is 32-bit clean. There is a neat extension called Savvy that will tell you if a program is 32-bit clean (look in the Get Info box). You can get Savvy from America Online or CompuServe (GO MACSEVEN and look in Library 2).

Don't forget the other stuff on the disks. There are lots more goodies on the system software installation disks (both System 6 and System 7) that the Installer doesn't install. Check the Tidbits disk to see if you want to put any of them on your hard disk after the installation's done. There's Apple File Exchange, for example, which lets you transfer DOS files to your Mac and vice versa. There's also the LaserWriter Font Utility, which is invaluable for downloading PostScript fonts, turning the printer's startup page on and off, and so forth. And Disk First Aid is a handy utility to keep on your hard disk for repairing damaged floppies. On the Fonts disk with System 7.1 are the Apple Classic fonts—those weird bitmapped fonts like San Francisco, Venice and Mobile.

GENERAL INSTALLATION TIPS

These next tips apply to situations where you're replacing corrupted system software, not necessarily upgrading from one system to a newer one.

Trash your old System file when you install a new one. The safest way to make sure you get an uncorrupted System is to trash the old one. Drag the current System file to the desktop or put it in another folder. You can't trash it when it's still the current System, but you can start from a floppy disk, trash the old System, and then install the new one.

Reinstalling corrupted Finder files. From time to time, the Finder may get corrupted. You'll suspect this when you've been having lots of crashes. Instead of reinstalling everything, just trash the Finder file and copy a new one onto your startup disk.

Unfortunately, when you do this, you'll lose any customizing you've done to the Finder, like Command-key shortcuts for menu items. For this reason, you should keep a copy of your custom-tailored Finder on a spare floppy or in a spare parts folder so you can reinstall it later, if the Finder you're using gets corrupted.

Keep the old System file on hand. The System file contains all your fonts and sounds, and if you trash it, you'll have to reinstall them all. To save yourself the trouble, move the System file to another folder if you have to reinstall system software. After you've installed the new system software, open the old System file and copy the fonts (in Systems 6 and 7.0) and sounds to the new System Folder. Or use a suitcase program to store these items. Either of these tricks will save you hours of hunting for fonts and sounds.

You can also keep a compressed version of your System file on a floppy disk for retrieving fonts and sounds if your current System file gets corrupted (see the preceding tip). The Finder will fit handily on a floppy, but a System file usually won't unless you compress it or unless you're using System 6 with only a few fonts and other goodies.

Improving installations. If you have MountImage and Apple DiskCopy 4.2 or greater, you can speed up installations. Frankly, some applications have rather sloppy installers that make you swap disks in and out too many times. You'll also need some free RAM to use this trick—a little more than the capacity of the Install disk (a bit over 800k for a double-sided disk, and a bit over 1.44 Mb for a high-density disk). And it should be real RAM, not virtual memory.

First, check to see if you need to trash any old Preferences folders or whatever before you start the installation (check the Read Me document that comes with the program you're installing). Then launch DiskCopy and insert the installation disk so that it gets read into memory. Click Read Master Floppy. Then choose Save Disk Image from the File menu and quit from DiskCopy.

Start MountImage. Click on the first disk icon (Figure A-1) and then click on the name of the installation disk image. That installation disk is now in RAM, and you can install from it without ever having to swap disks in and out of the floppy drive. It appears as a disk image icon on your desktop.

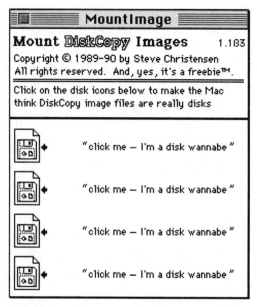

Figure A-1: MountImage lets you click on DiskCopy images to mount them.

You can do this trick with a whole set of installation floppies if you have enough RAM.

Thanks to Dave Axler, Mac Utilities Forum, America Online, for this tip and the next two.

Installing a minimal system on a floppy with MountImage. If you need to create a minimal system on a floppy disk, try this trick. Use MountImage to create a floppy in memory. Then, in the Installer, choose that disk to install on. When the installation's done, fire up Apple Disk Copy to create your real floppy. You'll save lots and lots of disk swapping, especially if you have only one floppy drive.

What you get with a minimal installation. If you install a minimum system via the Installer, you get only the System, the Finder and the basic fonts. What you see is a little misleading, because there'll be folders for extensions and other things—but they're empty.

Compressed installation files? Lightning fast with a RAM disk. Also, if you have a RAM disk utility and the files you're installing have been compressed, you'll find that it's much faster to install to a RAM disk, because all the decompression will take place in RAM at lightning-fast speed. Just be sure that you create a RAM disk big enough to hold both the compressed and decompressed files (see Chapter 9, "Memory Demystified," for how to create a RAM disk).

With all these RAM drive tricks, use real RAM. You'll wind up doing a lot of disk swapping—which is what you were trying to avoid—if you're trying to use virtual memory as RAM when doing these tricks. Virtual memory is disk memory. Use real RAM.

System 7 TuneUp—when to use it? If you're still running System 7.0, get the latest version of System 7 TuneUp and run it. You can get it from an online service, bulletin board, or user group. TuneUp fixes a mysterious disappearing folder bug, speeds up the Finder's copying process and gives you better printer drivers. If you have to reinstall System 7, run TuneUp on it again.

How can you tell whether TuneUp's installed? Check the system software version in the About This Macintosh dialog box. There'll be a tiny dot next to it (see Figure A-2).

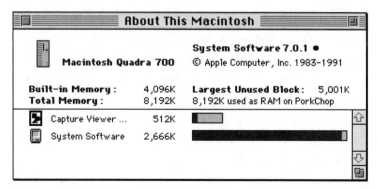

Figure A-2: The dot in the upper-right corner indicates that TuneUp's installed.

If you have to replace your system software on any occasion, run TuneUp again after it's reinstalled. TuneUp doesn't "stick."

If you're running System 7.1, you don't have to use TuneUp. The features TuneUp provides are built in.

Copying the System disks. If you want to make backup copies of your system software disks, be sure to use a disk copying program that makes a track-by-track copy. DiskCopy 4.2 or greater is ideal for making disk copies, and it's fast, too, because it reads the whole disk into RAM and then writes it out. (You have to have 2 Mb of RAM to use it.) DiskDup+ is a shareware program that does much the same thing, and FastCopy does it too (it's part of MacTools Deluxe).

After you've installed your system software, trash any printer drivers you don't need. Using Easy Install puts all the printer drivers on your hard disk. If you don't have an ImageWriter or a Style-Writer, trash the icon for those printers to pick up around 75k of hard disk space for each printer icon you delete from the System Folder.

Your Scrapbook isn't replaced when you reinstall. If you have a Scrapbook with anything in it in your System Folder when you install new system software, the Installer doesn't replace it with the new Scrapbook. There are usually neat new things in the Scrapbook that comes with a new system version, so unless there's something you can't live without in your old Scrapbook, trash it before you install the new system, copy out the can't-live-without item, or rename that Scrapbook something besides "Scrapbook." If you need to merge Scrapbooks often, get a utility such as SmartScrap from Solutions International that will let you combine Scrapbooks.

Thanks to Eric Apgar, Apple Worldwide Technical Assistance.

WHERE TO GO FROM HERE

I f you're interested in pursuing other sources of information about the Mac, you should make contact with other people who use Macs every day. User groups and online services are the best places to find people who love Macs.

Unless a phone number specifically says "BBS," that number is for voice conversations—to find out more about how to sign up, log on to their system, get a catalog of products, and things like that.

USER GROUPS

User groups are a great source of information and help. Many of them maintain electronic bulletin boards and publish newsletters of members' tips and tricks, too.

East Coast

The Boston Computer Society/Macintosh (BCS/MAC)
617/864-1700
BBS: 617/864-0712

New York Mac User Group (NYMUG)
212/473-1600

Washington, D.C., area

Washington Apple Pi
301/654-8060

West Coast

Berkeley Macintosh User Group (BMUG)
510/549-2684
BBS: 510/849-2684

Los Angeles Macintosh User Group (LAMG)
310/278-5264

USC Mac User Group
213/937-4082

For more information on user groups, or to find one near you, call Apple's User Group Information number, 800/538-9696.

CALLING APPLE

Apple Customer Assistance Center

800/776-2333

There are also individual toll-free numbers for products that Apple supports, such as Macintosh PC File exchange. Check the documentation that came with your product (the stuff in the box that I hope you didn't throw away), as you will be asked for your private access code.

ONLINE SERVICES

My advice is: get a modem and join one. America Online's interface is most like the Mac's, so that might be the best bet if you're just starting out.

America Online
8619 Westwood Center Dr.
Vienna, VA 22182-2285
800/827-6364

CompuServe
5000 Arlington Centre Blvd.
Columbus, OH 43220
800/848-8990

GEnie
401 N. Washington St.
Rockville, MD 20850
800/638-9636

MAIL ORDER HOUSES

I have ordered many times from both MacConnection and MacWarehouse, with absolutely no complaints. If you get any of the Mac magazines (*MacUser*, *Macworld* and so forth), you'll have no trouble finding many other mail order houses, all of which advertise in each issue.

MacConnection
14 Mills St.
Marlow, NH 03456
800/800-3333

MacWarehouse
1720 Oak St.
Lakewood, NJ 08701
800/255-6227

MAGAZINES

Mac magazines are a great resource. Even if you don't read the articles, you'll find current street prices for all the popular hardware and software that's available. They're filled with up-to-date tips and reviews, too. Here are a couple of the biggest magazines. You can get a better subscription rate than the retail prices I've listed here by sending in the business reply cards from the latest issues.

Macworld

The Mac magazine that's been around longest, and one of the best. $24.95/year.
Subscription number: 800/234-1038
Contact editors via America Online (keyword Macworld)

MacUser

Another great Mac magazine. It probably has more product reviews than *Macworld*; it's hard to say. $27/year.
Subscription number: 800/627-2247
Contact editors via CompuServe (go ZMAC)

MacWEEK

Kind of expensive ($99/year for 44 issues), but the industry's gossip sheet; also known familiarly as MacLeak.
Subscription number: 609/461-2100

INDEX

A

Abbreviations, in telecommunications sessions   239-40
About the Finder Easter Egg   70-71
About This Macintosh   249, 255, 263, 288-90
Accent marks   209
Access, restricting on a network   223
Access PC (Insignia Solutions)   126
Adobe Photoshop Easter Egg   75
Adobe Type Manager (ATM)   202, 205-7, 255
After Dark (Berkeley Systems)   63, 255
AIFF (Audio Interchange File Format)   165
Aitken, Kevin   80
Alarm Clock   152
    copying time from   147
    ringing   53
Alias, removing the string   98
Aliases
    disk space for   2
    in Apple menu   32
    of control panels   144
    of file servers   228
    of printer drivers   195
    and SCSI devices   232
    sharing   225
    tricks for   2-6
Allocating memory to the Finder   247-49
Alphabetical order, in Apple menu   35
Alphabetizing icons   9-10
America Online   234-35, 293
Animated cursors   97
Apgar, Eric   30, 65, 77, 100, 128, 133, 141, 161, 214, 228, 229, 252, 290
Apple Classic fonts   204, 287
Apple Customer Assistance number   292
Apple fax modem Easter Egg   74
Apple File Exchange   126, 237, 241, 243, 237, 285
    formatting disks with   130
Apple HD SC Setup utility   79-80, 137, 267

using to gain disk space   140
Apple Icon Colors   111
Apple logo symbol   207
Apple menu
    alias of Clipboard in   6
    Apple symbol in   33
    flashing   53
    icon   147
    putting Trash in   5
    and PrintMonitor   194
    tricks for   32-38
Apple Menu Items folder, making alias of   32-33
AppleShare   218
AppleTalk   252
    and printing   193
AppleTalk Remote Access   229
Application busy or missing message   270
ApplicationMenu (shareware)   52
Applications
    copying on a network   225
    increasing memory allocation in   250-51, 275
    installing fonts in   205
Applications folder, creating an   2
Applications menu (System 7)   31
    blinking   195
    tricks for   52-53
Applicon   52
Arrow cursor   95
ASCII format   235
At Ease   10-12, 252
    and PowerBooks   156
ATM (Adobe Type Manager)   202, 205-7, 255
AutoDoubler (Fifth Generation)   133-34, 157
Automatic network connecting   224
Axler, Dave   287

B

Background copying   26
Background printing   141, 194, 252
Backgrounder, placement of   192
Backlighting, on PowerBooks   154, 158

Backups
  importance of   124
  using Find command for   43
Bad F-line instructions   276
Balloon Help   49
  Easter Egg in   72
Batch copying   42
Bates, Roger D.   262
Batista, Ricardo   67
Battery control panel, PowerBook   156
Baud rates   239
Baya, Harry   269
Becker, Lofty   265
Beep, System 7   38
Bitmapped fonts   200, 203, 204
  and ATM   206
Bitmapped graphics, printing   212
Black and white screens   141
Black terminators   233
BMUG   292
Bombs, when switching fonts   210
Boot bong, turning down   156
Boston Computer Society   291
Brightness   146
Bulk erasing   127
Bullet symbol   13, 34, 208
Bulletin board folders   221-23
Bus errors   275

C

Cables, and SCSI devices   232-34
Cache controls   260
Cache Switch control panel Easter
  Egg   72
Call Waiting, disabling   238
Canvas   101
Caps Lock extension   158-59
Caps Lock, turning off   174
Capture (Mainstay)   79, 243
Carpetbagger (shareware)   271
Carriage return characters   243
Cat icon   135
Chain, SCSI   229, 232
Check mark symbol   207
CheckList (ElseWare)   211
Chicago font, symbols in   201, 207-8

Chips, installing RAM   253-54
Chooser   193
  using with networks   219
Classic II   12
Clean Up command   9
Clendining, Kerry   34
ClickChange (Dubl-Click
  Software)   63, 88
Clipboard, alias of   6
CloseView control panel 144
Closing open windows   44
CODE resource   99
Color control panel   145
  Easter Egg in   72
Color map   38, 73
Color menu (System 6)   31
Color wheel (color picker)   47
  secrets of   145-46
Color-matching icons and disks   46
ColorDesk (shareware)   101
Coloring icons   104-5, 108-13
Colors
  in Apple menu   36
  in startup screen   103
Command key
  assignments   54-55
  menu shortcuts, creating   53-62
  symbol   207
  using   2
Command-clicking   24-25
Command-D, to go to the desktop   27
Command-dragging icons   45
Command-O (Open)   24
Command-period, to cancel an
  operation   24, 67
Command-S, in Disk First Aid   132
Command-W
  to close dialog boxes and
    windows   22, 25
  with Find   25
Command-Y (Put Away)   21, 22
  for disk ejecting   127-28
Comments, in Get Info boxes   17-18
Compact Pro   133-34, 236
Compatibility Checker   284
Compressed files   235
Compression utilities   133, 157-58

CompuServe 293
CompuServe Information
    Manager 235
Control panels
    putting on Apple menu 37
    renaming 144
    tricks 143-53
    use of memory 254-55
Converting fonts 201
Copying
    disks 128-29
    icon names 10
    icons 8
    in the background 26
    programs on a network 225
Copyright symbol 208
Corless, "Pete" 265
Courier font 202
Creator codes 183-85
Crosshair cursor 95
CURS resource 95
Cursor Animator (shareware) 97
Cursors, editing 95-97

D

Dagger symbol 208
Dashes 208, 209-10
Data fork 86
DateKey (shareware) 78
Davis-Charles, Spring 48
Deleting
    fonts 201-2, 210
    locked files 48
Desk accessories
    copying and pasting with 147
    installing in applications 149
Desktop
    fitting more icons onto 14-15
    getting to from Open and Save As
        dialogs 5
    going to 27
    moving found files to 39
    organizing 3, 6
    rebuilding the invisible 64-66, 67,
        83, 130, 268, 269-70
Desktop pattern, changing 89-93
Desktop DB file 141

Desktop DF file 141
Desktop folder 83
    creating 37
Desktop Manager extension 83
Desktop vs. desktop 120, 140
DeskZap 6
Diacritical marks 209
Dialog boxes
    adding color to 108-9
    editing icons in 105-8
    moving 26-27
    shortcuts in 27
Diamond symbol 34, 207
Disabling extensions on startup 64,
    67, 146
Disconnecting from a network 226-27
Disinfectant
    Easter Egg in 76
    sound in 172
Disk caches 247, 259-62
Disk capacities 126, 128, 140
Disk compression utilities 157-58
Disk drivers 275
Disk images 129
DiskCopy 128-29, 286-87, 289
Disk First Aid 81, 131-32, 266-67,
    268, 278, 285
Disk Tools disk 131, 256, 266
    for startup (System 7) 69
DiskDoubler (Fifth
    Generation) 133-34, 236, 255
DiskDup+ (shareware) 289
Disks. *See* Floppy disks; Hard disks
DiskTop (CE Software) 6, 186, 278
Dismounting disks 21
DITL resource 212
Dividers
    creating in icon windows 13
    using in Apple menu 35-36
Documents
    formatting for different
        printers 197-98
    opening from the Finder 24
DOS disk readers 125-26
DOS disks
    formatting on Macs 242
    initializing (formatting) 139-40

DOS Mounter (Dayna)   126, 237, 242
Double-density disks   126
Downloading
    files   237
    fonts   200
    PostScript files   196
    sounds   167
Dragging and dropping to open
    files   24, 87
Dragging items to System Folder
    (System 7)   29-30
Dragging operation, stopping   20
Dragging, for selecting items   19-20
Drivers, for hard disks,
    updating   136-37
DSAT resource   68
Duplicate command   8

E

Easter Eggs   63-64, 70-77
Easy Access control panel   147
    indicator of   53
    using when mouse freezes   26
EasyPlay   160
Editing sounds   168-69
Eject Disk command
    (Command-E)   21
Ejecting disks with Command-Y   127
Ellipsis symbol   208
Em dash   208, 209-10
Emoticons   240-41
Empty Folder vs. New Folder   38-39
Empty Trash, assigning to
    Command-T   61
En dash   208, 209-10
Envelopes, printing   197
EPS (Encapsulated
    PostScript)   212, 243
Erasing floppy disks   127
Error numbers   265
Esc key
    alternate for   65
    swapping with tilde   158
Ettore, Riccardo   164

Excel 3.0 Easter Egg   75
Exiting with Force Quit   65
Expanded folders, compressing   42
Extensions
    bypassing   64, 67, 146, 249,
        252, 268
    for compressed files   135
    use of memory   254-55
Extensions folder, for printer
    fonts   202, 205
Extensions Manager   67, 268, 271-72
Eyedropper tool   112

F

FastCopy (MacTools Deluxe)   289
Fax, printing via on PowerBook   198
Faxing   244
FDHD drives (SuperDrives)   125-26,
    153, 241
Feldman, David N.   74
File menu, tricks for   38-44
File names, protecting from
    change   187
File servers   219, 228
File sharing   141, 249, 252
    between PowerBooks   157
File transfer speeds   239
File transfers   157
Files, recovering   268
Find command   2, 39-43
Find File desk accessory (System 6)   39
Finder   1-30
    "clean" copy of   276
    editing   54, 89
    increasing memory size in   247-49
    names in   120
    navigating   24-25
    numbers in   9
    printing from   192
    replacing corrupted   268, 276,
        285-86
    selecting items in   19-21
    speeding up   26, 27-28, 141
Finder icon, flashing   53

Finder menus
  changing in System 6   56-57
  System 6 vs. System 7   31
Finder windows, closing   28-29
FKEYs   77-79, 157, 176, 271
  installing in System file   78
Flash-It (shareware)   79
Flashing
  Apple menu icon   53
  Application menu   53
  Finder icon   53
  PrintMonitor icon   195
FlipTIFF   243
Floppy disk icon, changing   129
Floppy disks
  aliases on   4-5
  care of   125
  ejecting   21, 77, 127-28
  problems, with PowerBooks   153
  rebuilding Desktop on   128
  tricks for   126-33
Floppy drive, bypassing   64, 66
fmenu resource   57
Folder icons, changing   18-19
Folders
  calculating size   29, 141
  expanding and compressing   28
  looking in   24-25
  making aliases of   5
  naming   13-14
  organizing   1-2, 6
  trashing reluctant   48
Font cache, in ATM   205
Font Downloader   196
Font managers   203
Font substitution   213
Font suitcases. *See* Suitcases
Font/DA Mover   144, 203, 205
  using to install DAs   148-50
FontMonger (Ares Software)   201
Fonts   199-211
  changing in Finder   45
  colored labels for   47-48
  deleting   201-2, 206, 210
  downloading   200
  folder   201
  order in which Mac uses   200-201, 202

switching, on PowerBooks   158
  weird   204, 285
Fonts folder   201
  in System 7.1   78
Force Quit   65
Foreign-language keyboards   51-52
Formatter Five (Software
  Architects)   80
Formatting documents for
  printers   197-98
Frozen mouse   26

G

Generic icons, replacing   17
Geneva, using as Finder font   27-28
GEnie   293
Get Info boxes
  comments in   17-18
  for finding alias originals   4
  replacing icons with   18
Gibson, Robert   15, 24
Goodman, Bill   236
Greenwich Mean Time, in Map   152
Grid, using for icons   44-45
Guests, allowing on a network   220

H

HAM (Microseeds)   34
Hannah, Elise   237
Hansen, Hans   104
Hard disks
  care of   125
  changing icon of   135
  formatting   136-38
  making alias of   6
  organizing   1-2
  partitioning   79-80
  reclaiming space on   140
  sharing on a network   220, 226
  SCSI ID numbers of   230
  tricks for   133-39
Headers, in PostScript files   214
Help menu (System 7)   31
  tricks for   48-49

Helping Hand   29-30
Hexadecimal format, in fmenu
    resource   57, 61-62
Hide Others, in Finder   25
Hiding windows   25
High-density disks   126
Holzgrafe, Rick   52
Hot spot
    in cursor   97
    on pointer   20
Hue   146
HyperCard
    art stacks in   135
    Easter Egg in   76
    setting to higher levels   180-81
    sound   163-64

I

I-beam cursor   95
icl4 resource   110
icl8 resource   110
ICN# resource   111-12
Icon collections, using   113-120
Icon names, copying   10
Icon tricks   7-19
Icons
    alphabetizing   9-10
    blinking   194-95
    colons in names   9
    editing   104-20
    repairing   278
    replacing   17-19
iCONtraption   104
ID numbers, for SCSI devices   230
Imagery   243
ImageWriter II cable   242
ImageWriters   197, 198, 200
    and screen shots   77
In box folders   221-23
INITs, disabling   64
Installation tips   281-90
Installing
    desk accessories   144
    fonts   202, 205
    RAM   253-54
Internal hard disk, bypassing   64, 66

International menu
    (System 7.1)   49-52, 178
Interrupt switch   71, 277-78
Invisible
    files   186-87
    folders   6, 186
    labels   17
itlc resource   50, 178

K

KCHR resources   174-78
Kendig, Brian   77
Key Caps desk accessory   179-80, 207
Keyboard
    selecting with (System 7)   20-21
    shortcuts, for Application
        menu   53
    switching between   51-52, 178
Keyboard icons, creating   178-79
Keyboard layouts, viewing
    icon of   49-52
Keys, reassigning   174-77
Knight, Holly   272
Knuttila, Jorn   46, 127

L

Label menu (System 7)   31, 46
    changing colors on   46
Labels (System 7)   17
Labels control panel   145
Laser Prep, placement of   192
Laser printer problems   198
LaserWriter Font Utility   285
LaserWriter SC   200
LaserWriter Utility   196, 200
LaserWriters, naming   196-97
Lau, Raymond   134
Launch pad, creating a   15
LAYOUT (shareware)   45, 88
LC II   12
    startup sound   70
Ligatures   209
Line feed characters   243
Linotronic output   212, 214
Lists, arranging items in   8

Local time, in Map control panel   152
Localtalk Connector Kit   217
Lockable power switch   66
Locked files, deleting   48
Locking floppy disks   127
Los Angeles Macintosh Users
   Group   292
Lost files, recovering   268
Low-memory situations   251-52

M

Mac Classic
   Easter Egg   71
   startup sound   70
Mac II
   sounds   163-64
   startup sound   70
Mac IIci Easter Egg   71
Mac IIfx Easter Egg   71
Mac IIsi, sound problem with   174
Mac Plus
   Easter Egg   71
   startup sound   70
Mac Shareware 500   162
Mac Shareware 500 Library (America
   Online)   163
Mac Tools (Central Point
   Software)   258
MacBinary   237
MacConnection   293
Macintosh Memory Guide   247, 253
Macintosh PC Exchange   126, 237,
   241, 242
MacLink/Plus   242
MacPaint   101
   screen shots to   181-82
MacRecorder   167
MacSink (shareware)   243
MacTools (Central Point Software)   22
MacUser   294
MacWarehouse   294
MacWEEK   294
Macworld   294
Mail order houses   293-94
Mailbox folders   223

Make Alias   2
   assigning to Command-M   57-69
Map control panel
   tricks   151-52
   Easter Eggs   73-74
Marquee tool   20, 112
Mask, in cursor   97
MasterJuggler (ALSoft)   162,
   166, 271
Mathematical symbols   209
Maxima (Connectix)   155, 261
Memory   245-64
   allocating Finder   277
   allocation, checking   249
Memory control panel 257, 263
   Easter Egg   72
MenuChoice (shareware)   34
Message folders   221-23
Messages
   changing in Finder   120-22
   on desktop   15-16
Metamorphosis Professional
   (Altsys)   210
Microphone II   238
Microphones, built-in   162, 167
Microsoft Word
   creator code   184-85
   Easter Egg, version 5   74
   Easter Egg, version 4   74
   sound in   173
   thesaurus in   149
Middle Of Nowhere   73
Mileage, on Map control panel   151
Minimal installations   282-83, 287-88
Minneapolis, as middle of nowhere   73
Mode32   258
Modems   234-41
   speed of   239
Monitors, switching startup   150-51
Monitors control panel   141
   Easter Egg   72
More Disk Space (Alysis)   133
Morris, Joe   77
MountImage (freeware)   129, 286-88
Mouse
   frozen   26
   picking up   153

Mouse Keys   147
Movies, playing   160-61
MultiFinder   1
   background printing   194

N

Name view   9
Namer   197
Naming
   icons   7-8, 10
   your printer   196-97
Navigator (CompuServe)   235, 237
Network printing   192
Networking   217-29
   connecting to   219, 224, 228
   mixed System 6 and 7   133
   registering users   219, 220
New Folder command   54
New York Mac Users Group   292
Norton Utilities (Symantec)   267,
   270, 278
Note Pad, as startup item   16
Novell NetWare   218
Now Utilities (Now Software)   255
NowMenus   34
Numbers
   using in the Finder   9
   using in lists   8

O

O'Connor, Michael C.   45, 88,
   160, 161
Office on a disk trick   227
One-handed typing with Sticky
   Keys   148-49
Open dialog box shortcuts   24-25
Optima (Connectix)   247
Option key symbol   207
Option key, using to trash items   22
Option-8, for bullet   13, 34
Option-clicking   28-29
Option-Command-E, to eject disks   21
Option-opening windows   43
Option-Shift-K (Apple Symbol)   33
Option-Shift-V (diamond)   34

Option-switching applications   53
Originals, of aliases   4
Out of memory messages   247, 251-52

P

Page Setup dialog box   195
Page sizes, and printers   198
PageMaker (Aldus)   211
   and memory   251
   faster saves in   185-86
Partitioning a disk   79-80, 259
Passwords   224, 229
PAT resource   93
PB Sleep FKEY   155
PC
   disks, formatting   130
   files   237
   transferring files to and
     from   241-42
PDEF resource   215
Performas   12-13
   starting from floppy   69
Peter the Bugman   77
Phone lines, noise on   239
PhoneNET (Farallon)   157
Photoshop (Adobe)   216
   Easter Egg   75
   using to create icons   105
PICT Compressor   159
PICT resource   102
PICT screen shots   77
Pig mode   75-76
PixelPaint   101
PKZIP   237
Platinum terminators   233
PMMU (Paged memory management
   unit)   258
Polic, Robert   231
PorkChop   10, 135
Post-It notes, creating   15
Poston, Tom   104
PostScript files
   creating   214
   downloading   196
PostScript fonts   199-202, 205, 211
PostScript graphics, faxing   244

PostScript-only system 201
Potkin, Noah 104
Power strips, using with SCSIs 230
Power surges 125
Power switch, lockable 66
Power-Saver option 154
PowerBooks 153-59
   and aliases on floppies 5
   and At Ease 12
   conserving battery power 153-55
   Easter Egg 72
   installing system on 284
   metal detectors and 159
   printing on via fax 198
   and SCSI connectors 234
   Sleep mode 154
   startup sound 70, 156
ppat resource 90
PRAM, clearing 64, 274
Precision Bitmap Alignment 212
Preferences folders, trashing 286
Prevost, Ruffin 162
Print color, changing the 215
Print spooling 194
Print Window command 195
Printer drivers
   deleting 292
   using aliases of 195
Printer fonts 199, 203, 205
Printer port, using for file
   transfers 157
Printing 191-216
   draft 197
   number of copies,
     changing 212-13
   to disk 214-15
PrintMonitor
   on Apple menu 194
   flashing 53, 195
   placement of 192
Programmer's switch 71, 277-78
Proofing documents 212
Protocols, file transfer 235
Put Away (Command-Y) 39
Puzzle
   Easter Egg 72
   hidden 186

Q

Quadra startup sound 70, 156
QuarkPrint 211
QuickDraw printers 200
QuicKeys 78
   Easter Egg 75
QuickTime 255
   Easter Eggs 75, 159
   movie, as startup movie 103
   sounds 165
   Starter Kit 159
   tips 159-61
Quotation marks 208

R

Radio buttons 27
RAM (random-access memory) 245
   and Finder 1
   freeing up 252
RAM caches 259. *See also* Disk caches
RAM creep 256
RAM disks 247, 252, 259-62
   installing with 286-88
   on PowerBooks 155
RamDisk+ (shareware) 262
Random-access memory. *See* RAM
Read Mes, making 187
Read-only memory (ROM) 246
Reassigning creator codes 184-85
Rebuilding the Desktop 64-66, 67,
   83, 130, 268, 269-70
Registration mark symbol 208
Remapping keys 174-77
Renaming
   disks 132-33
   icons 7-8
Repair hotline, for PowerBooks 153
Repairing disks 131-32
ResEdit
   Easter Egg in 75
   general rules for using 86-88
ResEdit Complete 88
Resolution, when printing
   graphics 212

Resource
  fork 86
  types 86
Restart, assigning Command-R
  to 56, 61
Restarting the printer 191-92
ROM (read-only memory) 246
Rosenstein, Larry 52

S

San Francisco font 204
Saturation 146
Save As dialog box shortcuts 24-25
Saving, importance of 124
Schneider, Derrick 104
Scrapbook
  maintaining several 290
  pasting sounds in 166, 170
  using to copy icons 113
  using for transferring art 185
Screen fonts 141, 199
  and ATM 205
  deleting 206
  locating 42
Screen shots 19, 77, 215, 243
  in System 6 vs. 7 78
  printing 181, 183-84
Script Switcher (System 7.1) 51-52
Scroll bar, changing pattern of 93-97
SCSI drive
  bypassing 64, 66
  as startup disks 84
SCSI interface kit 234
SCSI port, and LaserWriter 196
SCSI Probe 231-32, 267
SCSI tricks 229-34
SE
  Easter Egg in 71
  startup sound 70
.sea extension 135, 235
Searching 2, 39-43
  criteria for 39-41
Selection rectangle, using 20
Service bureau tricks 211-12, 214
Shareware, obtaining 163
Sharing command 219
Sharing files. *See* Networking

Sharing Setup control panel 219,
  220-21
Shift key
  disabling extensions in
    System 7 67
  disabling Startup Items folder 16
Shift key symbol 207
Shortcuts, in dialog boxes 27
Shut Down, assigning to
  Command-K 59-60
Shut Down message, changing 68
SICN resources 178-79
Silbernik, Mary 277
SimAnt Easter Eggs 76
SIMMs 246, 253-54
SimplePlayer 159-60
.sit extension 135, 235
Sitka/TOPS network 237, 241-42
SIZE resource 248
Sleep mode, on PowerBooks 154
Small Icon, viewing by 19
Small type, faxing 244
SmartScrap (Solutions
  International) 290
Smokey 135
snd resources 169
SndConverter (shareware) 163-64
Somebody 135
Sound control panel 164, 167,
  170-72
  on PowerBook 156
Sound in System 7 38
Sound tricks 162-74
  downloading 167
  stealing sounds 169-72
  types of sounds 164-65
SoundEdit (Paracomp) 164-65, 172
SoundExtractor (shareware) 163, 172
SoundFix FKEY 174
SoundMaster (shareware) 63, 162-63,
  169, 172
SoundMover 164-65, 168-69, 172-73
Spaces
  sizes of 210
  using in Apple menu 34-35
  using in icon names
    (System 6) 8-9
Spare parts folders 276-77

Speakers, for Macs 174
Spell-checking, on PowerBooks 158
Startup combinations 64
Startup Disk control panel 138-39, 230
Startup disks 81
    making 266-67, 283
    switching 138-39
Startup items
    bypassing 64, 271-73. *See also*
        Extensions, bypassing
    loading order of 273-74
Startup Items folder 16
    and Apple Menu items
        folder 33, 37
Startup monitors, switching 150-51
Startup movie 103, 161
Startup page, suppressing 196
Startup screen, making 101-3
Startup sound 70, 104, 163
Stationery pads, creating 188-89
Stein, Adam 88
Sticky Keys 148-49
StuffIt 133-35
StuffIt Classic 134, 236
StuffIt Deluxe 134
StuffIt Lite 134
StuffIt SpaceSaver (Aladdin) 133-34,
    157
StyleWriters 194
Suitcase II (Fifth Generation) 42,
    167, 203, 271
Suitcases 203-4, 271
    and memory 250
    and System Folder 30
    using for sounds 166
    working with 144-45
SUM (Symantec) 22, 258
SunDesk (shareware) 104
Super Boomerang (Now
    Software) 255
SuperDisk 157
SuperDrives 125-26, 153, 241
Swapping floppy disks,
    stopping 126-27
Switching
    between Systems 6 and 7 79-84
    printers 195
Symbol font 210

Symbols 207-10
    assigning to keys 177
    using in Apple menu 33-34
Syquest drives, ejecting 138
System beep, creating 163, 166-67
System, putting on floppy 283,
    287-88
System Errors (freeware) 265
System file
    and fonts 201, 202
    Easter Egg in 72
    editing 89
    replacing 69, 285-86
    searching 42
System files 187
System Folder
    alias of 5
    adding fonts to 202, 204
    blessed 82
    dragging items to 29-30
    installing on RAM disk 155, 262
    multiple copies of 82-83
System Picker (freeware) 80
System 6
    changing Finder menus in 56-57
    and MultiFinder 1
    rebuilding Desktop in 6
    screen shots in 78
    starting from floppy 69
    startup disk 81
System 6 and 7
    on a network 192, 218
    switching between 79-84
System 7
    installing 282
    screen shots in 78-79
    sounds 164
    starting from floppy 69
    startup disk 81, 84
System 7 Pack! 88
System 7 TuneUp 252, 288-89
System 7.0P 12
System 7.1
    and font suitcases 201, 204
    installing FKEY in Fonts folder 78
    and International menu 49-52
    starting from a floppy 256
    startup disk for 283

System 7.1P 12
System Tools disk 69, 266
Systems, switching 79-84
Systems, corrupted 268

T

Tabs, using instead of spaces 210
Tah-Dah, stealing from
    Puzzle 171-72
Talking Moose 63
TeachText
    Easter Egg 75
    finding extras 43
    limitations of 183
    nasty trick for 187
    and screen shots 78-79, 215
Teleprotectors 238
Tempo 78
Termination, in SCSI chains 231, 233
Terrell, Rob 77, 162
Testing folders, maintaining 269
The Little System 7.1 Book 283
Third-party formatters 138
32-bit addressing 246, 256, 258, 261,
    262-64
32-bit clean programs 284-85
Tidbits disk 285
TIFF (Tagged Image File
    Format) 79, 243
Tilde key, swapping with Esc 158
Time, setting the 147
Time zones, in Map control panel 152
To-Do lists 16
Toner, for laser printers 199
TOPS network 237, 241-42
Torres, Fred 77
Trademark symbol 208
Transferring files
    from PCs 241-42
    to PowerBooks 157
Trash
    emptying 22-23, 278
    making aliases of 5
    moving (System 7) 48
    retrieving items from 22

    tricks 21-23
    using to disconnect from a
        network 227
Trash folder 83
Trash icons 117
TrashChute (freeware) 23
TrueType 199-202
TuneUp 252, 288-89
Tung, Kenny S. C. 74
Type 1 fonts 199, 205

U

UltraPaint 101
Unattended printing 192-94
Undo command 7
UnStuffIt 134
USC Mac User Group 292
User groups 291-92
Users & Groups control panel 219
Utilities disk, for startup
    (Performa) 69

V

Viewing by Kind 9
Views, changing in Finder
    (System 7) 46
Views control panel 44
Virtual memory 246, 256-59
VM Storage file 258
Voice annotations 173

W

Waite, Dave 65
Warnings, bypassing 22
Washington Apple Pi 292
Weird fonts 204, 285
White box tricks 13-15, 17, 36
Williams, Robin 187
Windows
    closing 28-29, 44
    hiding 25
    Trash 21-22
    zooming 99-100, 141

Word
    creator code   183-85
    Easter Eggs in   74
    sounds in   173
WordPerfect   159-60
    creator code   183-85
World map, in System 7   38
WorldScripts (System 7.1)   51-52
Wristwatch cursor   95
WriteNow 2.2 Easter Egg   75

X

XMODEM   235

Y

YMODEM   235

Z

Zapf Dingbats   209
Zapping the PRAM   64
Zen and the Art of Resource
    Editing   88, 104
ZMODEM   235

COLOPHON

Voodoo Mac was produced on a Macintosh Quadra 700, using Aldus PageMaker 4.2. Body text is set in Digital Typeface Corporation (DTC) Galliard Roman, tip and trap names, running heads and subheads are DTC Optimum Bold, chapter heads are Adobe Lithos Bold and folios are set in Adobe Revue. Screen shots were created with Capture 4.

Prevost & Terrell $39.95
376 pages, 4 disks

The Ultimate Mac Shareware Resource!

W hether you're a shareware veteran or skeptic, this book is required reading. Authors Ruffin Prevost, Rob Terrell and a team of impartial reviewers have carefully examined thousands of programs and handpicked the best. The only comprehensive guide to 500 of the best Mac shareware programs, *The Mac Shareware 500* is a four-disk, 376 page set offering users a program overview, tips for shareware sources, extensive operating instructions and much more.

The Mac Shareware 500 also provides invaluable information on

- ✳ The many different varieties of shareware, including an in-depth look at the politics and ethics of the shareware community.
- ✳ The best sources for acquiring shareware, whether you're buying direct from the author, receiving it through a user group or disk duplication service, or downloading it from your favorite online service.
- ✳ Checking your shareware for viruses, quickly and easily.
- ✳ Solving compatibility problems.

The book is packaged with three disks of the authors' top program picks from a variety of shareware categories, including business, games, clip art, fonts, utilities and more.

With the purchase of this book, you'll also receive five hours of free time on America Online whether you're a new or current member.

Ready, Set, Play!

Every Mac aficionado's ideal amusement resource, *MacArcade* takes fun to new limits! You'll find the industry's best action-packed Mac shareware games in this one-of-a-kind book/disk set.

Mac pundit Don Rittner has carefully reviewed hundreds of shareware games, handpicking the top 40 programs loaded with show-stopping graphics and non-stop fun. This unique guide features everything you need for hours upon hours of unbeatable entertainment, including:

- ✳ Game summaries.
- ✳ Compatibility listings.
- ✳ How to get games for almost free!
- ✳ Hot game tips.

INSTANT GRATIFICATION!

MacArcade includes 2 high-density 1.4 Mb floppies packed with the best of the best, Rittner's top 10 games—including the classics that thousands of Mac users have been enjoying for years!

Turn to *MacArcade* for outlandish, recession-proof, virus-free fun and amusement on your Mac!

To begin enjoying the best shareware games around, use the order form in the back of this book or call/write Ventana Press, P.O. Box 2468, Chapel Hill, NC 27515. (919)942-0220; (800)743-5369; FAX:(800)877-7955.

TO ORDER additional copies of *Voodoo Mac* or any other Ventana Press book, please fill out this order form and return it to us for quick shipment.

	Quantity	Price			Total
Voodoo Mac	_____	x	$21.95	=	$_____
MacArcade	_____	x	$27.95	=	$_____
The Mac Shareware 500—A Book/Disk Set	_____	x	$39.95	=	$_____
The System 7 Book, Second Edition	_____	x	$24.95	=	$_____
The Official America Online Membership Kit & Tour Guide: Mac Edition	_____	x	$34.95	=	$_____

Shipping: Please add $4.50/first book for standard UPS, $1.35/book thereafter;
$8.25/book UPS "two-day air," $2.25/book thereafter.
For Canada, add $8.10/book. $_____

Send C.O.D. (add $4.50 to shipping charges) $_____
North Carolina residents add 6% sales tax $_____

                                                              Total $_____

Name _____ Co. _____

Address (No PO Box) _____

City _____ State _____ Zip _____

Daytime telephone _____

____ VISA ____ MC Acc't # _____

Exp. Date _____ Interbank # _____

Signature _____

Please mail or fax to:
Ventana Press, PO Box 2468, Chapel Hill, NC 27515
919/942-0220; 800/743-5369 (orders only); FAX: 800/877-7955

FINALLY! Mac News You Can Use
From a Name You Can Trust!

If you keep up with magazines and trade publications about the Macintosh, you may have noticed how it's sometimes hard to tell the news from the snooze. But now you've got a source you can rely on. Because Ventana Press accepts no advertisements in our newsletters, we won't be swayed by the market propaganda. You'll get the straight dope on the things that matter to Mac users, compiled by the best writers in the business...our authors.

Free Issues
The Ventana
Mac Update

In your two free issues of *The Ventana Mac Update*, you'll get the facts—and just the facts—on all the hot topics: the inside track on System 7, tips and tricks that will make anyone a power user, shareware bargains, and impartial hardware and software reviews.

If you purchased *Voodoo Mac* directly from Ventana Press, you'll receive *The Ventana Mac Update* automatically. If you bought the book elsewhere, complete the form below and return it to: Ventana Press, PO Box 2468, Chapel Hill, NC 27515. Fax 919/942-1140.

Order card for *The Ventana Mac Update*. Please send me two free updates on the latest news in the Macintosh community:

Name _____

Company _____

Address _____

City _____ State _____ Zip _____

Country _____ Telephone _____

VM